# THE AUDI QUATTRO BOOK

*Other books by this author:*

Jaguar XJ6 Restoration Manual
Range Rover Restoration Manual
Jaguar XK Engine
In Car Entertainment Manual
Classic Car Electrical Systems Repair Manual

*Co-written with Lindsay Porter:*

Improve & Modify Series
    Escort & Orion
    Fiesta
    Golf/Jetta
    MGB
    Capri
    Peugeot 205

*Co-written with Lindsay Porter, Tom Falconer and John Pfanstiehl:*

Chevrolet Corvette Purchase and Restoration Manual

# THE AUDI
# QUATTRO
# BOOK

**Buying, repairing and tuning**

## DAVE POLLARD

First published 1998
Reprinted 2000

British Library cataloguing-in-publication data:
A catalogue record for this book is
available from the British Library.

ISBN 1 85960 403 X

Library of Congress catalog card no. 97-77759

Haynes North America Inc.
861 Lawrence Drive, Newbury Park,
California 91320, USA.

Published by Haynes Publishing, Sparkford,
Nr Yeovil, Somerset BA22 7JJ, UK.

Tel: 01963 440635 Fax: 01963 440001
Int. tel: +44 1963 440635
Int. fax: +44 1963 440001
E-mail: sales@haynes-manuals.co.uk
Web site: www.haynes.co.uk

Designed & typeset by G&M, Raunds, Northamptonshire
Printed in Great Britain by J. H. Haynes & Co., Ltd

**Jurisdictions which have strict emission control laws may consider any modification
to a vehicle to be an infringement of those laws. You are advised to check with the
appropriate body or authority whether your proposed modification complies fully with
the law. The publishers accept no liability in this regard.**

**While every effort is taken to ensure the accuracy of the information given in this
book, no liability can be accepted by the author or publishers for any loss, damage or
injury caused by errors in, or omissions from, the information given.**

# Contents

Acknowledgements 7
Introduction 9

## 1 A brief history of the four rings 11
Pre-production – from nothing to everything 17
Quattro connections 18

## 2 Road car heritage 20
First encounters 20
Original dimensions 21
Preaching to the converted 31
Price progression 32
Driving the quattro 32
The Sport quattro 33
An Englishman in Ingolstadt 38
Creating the quattro 38
Show and go 38
Two that got away … 38
… and two that didn't! 39
Audi S2 – pretender to the crown 44
UK quattro sales 46

## 3 The competition connection 48
Rallying as it was 48
World Rally Championship results 53
To America – success in TransAm and IMSA tarmac racing 61

The tarmac terrors – European success from 1990 to 1996 63
European Touring car specifications 64
Audi European Touring Car results 67

## 4 The quattro in detail 68
The 10v engine 68
The 20v engine 73
More about fuel systems 76

## Quattros in colour 81–96
The cooling system 97
The exhaust system 102
Transmission 104
Brakes 107
Suspension and steering 112
Bodywork 114
Interior and electrical 117
Seat belts 121
Wheels and tyres 122
Audi high performance driving courses 127

## 5 Buying a quattro 128
Checking the bodywork 131
Checking the engine 134
Checking the transmission 138
Checking the suspension, wheels and tyres 138

Checking the brakes 141
Checking the interior 141
'Driving test' 143
Buying a Sport quattro 145
Quattro buying checklist 145

## 6 Tuning 147
BR Motorsport 148
20v options 148
Chips with everything 148

## 7 Security 152
Thatcham 152
Insurance 152
Getting physical 153
Central deadlocking 156
Electronic alarms 157
Tag, you're it! 159

**Appendix 1**
Workshop procedures and safety first 165

**Appendix 2**
Chassis number interpretation 168

**Appendix 3**
English/American terminology 169

**Appendix 4**
Useful names and addresses 170

Index 175

# Acknowledgements

I received a great deal of help in writing this book, most notably with archive information and period photos. I must especially thank Nigel Walker of Audi Sport UK; Paula Gillard and David Ingram of Audi UK; Neil Birkett, editor of *VW Motoring* magazine, and fellow authors Robin Wager and Lindsay Porter for digging through reams of paperwork and dozens of dusty old filing cabinets on my behalf. David Preece, chairman of the Quattro Owners Club, proved time and again the value of being a club member – when he didn't know an answer (not very often!) he knew a man who did.

Help was also forthcoming from others in terms of information given, brains picked and photos taken, and those most in the firing line were:

AM Cars
Audi Sport PR

Autofilm Direct
Robert Bosch GmbH

BR Motorsport
C & R Enterprises
Clarke International
Datatag/Meta
Demon Tweeks
Goodyear GB Limited

Adam Marsden
Martyn and Teresa Pass
David Cooper
Ruth Holubecki and Stefan Buchsteiner
Brian Ricketts
John Russell
Ross Bernard
Martine Layland
Steve Bell
Trina Brindley and Katy Leese

GT Auto Alarms

Hella Ltd

Manton Software
Pristine
Sachs Boge
Sempal
Serck Marston
Superchips
Sykes-Pickavant

Wayside Garage

Blair McWilliam and Peter Mouncer
Chris Marshall and Paul Baker
Chris Brown
David James
Jerry Banks
Matthew Morris
Tony Lewis
Ian Sandford
Christine Whitworth
Patrick Pollard (no relation!)

As ever, my wife Ann was instrumental in preserving my sanity and helping pull the whole project together.

# Introduction

Every now and then a car arrives that grabs the attention like no other. In 1961 Jaguar stopped the world in its tracks when it unveiled the E-Type at the Geneva Motor Show. Boys, young and old, drooled and dreamed and a whole generation was affected by this most svelte of sports cars.

It could be coincidence or it could be fate, but almost 20 years later Switzerland once again played host to the unveiling of a car that had the motoring press and the public on its knees.

As practical as a Polo but as fast as a Ferrari, the Audi quattro fairly leapt from the show stand into 11 years of motor magazine hyperbole and it changed forever the face of World Championship rallying.

Within four seasons the Audi team had won the Manufacturers' World Championship and the Drivers' Championship – twice! – and, in doing so, overtook Ford and Lancia in terms of number of rallies won.

With the turbocharged quattro at the top of the tree, Audi spread the 4WD message across the whole of its range, prompting almost all other major car manufacturers to follow.

When the world and his brother said that 4WD was only of use on loose surfaces, Audi proved them wrong by winning the USA TransAm series first time out in an Audi 200 quattro, the German

Touring Car Championship two years running (an unprecedented feat) and latterly winning no fewer than seven Touring Car World Championships world-wide with the glorious A4 quattro Supertouring.

Dream cars, like idols, often have feet/tyres of clay, but not so Audi's 4WD wunder-car. Few vehicles so effortlessly blend exciting motoring performance with fuss-free mechanicals and massive levels of safety. And, unlike many so-called supercars, it is surprisingly practical to use on a day-to-day basis, being as happy on the school run as on an investigative trundle down to AM Cars in darkest Somerset.

Perfect? No, but its intriguing mix of good points (lots) and bad points (few) gives it a soul and wins the kind of enthusiasm that is displayed by Porsche 911 owners. It could be argued that enthusiasts will always find something good to say about their cars, but motoring journalists are usually not so easily impressed. The following quotes emphasise the 'rightness' of the quattro:

*'... a marvel that re-writes the motoring rule books ...'*
– Car

*'Getting back into an ordinary car feels like stepping back into the past.'*
– Autocar

*'The thing that sets the quattro apart is the ability to deploy massive power without drama. Here is none of the wheel-spinning heroics of the traditional supercar, but a steady flow of power and grip.'*
– Performance Car

*'... almost beyond belief in its combination of roadholding, handling, traction and performance, the 4WD quattro knows no peers.'*
– Motor Sport

*'... it's not often nowadays that I come back from driving a new car and say: "Well, that was fabulous!" But that's just what happened with the Audi quattro.'*
– Motor

*'Merely to read the specification of the Audi quattro is enough to leave one stunned. To drive it is to discover a new experience in motoring.'*
– Motor Sport

Throughout this book, the word 'quattro' is given a lower-case 'q' (unless it's part of a title and the whole word is upper case). This follows Audi's original decree. 'The quattro' has always meant the turbocharged, flared-arch coupé. However, confusion began to arise as more and more models gained Audi's

*Truly the stuff of legends, the quattro came rip-snorting from the rally tracks and special stages to the autobahns and B-roads to change forever the face of motoring.*

4WD system. So, it should be noted that any non-turbo quattro will be pre-fixed by its model name, eg Audi 80 quattro, Coupé quattro or A4 quattro.

In Germany, as Audi's S2 hit the market, the quattro became known as the Ur quattro – Ur (pronounced *oor*) being the German word for 'original'.

And in case you're *still* wondering, that world-famous piece of PR copy-writing, *Vorsprung durch Technik*, means Progress through Technology. As you'll see from what follows, it couldn't be more apt.

*Dave Pollard*
*Hertfordshire 1997*

A long-time Audi enthusiast, Dave Pollard has owned seven Audis over a 20-year period – a MKI 80 1.6 litre, a brace of MKII 80 1.8s, a MKII 80CD, a MKIII 80 quattro, a MKII 90 and finally a Tornado red, 10v 'WR' 2144cc quattro.

# Chapter 1

# A brief history of the four rings

The name Audi is synonymous with motoring innovation and technical achievement. For over 100 years, Audi (or one of the names that go to make up the company) has been extending the limits of motoring in such areas as aerodynamics, the 5-cylinder petrol engine, front-wheel drive and, of course, four-wheel drive.

The four rings logo on the front of every Audi represents the amalgamation of four German car-makers which took place in 1932. It was then, mostly because of financial problems, that Audi, DKW, Horch and Wanderer merged. Despite this coming together, for many years all four marques kept their names and individual identities whilst making the most of the available pooled resources.

The convolutions of the company we know today simply as Audi would alone be sufficient to fill a book (indeed, the company has done just that), so here are just a few of the milestones in a history that goes back to the dawn of the automobile. The details for NSU are separate as it was not absorbed until 1969.

## 1885
- The Wanderer company is founded and for nine years will sell cycles, motorcycles, heavy machinery and typewriters.

## 1899
- After working for Karl Benz, August Horch forms his own eponymously named company.

## 1900
- Horch applies for a patent for his 'jerk-free twin-cylinder engine'.

## 1901
- Horch produces the first car to bear his name – it has a top speed of 23kph.

## 1904
- First Wanderer prototype car produced (see 1911).
- The DKW company is founded by Rasmussen and Ernst – the initials are taken from a failed experimental steam engine (a *Dampf-Kraft-Wagen*). When the company later produces stationary engines to power models, the initials will also stand for *Das Knaben Wunsch* – a boy's dream.

## 1906
- A Horch car wins the second Herkomer Rally.

## 1908
- Horch's 'torpedo' coachwork is effective in increasing the top speed of some racing cars. He is one of the first to recognise the effects of aerodynamic drag and how it can be countered by the use of smooth designs.

## 1909
- Horch is forced to leave his own company but, undaunted, starts again. He calls his new company Audi – from the Latin *audire* 'to hear', prompted by his own name which, in German, means 'hark'.

## 1910
- The name Audi is accepted by the registrar of companies.

## 1911
- Horch wins the Austrian Automobile Club's Alpine Rally, driving his own Audi. Audi will repeat the win in 1912, 1913 and 1914.
- The Wanderer prototype design enters production as the Püppchen ('Poppet'), a 12hp model with a 1150cc, 4-cylinder, engine combined with the gearbox. It proves very successful and, with engine uprates to 1220cc and 1280cc, is to continue to sell until the end of WWI.

## 1914
- Top of the Horch range is the 6.43 litre, 4-cylinder, 25/60hp model, capable of nearly 70mph and featuring such luxuries as an electric starter and a dynamo.

## 1921

- The new 14/50 Audi model incorporates advanced features such as an aluminium cylinder block with pressed-in liners, ball-action gear shift and 4-wheel brakes – the first production car so-equipped (years later Audi scores another first with dual circuit, diagonally linked braking).

## 1923

- Audi starts to equip all its cars with 4-wheel braking.

- Wanderer announces a car with a 6/24hp engine.

## 1925

- The first DKW car (the DKW E206) is manufactured. It leads to the production of the E200 which is the first car in Germany to get exemption from road tax and driver's licence.

## 1926

- The Horch company produces the first ever German 8-cylinder car, the Type 303.

## 1927

- The first Wanderer car with LHD and 4-wheel brakes appears – the 6/30hp Type W 10. This is to be the mainstay of Wanderer's output for many years.
- After design revisions, the Horch 8-cylinder engine is installed in a new model – the Type 500.

## 1928

- Wanderer displays the new Type W11, with a 6-cylinder, 10/50hp engine.
- DKW markets its first production cars, a 2-seater roadster and a 3-seater convertible known as the Type 15. Both are powered by 2-stroke engines – quite a novelty.

## 1930

- At DKW, despite technical mastery and wide diversification (with popular and cheap motorcycles, a Framo 3-wheeled light van, a 500cc water-cooled motorcycle,

refrigerators and a 2-stroke car) the company's bank has to appoint an administrator to try to make the accounts balance.
- Audi launches the Dresden, with a 3838cc 6-cylinder engine producing 75hp.

## 1931

- DKW takes centre stage at the Berlin Motor Show with the DKW F1 – the first production car with front-wheel drive. It will be 40 years before this feature becomes commonplace for other marques and three years before it is seen on the Citroën Traction Avant. (Audi is also first with negative roll radius self-stabilising steering.)
- Wanderer hires a freelance motoring design consultant – Ferdinand Porsche. He designs some new cars with 1.7 litre and 2 litre 6-cylinder engines which see service in the W21, W22, W50 and the W25K, a Roots supercharged version, producing 85bhp and equipped with independent suspension.
- At the Paris Motor Show, Horch displays its latest range-leader, the 12-cylinder Type 670.

## AUTO UNION AG

## 1932

- The amalgamation of the four

*Note the four rings on the grille, symbolising the amalgamation of the four companies in 1932. Note also the 'W' Wanderer emblem at the top of the grille.*

companies (Wanderer, Audi, Horch and DKW) is finally completed, the eventual company having some

*The 16-cylinder Auto Union racing car is arguably one of the most famous in the world. Its 6010cc engine was supercharged and developed 520bhp at 5000rpm. Top speed depended on the gearing, but it was capable of over 200mph.*

20,000 employees. The product of the new concern is the 'Front', a development of the 1931 DKW prototype. The front-wheel drive car featured a Wanderer 2 litre 6-cylinder engine, DKW-designed transmission, a central box chassis and a new advanced rear axle design.

## 1933
- Seven Front models are entered in a round-Germany race and pick up all the major awards.

## 1934
- Birth of the Auto Union 'P-Car', designed by Ferdinand Porsche, the world's first mid-engined racing car. It is powered by a 4.3 litre, 295bhp, V16 engine which sits in a tubular space frame fitted with torsion bar suspension. This year it breaks seven world records. Hans Stuck, father of the current Audi star, wins the German Hill Climb Championship and dominates road racing and

*The Horch 853 started production in 1935 with a 4911cc straight eight engine which initially produced 100bhp, but by the time this particular car hit the road in 1938 the power output was 120bhp at 3600rpm. Top speed was around 140kph (approx. 87mph).*

hill climbing throughout the 1930s.

## 1935
- Auto Union wins 34 gold and 45 silver awards in reliability trials.
- The attractive Horch Type 835 is launched, with an 8-cylinder in-line engine producing first 100bhp and later 120bhp.
- DKW introduces the F5 Front model series.

## 1936
- Bernd Rosemeyer wins three Grand Prix to clinch the European GP title in

*In 1933, the front-wheel drive Audi Front preceded Citroën's acclaimed Traction Avant by a couple of years. It had a 6-cylinder in-line engine of 1950cc which produced 40bhp at 3500rpm. Top speed was 100kph (approx. 62mph).*

*The 1936 Wanderer W25K had a 6-cylinder in-line engine of 1950cc featuring a Roots compressor. It produced 85bhp at 4000rpm and had a top speed of 145kph (approx. 90mph).*

*Horch 853A built in 1938*

*Wanderer W.25K built in 1936*

*This is H. P. Müller taking part in the European Mountain Championship at Grossglockner in 1939.*

the 6-litre, 520bhp, V16 'Silver Arrow'.

### 1937

- Bernd Rosemeyer uses a streamlined version of the Silver Arrow to set a new world public road speed record, averaging 254mph (406kph). The following year he is to up the ante by cracking 273mph (436kph).

### 1939

- The Audi 920, with a 3.2 litre 6-cylinder engine and RWD, replaces the Audi Front.

## AUTO UNION GmbH

### 1950

- Production of the DKW 125cc motorcycle and the post-war high-speed truck commences in Ingolstadt.

### 1951

- Two new motorcycles are launched – the RT200 and the RT250.

### 1953

- The Auto Union DKW Sonderklasse

Type F91 is launched with a 3-cylinder 2-stroke engine. A total of 230,000 are to be produced.

### 1954

- Production of the Type F91 increases to one car every four minutes.

### 1955

- The 2-stroke-engined Munga 'jeep' starts production – the odd name is an acronym of German words meaning 'multi-purpose universal off-road vehicle with all-wheel drive'.

### 1957

- Auto Union GmbH is the first German car-maker to fit its cars with the 'Saxomat' automatic clutch.

### 1958

- Daimler Benz takes an 85 per cent stake in the Auto Union company, and the manufacturing plant at Ingolstadt is built.

### 1959

- The DKW Junior is launched, and becomes one of the best-sellers in its class.
- The AU 1000 is launched, featuring a panoramic windscreen.

### 1960

- The 500,000th Auto Union/DKW car built within a decade comes off the production line.
- Auto Union and DKW cars win 24 national and international race championships.

### 1962

- The plant at Düsseldorf is taken over by Daimler-Benz, and Auto Union

*With a synthetic body shell, DKW's sharp-suited Monza sports car was powered by a 3-cylinder 980cc 2-stroke engine producing 50bhp at 4500rpm. Its top speed was 135kph (approx. 83mph).*

production is moved to a new plant in Ingolstadt.

## 1965
- The first post-war 4-stroke Audi is manufactured – developed from the DKW F102 2-stroke car, it marks both the beginning and the end of an era.
- VW Beetles are assembled at Ingolstadt – 61,830 of them.

## 1966
- New cars include the Audi Variant, Audi 80 and Audi Super 90.
- Production of the DKW F102 ends.

## 1968
- The Audi 60, with a 1.5 litre, 50bhp, engine, is a huge success. A 60bhp version for export is shown at the Geneva Motor Show.
- The MKI Audi 100 is launched in three versions, producing 80, 90 and 100bhp.
- Munga production ceases.

## 1969
- NSU becomes part of the Auto Union GmbH, the resulting concern being called Audi NSU Auto Union AG.
- VW Beetle production at Ingolstadt ceases, and the lines are given over completely to Audi production.

## NSU

## 1873
- NSU company founded – to manufacture knitting machines – and is called *Neckarsulm Strickaschinene Fabrik* (literally, the Neckarsulm Knitting Machine Factory).

## 1892
- Using the letters from its home town (NeckarSUlm), *Neckarsulm Strickaschinene Fabrik* changes its name to NSU; now producing cycles and motorcycles.

## 1925
- In 1925 and the following year, an NSU 6-cylinder racer beats the mighty Mercedes and Bugatti teams to win the German Grand Prix.

## 1927
- NSU becomes the first German motorcycle manufacturer to introduce conveyor-belt assembly methods.

## 1929
- The recession hits NSU badly and they forgo car production, delivering only motorcycles for the next 30 years. The car plant is sold to the Italian Fiat concern.

## 1934
- Ferdinand Porsche develops three Volkswagen prototypes for NSU, named Porsche Type 32.

## 1949
- The 98cc NSU Fox is the first motorcycle produced since the war.

## 1951
- Wilhelm Hertz sets a world motorcycle speed record on his supercharged 500cc NSU machine, hitting 290kph.

## 1954
- NSU Motorenwerke, by now the largest motorcycle factory in the world, produces the remarkable NSU 'Flying Deckchair', which sets a two-wheeler world speed record of 339kph with an engine of only 100cc. It has the lowest drag coefficient ever achieved for a vehicle of this type.

## 1957
- NSU once more returns to car production, with the small 'Prinz' model.

## 1959
- After some nine years in the development process, the NSU/Wankel rotary piston engine is revealed to the Press.

## 1961
- The new Prinz 4 model is launched, with a 600cc engine developing 30bhp.

## 1964
- The Prinz 1000 is launched, the first of a new series, with 4-stroke, 4-cylinder engines.
- The Spider is launched, the world's first production car fitted with a Wankel rotary piston engine.

## 1967
- The stunning, space-age 115bhp NSU Ro80 is unveiled. Advanced aerodynamic styling and semi-automatic gearbox are marred only by the Wankel engine's reputation for unreliability.

## 1969
- The merger with Auto Union GmbH takes place.

## 1972
- The Audi 80 collects four Car of the Year awards – in London, Stockholm, Kronberg and Belgrade.

## 1973
- The 1,000,000th Audi since 1965 is produced – it is also the 100,000th Audi 80.
- The 100bhp Audi 80 GT is launched.

## 1975
- Production of the Porsche 924 commences at the Neckarsulm plant (to be joined later by the more powerful 944 model).

## 1976
- In an effort to produce 6-cylinder performance with 4-cylinder economy, Audi is the first company to mass-produce a 5-cylinder petrol (as opposed to diesel) engine.

## 1977
- Production of the NSU Ro80 ceases.

## 1978
- The MKII Audi 80 is launched.
- A significant event – Audi begins the production of the 4WD Volkswagen

Iltis military vehicle at the Ingolstadt production facility.

## 1980

- The Audi quattro is launched at the Geneva Motor Show: the first high-performance production car built on the four wheel drive principle. (4WD spreads the power across all wheels, resulting in improved handling, greater stability, better traction and, thus, greater safety.)
- The Audi 200 is Europe's most powerful production front-wheel drive car.

## 1981

- The quattro enters rallying and, though beset by mechanical maladies, it fires a warning shot across the bows of the established teams, winning three World Championship rallies, including the first ever win for a woman – Michèle Mouton in San Remo.

## 1982

- Audi introduces the new 100 model with its world-beating Cd (drag coefficient) of 0.30 – incredible for a large luxury class vehicle.
- In rallying, the 4WD quattro proves its worth with the Audi Sport team winning the Manufacturers World Rally Championship. Audi's Michèle Mouton almost clinches the driver's title.
- The first non-turbo quattro, the 5-cylinder Audi 80, is launched.

## 1983

- Audi is the first German manufacturer to receive a general operating permit for cars with catalytic converter technology to clean exhaust fumes.
- In rallying, the quattro triumphs again, this time with a Drivers' World Championship title for Hannu Mikkola.
- The Audi 100 is voted Car of the Year.
- The homologation special, short wheelbase Audi Sport quattro is launched, with a very limited production run.

## 1984

- The quattro strikes gold by winning both the Manufacturers' World Rally Championship and the Rally Drivers' World Championship with Stig Blomqvist.
- The Audi model range is revamped, with the Audi 80 only being fitted with 4-cylinder engines and the Audi 90 using 5-cylinder units.

## 1985

- The company was renamed Audi AG.
- Walter Röhrl scores the first Sport quattro rally victory in San Remo.
- Michèle Mouton brings her Sport quattro home first in the American Pikes Peak climb.

## 1986

- Audi's pioneering fully-galvanized bodies are now guaranteed for ten years. The company is awarded the German industry's Innovation Prize for its ability to develop and realise new ideas.
- After the tragic accident in Portugal, Audi withdraws from Group B rallying.

## 1987

- The brilliantly simple Procon-ten safety system is introduced. In the event of a serious accident, this system puts extra tension on the seatbelts and contracts the steering column, pulling it forward and away from the driver's head, all within a fraction of a second.

## 1988

- The new 32 valve V8 is launched, which – for the very first time – links quattro all-wheel-drive with an automatic four-speed gearbox.
- In the USA, the mighty 200 quattro racer takes the TransAm title first time out.

## 1989

- Despite missing the first three races, the Audi 90 quattro racer almost clinches the American IMSA GTO title.

## 1990

- With Hans-Joachim Stuck at the wheel, the V8 quattro wins the German Touring Car Championship.
- Catalytic converters become standard equipment in all Audi cars in countries where lead-free petrol is available.
- On 9 January the 7,000,000th Audi (since 1965) is produced.
- The Audi quattro celebrates ten years in production – original production estimates were for a short run of just 400 cars!

## 1991

- Audi causes sensations at both the Frankfurt and Tokyo motor shows by showing two incredible, all-aluminium, design studies – the quattro Spyder and the Avus quattro.
- Frank Biela drives the V8 quattro to victory in the German Touring Car Championship.
- Because production capacity is required for the Audi 100, production of the Porsche 944 at Ingolstadt ceases.
- Audi quattro 20v ceases production – total since 1980 is 11,452.

## 1993

- Audi lifts more eyebrows as they show the Aluminium Space Frame (ASF) concept car with a 4.8 litre, 12-cylinder, 60-valve engine in a 'W' formation (260kW at 6300 and 480Nm at 3500).
- Frank Biela wins the French Touring Car Championship in an Audi 80 quattro.

## 1994

- Audi introduces a new model designation with A8, A6 and A4 effectively replacing the V8, 100/200 and 80/90 respectively.
- Emanuele Pirro wins the Italian Touring Car Championship in an Audi 80 Competition.

## 1995

- Emanuele Pirro repeats his success in the Italian Touring Car

Championship, this time driving an A4 quattro Supertouring.

- Frank Biela wins the FIA Touring Car World Cup driving an A4 quattro Supertouring.

## 1996

- Audi launches the all new Audi A3 models in Luxembourg.
- The A4 quattro Supertouring racer rules the Touring Car Championships, winning every one they enter, namely the Australian, Belgian, British, German, Italian, South African and Spanish.

## PRE-PRODUCTION – FROM NOTHING TO EVERYTHING

As has already been seen, Audi (at first individually and then as a part of Auto-Union) has always been at the forefront of technology. For example, at one point Audi was producing the fastest 1600 4-door saloon on sale in the UK (the MKI Audi 80). And, for the second-generation Audi 100, the company introduced the world's first mass-production 5-cylinder engine in 1976, aiming to combine the smoothness, torque and power of a 6-cylinder unit with the fuel-consumption benefits of a 4-cylinder engine – this, remember, was at the height of the fuel crisis. To prove its durability and performance capabilities, the unusual engine was turbocharged, fitted into an unsuspecting Audi 100 and packed off to the Talladega Speedway in Alabama, USA, where it set ten world speed records. Back in Europe, it established two new world benchmarks for 800km and 1000km at Italy's famous Nardo test track. Despite a general air of scepticism, the effort put into the 5-cylinder engine in general, and turbocharging in particular, was eventually to prove very useful indeed.

As the 1980s approached, Audi looked long and hard at itself and its compatriot competitors. Porsche, of course, was world-renowned as a maker of high-quality sports cars, BMW was well on the way to becoming *the*

stylish quality German car to have if you couldn't afford one from Mercedes, the company which had carved itself an expensive niche at the top of the tree. Audi needed a way to bring its cars and technical innovations to the public's attention; and it needed to change its image from what at the time was, quite simply, that of an old man's car.

It didn't call for a genius to work out that the best way to achieve this was via motorsport; to get into the white-hot arena of competitive motoring – and win. But which discipline? Formula 1 was (and still is) massively expensive and would not, in any case, really put across the image Audi required; and Touring Car racing had yet to achieve the world-wide popularity it now enjoys. The answer lay in rallying, a sport where the cars bore at least a passing resemblance to the vehicles the general public could buy in the showroom.

For years Audi had subjected its models to severe-weather tests during the long, hard winters in Finland. It was during one such testing session that Audi's Jörg Bensinger realised that, despite the vicious weather conditions, the fastest and most driveable car on the fleet was usually a simple support vehicle – the VW Iltis. This had been developed by Audi for its partner at the company's Ingolstadt HQ, and it used the same 4-cylinder transaxle engine as the contemporary Audi 80.

Perhaps this could be the start of something big? Certainly, he thought it had to be worth investigating further. Having discussed it with Audi's development chief (and grandson of Ferdinand Porsche) Ferdinand Piëch, he received the OK to go ahead with a prototype car.

## March 1977

A 4WD Audi appears on Audi's records for the first time, coded as the A1. An Audi 80 is equipped as a mobile test bed with the relevant new 4WD components, and soon the rough and ready prototype begins to show its mettle. During one test it scuttled up a winter

pass with an incline of 20 degrees – on summer tyres!

## September 1997

The A1 is allocated a development number, and expenditure on it is officially sanctioned. Later on, the project is given the code number EA262.

## November 1977

The first A1 is put on the road and formally documented as a production project.

## January 1978

Sales director, Dr Werner Schmidt, and head of marketing, Edgar von Schenck, talk about the A1 to Audi development engineers in the lounge of the Hotel Seewirt in Turrach, Austria. The following day they witness the now famous and *very* convincing demonstration of the first prototype in severe winter conditions on Europe's steepest mountain road – the Turracher Hohe – which has gradients of up to 23 per cent. The car runs on ordinary summer tyres with no snow chains. Needless to say, it romps up the hill with no trouble at all and gains yet more converts to the 4WD cause.

## April 1978

At Germany's Hockenheim GP circuit the A1 surprised even its designers. With an engine tuned to only 160bhp, it returns lap times only slightly slower than those recorded by cars with up to 240bhp on tap. In truth, this would be expected on a wet track, but on dry tarmac it is nothing short of astounding, and certainly a key result in the quattro's development.

## May 1978

The Product Strategy Commission, chaired by Volkswagen AG engineering director, Dr Ernst Fiala, gives the go-ahead for completing development of the A1 up to the production stage.

## Summer 1978

The Gaimersheim fire brigade turns its hoses on the side of a hill to produce a sea of mud. Toni Schmucker, chairman of the VW board, tackles the muddy hill in several vehicles with different transmission layouts. Not surprisingly, the A1 is the only one to reach the top and, also without surprise, the chairman becomes another convert.

## Summer 1979

Development of the car progresses to the stage where it becomes the A2. Another Audi 80 is used to test the mechanical components. A fire starts in one prototype during trials in the Sahara desert. It is traced to a fuel line which has burst while using a 286bhp competition engine to test the car to its limits.

## September 1979

Hannu Mikkola, a Finnish world-class professional rally driver, makes the trip

*Ironically, the turbocharged Audi 200 did not go on sale in the UK until April 1980 – a month after the quattro's launch in Switzerland. Priced at £12,950, the importers reckoned on selling a thousand during the rest of the year, and they made much of its high performance, reasonable fuel consumption (a claimed average of 24mpg) and its high specification – air conditioning was the only listed option. Note the twin headlamps, also featured on the quattro.*

to Ingolstadt to find out about the latest developments. After a test drive in the prototype quattro he declares that he would be willing to drive the car as soon as it is ready for rallying. A canny move if ever there were one.

## 1980

The ultimate test of man and machine could truly be said to be the 10,000 mile Paris–Dakar rally. Audi enters four Iltis 4WDs for the event, one of which is equipped with a 5-cylinder engine, and all of which, of course, have what is essentially the quattro drivetrain. To finish at all is a great achievement and the Iltis quartet take first, second, fourth and ninth places. Any lingering doubts about the longevity of such a complex drive system are surely swept away by this.

## March 1980

Expecting that the specified homologation production run of 400 cars will be the total requirement, Audi shows the quattro at the Geneva Motor Show. The Press and public are stunned – but no more than Audi! It soon becomes apparent that not only will the company's acknowledged aim to bring 4WD across the whole range be achievable, but also that there will be a need for more than the 400 versions

of the turbocharged homologation special. Many more, in fact, as we shall see.

## QUATTRO CONNECTIONS

### Jensen Interceptor FF

Though Audi was the first company to make 4WD road-going cars commercially viable, the concept had been tried before. Back in the mists of 1964 there were rumours at the London Motor Show that small British motor manufacturer Jensen was to be involved with a 4WD sports car of some description. At the time they were producing their own CV8 (complete with 6.3 litre Chrysler V8 engine) as well as the Tiger for Sunbeam and chassis and bodies for the Austin Healey 3000. Though the rumours were denied, the company, in conjunction with Ferguson, produced in the following year a prototype 4WD version of the CV8, with a slightly longer (by 5 inches) wheelbase and Dunlop Maxaret anti-lock brakes – a system developed from contemporary aircraft technology, but relatively crude by modern standards. It didn't go into production, but in 1966 an FF (Ferguson Formula) version of the newly-announced Jensen Interceptor was offered. It was hardly a sales success, and by the time production

ceased in 1971 only 387 cars had been made. Its top speed of 137mph was the same as the early quattros, and the 0–60 time of 8.1 seconds was very respectable, though in doing so the thirsty Chrysler V8 engine could only deliver around 10/12mpg.

### Audi 200 Turbo

It was in 1979 that Audi first put a tur-bocharged car into production – the 200. This was basically a more up-market version of the Audi 100 4-door saloon, loaded with goodies and electric everything. It featured Bosch K-Jetronic fuel injection, an aluminium cylinder head and a KKK turbocharger, enabling it to produce 170bhp at a heady 5300rpm. Though it could hardly be said to be refined (especially when compared with similarly-priced luxury cars from the likes of Mercedes and Jaguar), it was fast enough, and with a 3-speed auto could reach 60mph from rest in 9.4 seconds and hit a maximum speed of around 126mph.

### The VW Iltis

Though badged a VW, the Iltis was designed and built (at Ingolstadt) by Audi following a direct commission from the West German defence committee. The vehicle was to replace the DKW Munga and was to be, effectively, a Land Rover equivalent – a go-anywhere vehicle, with ruggedness, reliability and huge ground-clearance built-in. The power plant was not unusual, in that it utilised the 1.7 litre unit already being used in the Audi 80 and its close cousin the VW Passat. The 4WD system was something different, though. Most conventional off-road vehicles of this sort featured a transfer box to put the drive to both ends of the vehicle, despite the fact that this added plenty of weight and

complexity, and increased fuel costs. Audi took the drive to the rear wheels by using a hollow output shaft, a simple and very effective solution and one which was soon to revolutionise the motoring world, especially World Championship rallying.

*Top The VW (née Audi) Iltis is an oddity from any angle and ... (Courtesy Neil Birkett)*

*Above ... a most unlikely starting point for one of the world's greatest rally cars. But that's the way it is! (Courtesy Neil Birkett)*

# Chapter 2

# Road car heritage

The Audi quattro was unveiled to a suitably awed public and Press at the Geneva Motor Show in March 1980. The car's in-line 5-cylinder, 10 valve, SOHC, turbocharged 2144cc engine had a power output of 200bhp at 5500rpm and torque of 210lb/ft at 3500rpm, with a quoted maximum speed of 138mph and acceleration of 0–60mph in 7.1 seconds. The engine, with alloy head and iron cylinder block, was mounted at 27.5 degrees from the vertical and had a compression ratio of 7:1. It was fitted with Bosch K-Jetronic fuel injection and a KKK turbocharger with 0.85 bar max. boost limited by wastegate. Transmission was by permanent 4WD and the electro-pneumatic centre and rear differentials could be locked manually by twin lever-operated cables.

All the first models were fitted with the four-spoke steering wheel taken from the Audi 200T, with the word 'turbo' embossed at the centre. The analogue dash was 'borrowed' from the Audi 80, but because of the inclusion of the turbo boost gauge there was no room for a water temperature gauge – a great worry for serious drivers of a car like this, on which the manufacturers had paid great attention to the need for extra cooling.

It's worth remembering that, since this was a handbuilt car, the makers were free to adapt and change almost at will as feedback from owners and the research department filtered through. In many cases it is possible to find that improvements listed for a new model year actually first started appearing on the last models of the expiring year.

## FIRST ENCOUNTERS

Brian Ricketts, quattro guru of BR Motorsport, recalls his first encounter with the beast:

'In 1980 I was involved in preparing the Works Audi 80 touring cars for Audi UK Ltd, which were driven by Stirling Moss, Richard Lloyd and Tony Lanfranchi. This gave me the great excuse to visit Audi's factory at Ingolstadt in southern Germany with Vic Elford who, after his celebrated exploits rallying a Works Porsche and an outing or two in Formula One for Cooper, had become our team manager. The purpose of the trip was to pick up some parts for the race cars, and we were travelling in a venerable VW Type 2 van, from which Vic wrung its modest best.

'Arriving (eventually) at the factory gates, we were greeted by Jurgen Stockmar, Audi's leading development engineer, who gave us a guided tour of the Audi 80 production line before ushering us into the inner sanctum of the Development Division, where he worked. The coupé had not then been launched, but all around were Audi 80 fastback body shells, and in the Engine Development Department he showed us all sorts of intriguing devices, many of which have never seen the light of day (keep hoping!).

'It was in the Competition Department (very small in those days), that we were introduced to Freddy Kottulinski, who doubled as a test driver for Audi when he was not rallying. Proudly, he showed us a truly bizarre creation – a VW/Audi Iltis built for the German army, into which he had somehow managed to squeeze a turbocharged 5-cylinder Audi engine before taking it rallying in the desert with remarkable success. Silently, I contemplated the bravery of Freddy's intrepid navigator.

'He then announced that Audi had just acquired an old supermarket down the road which was to become their new competitions department, where they would develop and run a new rally car.

'"Would you like a little treat?" asked Freddy excitedly, and he disappeared into the factory complex.

'He reappeared a few minutes later driving a rusty red coloured vehicle bearing one of the body shells we had seen earlier, but this one featured flared arches and wide wheels. "What on earth's that?" asked Vic. "Something special," said Freddy. "Want a ride?" You bet we did!

'Off we went, heading for a test track somewhere behind the Audi factory, Vic in the front seat and me bundled into the back. When we arrived I noticed with innocent unconcern that it comprised a series of dirt tracks and gravel roads. As he engaged the diff locks, Freddy, of course, was determined to impress a former ace like Vic, leaving me to strap myself in and fend for myself. It was an awesome demonstration. It was the first Ur quattro and I became an instant convert.'

The car was first available in the UK in March 1981 priced at £14,500. VAG imported a total of only 163 LHD cars, with chassis numbers starting from 85 BA90099. A complete specification included central locking, electric windows and relatively skinny 5-stud (as on the Audi 100) Ronal 6J x 15in wheels with 205/60HR 15 tyres, which were usually Goodyear. One of the options was for 7J Fuchs alloys fitted with 205/55 15 tyres, a particularly apt option as the Fuchs wheels were regularly to be seen on the rally quattros on loose surface stages.

The bluff shape of the quattro gave it a drag coefficient (Cd) of 0.43. At its launch this was pretty average, but with the super smooth Audi 100 launch on the horizon and Audi about to boast about its Cd of just 0.30, it was deemed politic not to make too much of the quattro's Cd. The gear change was distinctly notchy (something of an Audi trademark) and the transmission ratios came in for some criticism because of the gap between 2nd and 3rd.

Much was made of the car's ability to offer stunning performance but still turn in reasonable fuel consumption. The official figures were: urban cycle 18mpg; constant 56mph 35.7mpg; constant 75mph 27.1mpg. It was also emphasised that, although it was a coupé and very fast, it could still carry

four passengers with ease – in truth, the fifth occupant, sitting on the bulge in the rear seat, would not have been particularly comfortable.

The headlamps were halogen, double rectangle with headlamp washers as standard (in the UK) and with fog lamps built into the lower front valance. The windscreen included a green anti-glare strip. At the rear, the fluorescent strip running across the boot was red (later it was black) and had an integrated fog lamp.

The diagonally-split braking system was not ABS, but there was a disc at each corner operated by single pot callipers.

## ORIGINAL DIMENSIONS

| | |
|---|---|
| Length | 173.4in (4404mm) |
| Width | 67.8in (1722mm) |
| Height | 52.9in (1343mm) |
| Wheelbase | 99.3in (2522mm) |
| Track (front/rear) | 55.9in/57.4in |
| | (1419mm/1457mm) |
| Turning circle | 37ft |
| Luggage capacity | 13.8 cu/ft |
| Kerb weight | 2844lb (1291kg) |

Audi UK expected to sell 200/300 a year despite being only available in left-hand drive (LHD), and predicted that the world-wide sales would run at 2,500 a year. Initially, although all 350 Audi dealers were authorised to undertake routine service items, the importers appointed six dealers as specialist quattro centres, each of which operated a quattro demonstrator and were specially trained to carry out major servicing and repairs. The six were: Jack Barclay European, London; Dovercourt, St Johns Wood, London; Central Garage (Surrey) Ltd, Cobham; Smithfield Garage, Birmingham; Massingberd, Harrogate; and Ian Skelly, Glasgow. As can be seen, there were huge areas of the country that were mega-miles from a specialist.

Reflecting the demand for the car, it was announced on 22 October 1982 that right-hand drive (RHD) versions of the quattro would be available for the UK market, and Audi's sales expecta-

tions were raised to 400 a year. The first UK RHD chassis number was 85 DA 900556. At this stage the quattro was still unique – it was the only production car to have permanent 4WD not designed for off-road use – and its rallying successes were being used to great effect in the sales effort. The car had already notched up more than 100 international victories and had clinched national championships in America, Sweden, Germany and Austria.

Improvements for the 1983 model were the introduction of single-piece Cibié lights, rather than the twin lamps of the original models, and rear suspension revisions to make for better handling. The differential locks were upgraded to a single-knob vacuum operation from the end of the year, and the rear axle geometry was slightly modified so that toe-in variations under all road conditions were even smaller. The upshot was that handling, straight-line stability and resistance to cross-winds were all improved. Because of this the rear stabiliser bar was deleted and the front stabiliser bar was mounted on special links for better insulation against vibration.

For the 1984 model, Bosch ABS anti-lock brakes were fitted as standard to improve safety and general driveability. However, when either of the diff locks was engaged, the ABS would automatically be cut-out. The transmission also featured modified 3rd and 4th gear ratios.

A digital dashboard was installed, which included the Audi Autocheck system. The information was displayed in green on three rectangular glass fluorescent 'tubes'. The display showed two rows of five standard warning lights at either side of the odometer and trip meter. On the left the lights were: ABS, acoustic check system (electronic voice), engine oil pressure, alternator, emergency (hazard) lights. On the right they were: rear fog lamp, high beam, turn signals, heated rear window, handbrake/brake fluid. The awkward-to-use switchgear around the instrument binnacle was replaced in common with related vehicles in the Audi range. The

Audi sought to push the quattro's up-market image right from the start, intimating that it would be useful for the rich, horsey set – from pulling that horse box on muddy ground to …

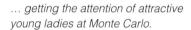

… getting the attention of attractive young ladies at Monte Carlo.

Most quattros (of any vintage) were fitted with Ronal alloy wheels, but an option to the original 6J Ronals were these 5-spoke, 7J Fuchs alloys. They were also used on rally quattros on loose-surface stages.

Right *The dash mirrored that of the contemporary Audi 80, save for the diff lock indicators below the Blaupunkt Coburg push-button radio/cassette deck. The 'turbo' wheel was taken from the Audi 200.*

Below right *Though the dash and control layout may have been sombre, the rest of the interior trim was '70s garish, to say the least.*

Below *The rear of the car was changed over the years. This shows the original set up of normal-coloured (red/amber) tail lamps. The boot lid had a red prismatic 'coupé' strip along its lower edge and badging was stick-on; top left was 'Audi' and top right was 'quattro'. There was a red reflector set into the top of the plastic rear bumper and the boot lid spoiler was black.*

Bottom right *The rear side glass was etched with the 'quattro' script until 1984 (although some 1985 models featured it as stocks were used up). Note the period sticker – a later addition – declaring Audi as 1982 world rally champions (the manufacturers' title).*

new switches were much more satisfactory, easier to use and with rotary controls for the lighting and panel light rheostat. The steering wheel was replaced by the then current Audi 100 4-spoke wheel, and the wiper sweep was improved by using Audi 100 wiper arms and blades. The upholstery was redesigned to give an '80s (rather than a '70s) look to the car. The UK price was marked up to £17,051.

In spring 1984 RHD pattern windscreen wipers were finally fitted. The suspension (springs/dampers) was uprated and the car was lowered by 20mm (3/4in). Wider Ronal alloy wheels (8J) were fitted instead of the relatively narrow 6J versions. The new wheels were fitted with Pirelli P700 tyres, 215/50 VR rating, in place of the previous 205/60 HR 15s. The wheel arches were 'doctored' to suit the extra width by the simple expedient of folding in part of the lip around the wing. Electric seat heating and leather trim were optional extras. The steering wheel changed to the more modern 'four-ring' model as used on other Audis of the time, albeit leather-rimmed for quattro application.

For 1985 Audi facelifted its 80/90 Coupé range, including the quattro. The front presented a smoother face with the Cibié light units sitting either side of the sloping centre grille section. The rear boot lid spoiler was colour-coded and the boot lid prismatic and rear lamp clusters were smoked black.

In his September 1984 road test of the '85 model for *Autosport*, Mike McCarthy was already suggesting that the quattro might be the Car of the Decade. He was right.

In spring 1985 the push-pull knob for the vacuum operated differential locks was replaced by a rotary control which

*The engine bay was crowded, to say the least.*

# Road car heritage

Right *The quattro was originally only available in the UK in LHD form from March 1981, but by the end of 1982 the factory had relented and also made it in RHD.*

Below right *Changes over the years were subtle. This 1984 car shows the RHD pattern wipers, single-piece Cibié headlamps and wider 8J x 15in Ronal alloy wheels. ABS had also been made standard by this time.*

Bottom right *In the US, the overall look of the quattro was ruined by the addition of huge 'safety' bumpers at front and rear. As might be expected, the specification of American cars was 'fully loaded', including as standard such luxuries as air conditioning.*

Below *Audi adverts had already developed the dry style for which they are famous. This one plays on the uniqueness of a 4WD road-car, as the opposition struggled to put their own four-by-fours into production.*

The quattro benefited from the general model range facelift of the 1985 model year. The radiator grille was given a sloping angle and at the rear …

… the rear lamps and prismatic were smoked black and the spoiler was colour-coded. The 'Audi' and 'quattro' badging stayed where it was, but now raised plastic lettering was used. The 4-ring logo in the centre was stick-on.

Inside the car, the much-improved switchgear around the binnacle was added, although with it …

*... came the controversial digital dash and synthesised warning system. The dash is seen here out of the car where it can be seen that it comprises three glass fluorescent 'bulbs' – break them at your peril!*

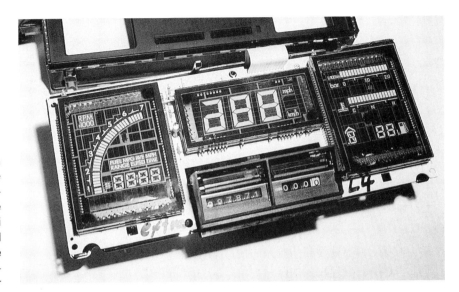

left, alongside it in the centre console, enough room for some extra gauges. However, there wasn't quite enough room for standard round analogue dials, so an LED-type bar graph volt-meter and oil temperature gauge were fitted. It's also possible that Audi thought that they would match in well with the digital dash arrangement. The gauges came in for the obvious comments that they were badly placed for the driver to see, but it's better to have them than not.

Some of the later 1986 models were fitted with twin hydraulic bonnet struts (replacing the single rod fitted since the launch).

In common with other 5-cylinder Audi engines, the capacity was increased to 2226cc and hydraulic tappets were introduced for the 1988 model. The compression ratio was raised from 7:1 to 8.6:1, a different ECU was fitted and the new smaller turbocharger was also water-cooled for increased reliability and reduced turbo lag. Power and torque remained at 200bhp and 210lb/ft, though both peak figures were available lower down the rev range. Engine cooling was improved and the quoted top speed was the same at 138mph, though the 0–60 acceleration time improved to 6.7 secs (from a previous quoted figure of 7.1 secs). Brake performance was upped with the introduction of front twin-pot callipers.

The instrument binnacle was slightly redesigned for improved clarity. The

*The console layout changed with the addition of digital bar graph LED warning lights for oil temperature and voltage, and the differentials were now locked by means of a two-position rotary switch. Note the ABS lock-out switch and (optional) seat-heating switches to the left of the steering wheel.*

By 1987 the rear end had changed once more – can you spot the omission? The central Audi rings have gone, but by 1988 …

… chrome was the thing to have. As you can see, the rings, plus the 'Audi quattro' nomenclature are all featured in raised chromed lettering. Torsen diff cars also got a fibreglass boot lid, usually recognisable by the 'rippled' effect when viewed at an angle.

The 1988 models got the 2226cc 'MB' engine with hydraulic tappets. The engine bay looked much the same, though give-aways are the extra pipery around the rear of the airflow sensor, and the use of a different power steering pump. Not visible, but very important was the change to a water-cooled turbocharger.

*It also gained the Torsen (torque-sensing) differential which necessitated yet another change in the centre console layout. This time the rotary switch was changed for a simple on/off switch to control the rear differential. Note the standard Blaupunkt Toronto radio/cassette deck. Though tame now, quattros were always fitted with top-notch Blaupunkt units as standard.*

digital dash layout was revised, with the semi-electronic mileage counter being deleted in favour of a full electronic version, and the unloved voice synthesiser bit the dust. The displays became LCD (liquid crystal) in semi-analogue and digital form, rather than the previous fluorescent type, and the turbo boost gauge was ditched. As previously, there was an on-board computer which could be switched from imperial to metric and which used the new electronic speedometer to add more functions than before. A tilt-only sunroof was fitted as standard. On the outside, interlocking Audi chrome rings replaced the stick-on badging of the previous models.

First appearing on the MKIII Audi 80/90 quattros, a Torsen (TORque-SENsing) central differential was fitted to the 4WD system, as opposed to the previous manual-lock, bevel type system. The new diff normally split the torque 50/50 between the front and rear axles but could vary it up to 25/75 or 75/25 if traction was reduced at either end. Unlike earlier models, the Torsen system did not affect the operation of ABS. The differential lock changed from a rotary control to an electronic push-on/push-off switch as used in the MKIII Audi 80/90/Coupé range. When selected, the ABS was deactivated but automatically reinstated when the speed exceeded more than 15mph.

The 20-valve cars were introduced for the 1990 model year and, though outwardly they appeared to be exactly the same as before, there were consid-

*The first series digital dash was junked (along with the voice) and a fully digital, LED dash was fitted.*

*The steel tilting (but not sliding) sunroof became standard. When not in use ...*

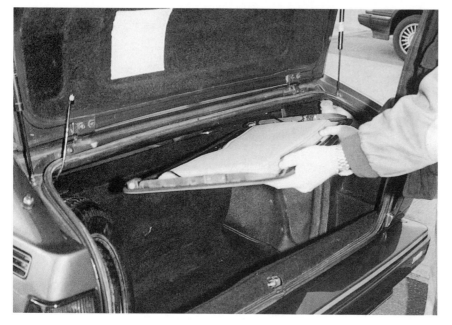

*... it could be removed totally and stored in a bracket under the rear parcel shelf, in the boot.*

*The quattro was often criticised for its lack of boot space, but it's not all bad; the author squeezed a Jaguar automatic gearbox in the back of his '85 model – with room to spare!*

*The same, but very, very different. At first glance, the 20v quattro appears identical to the 10v model, unless you look really hard …*

*… at the boot lid, where it's assumed that you now know it's an Audi quattro.*

erable engine changes. The twin cam unit used the crossflow aluminium cylinder head developed from the Sport quattro which, along with the impressive Bosch Motronic engine management system and an increase in compression ratio to 9.3:1, raised the power to 220bhp at 5,900rpm. More impressive was the torque – a whopping 228lb/ft of torque at just 1950rpm. All the valves were specially strengthened and the exhaust valves were sodium cooled.

Top speed was up to 142mph and the 0–60 time was cut to a Ferrari-esque 5.9 seconds. The increased torque meant that in-gear acceleration improved and, because of the need for less gear changing, so did fuel economy. Two three-way regulated catalytic converters were fitted which meant that the car could only ever be run on unleaded fuel. Inside, the part-leather trimmed seats had been redesigned to offer better anatomical support and had the quattro nomenclature written into the luxurious Jacquard satin trim. Electric seat heating and a superb leather-rimmed steering wheel (badged Audi and made by Personal) were standard. Leather was also used in the door trims, various compartments and storage trays. The carpet was the same hard-wearing wool compound used in the recently introduced top-of-the-range Audi V8.

## PREACHING TO THE CONVERTED

Though the first quattros imported were

*Inside the car, luxury reigned, with a (Personal) Audi Sport wheel and Jacquard-trimmed, part-leather seats with the quattro logo running through the squab and backrest.*

all LHD, several were converted to RHD, some more successfully than others. The most successful were those completed by GTi Engineering and David Sutton Motorsport (now Historic Motorsport). Brian Ricketts takes up the story:

'In 1981 I was co-owner of GTi Engineering at Silverstone, and because of our successes in racing the works Audi 80 cars we got requests from customers wanting a RHD quattro, not least because I had been the first to convert a MKI Golf GTi to RHD in the UK. However, Audi said that the quattro could not be produced in RHD form.

'Unfortunately, we did not have the resources to go out and buy this £14,500 supercar and pull it apart just to see if it could be done – with the real possibility that it couldn't. Happily, one of our frustrated customers came to see us and said he was willing to take the risk and did not mind what it cost.

'We completely stripped the car from the 'B' pillars forward; engine and gearbox, carpets, dashboard, steering, windscreen and wiring all had to be removed until the bulkhead was clear. We cut off all the LHD brackets and welded new ones to take the RHD components, including provision for a hydraulic clutch cylinder as the coupé parts only provided for a cable clutch. When we were sure we had moved everything, we had to weld up all the unwanted holes and repaint the bulkhead.

'The rebuild was straightforward, but I was amazed at the number of things that were different on a RHD car; the door mirrors were among the many items that we had not originally considered would need changing. Anyway the car started first time and drove really well, much to our relief – and no doubt even more to our customer's! We then drove the car to Audi's HQ at Milton Keynes and parked it right outside the main entrance. A large crowd soon gathered around it – quattros always had

this effect, even in LHD format.

'Within a week we received an order for two cars – one for the MD and one to be shipped to Ingolstadt.'

## PRICE PROGRESSION

Over its lifetime the price of the quattro more than doubled and, compared with similar cars (even other Audis), it always appeared expensive. It was, though, virtually a handbuilt car, and models came off the production line at an incredibly slow pace.

| At UK launch (LHD) | £14,500 |
| December 1981 | £15,037 |
| October 1982 | £17,051 |
| Sept 1983 | £17,721 |
| September 1984 | £20,401 |
| May 1985 | £22,615 |
| November 1985 | £23,273 |
| February 1986 | £24,204 |
| December 1986 | £26,346 |
| May 1987 | £28,110 |
| August 1988 | £30,199 |
| *March 1989 | £31,367 |
| **20v** | |
| 1989 | £32,995 |
| 1990 | £35,523 |

*In March 1989, Audi made the incredible move of reducing quattro prices across the range. You'll note, however, that the turbo quattro price just kept on rising.

By the time of its demise, the 20v quattro was almost £5,000 dearer than the S2 Coupé with the same engine installed. Unfortunately, this led to declining sales and gave Audi the opportunity it needed to axe the Ur quattro.

## DRIVING THE QUATTRO

The 4WD quattro was designed to be compatible with the average driver's natural reactions, and it feels similar to most FWD Audis. The original suspension set-up was for slight understeer, so that the cornering radius increases if speed is excessive and is tightened gently as the throttle is closed. Though

'enthusiastic' drivers claim to prefer oversteer, few of us can really lay claim to being capable of controlling a tail-happy 200bhp motor car, especially on public roads. If forcibly provoked, the quattro can be made to oversteer.

Straight line stability is better than a comparable FWD car and cross-wind susceptibility is as low. 4WD has no direct effect on aquaplaning behaviour, though it is possible to use narrower tyres – and of a softer compound – than for a similarly-powered 2WD car (because each tyre is only handling around 25 per cent of the power instead of 50 per cent). The wider the tyres, the more likely any car is to aquaplane.

### Braking

The braking capability is not increased by 4WD, but the point to remember is that the acceleration available with 4WD is much greater and it is easy for drivers to find themselves going much faster than they would normally. The laws of physics must be respected, because the car can only grip the road – to accelerate or brake – through four small patches of rubber, and whilst the acceleration and cornering capabilities are improved through doubling the number of driven wheels, the number of wheels braked remains the same!

### Economy

The extra components relating to the quattro 4WD system means that the car weighs around 75kg more than a FWD car and 30kg more than a RWD car. There are also unavoidable friction losses through additional bearings, gears, seals and oil churning. But, unlike conventional arrangements used in off-roaders and utility vehicles, the Audi transmission reduces these losses to an absolute minimum.

Audi carried out extensive tests during which a 4WD car was converted to 2WD by removing the drive shafts. The 4WD car showed a fuel consumption penalty of around 2.5 per cent at constant speeds of between 60 and 80mph. At a constant 100mph this difference was reduced to around 1 per cent.

The narrowing of this percentage results from the fact that when higher power levels are transmitted there is more tyre slip, and when only two wheels are driven the power loss increases much more sharply than when four wheels are driven. When driven hard, with heavy acceleration or on a slippery surface, the 4WD penalty can drop to zero or even turn into an economy advantage by comparison.

It should be noted that otherwise identical production engines can vary in absolute power output by +/- 5 per cent. A 6-cylinder engine typically uses 5–10 per cent more fuel than a 4-cylinder engine, and cars with automatic transmission use 15–20 per cent more fuel than similar vehicles with manual transmission. The average quattro owner is unlikely to be able to measure any extra fuel that might be used and, in truth, is not likely to be too worried about overall fuel consumption anyway.

## The real world

If we assume that most of us cannot drive as well as Mikkola or Mouton, such facts, figures and considerations are best reserved for pub conversations. The plain fact is that driving a quattro is a delight; a soul-stirring performance worthy of Porsche or Ferrari. A flick through just a few of the quoted comments of hard-bitten and hard-to-impress motoring journalists over the years will clearly show that this is not just the author's opinion. The quattro is a driver's car – one for those who truly enjoy the (fast diminishing) art of driving. The characteristic whistle of the turbo pre-empts a howling exhaust note as the power meets the torque and slings car and driver at the horizon with eye-widening velocity. Experienced quattro drivers will have long-since mastered the art of quick changes with the clunky gear shift and, with the engine still on song, the progress continues unabated. Cornering speeds are generally much higher than 'performance' 2WD cars, regardless of which end is driven, and in general allows a quattro to keep pace with more recent engine developments amongst the opposition.

Also, it transcends more exotic vehicles because its use is not limited to high days and holidays – 4WD means that rain (always a possibility in the UK) does little to hinder progress. And its general user-friendliness means that it doesn't get moody and unpleasant in heavy traffic.

The quattro can be most things to most people, flattering average driving and rewarding the skilled pilot like a 'sports' car should. At a time when jelly-mould, aerodynamic 'world cars' rule, driving pleasure has largely been lost. With a quattro you can join that elite band of drivers who know where to find it again. But beware – take liberties and the accident you will surely have will happen at a much higher speed than you would believe possible. If you *really* want to get the best from your quattro, contact the Quattro Owners Club for details of the track days and/or Audi UK for details of their quattro Driving Days, where expert tuition is available.

## THE SPORT QUATTRO

Often referred to incorrectly as the quattro Sport, the Sport quattro was truly a 'homologation special', produced in order that its rally counterpart could attempt to fend off the attentions of the space-framed specials produced by the opposition in the Group B category. Introduced at the 1983 Frankfurt Motor Show, it certainly pulled the eye, looking as if it had been the middle car in an autobahn pile-up! It was based on the WR-engined car and was only produced in LHD format. As far as can be ascertained, only one car was changed to RHD by, of course, David Sutton Motorsport (now Historic Motorsport).

## Styling

This most obvious difference between the Sport and the Ur quattro was achieved simply by hacking 320mm from the centre of the car, just behind the driver's door, and hacking the propshaft accordingly. The purpose was to give the rally cars more 'chuckability', something the long, nose-heavy original cars lacked. With a 55/45 front/rear weight split, the overall handling should have been much improved, although it took the advent of massive wings and spoilers to make the rally-going version handle as it should. The even wider flared arches just about covered the huge 9in Ronal alloy wheels shod with 235/45VR 15 Michelin (or 225/50VR Pirelli) rubber and resulted in the meanest looking road-going quattro ever.

In keeping with its rally heritage, steel was used more or less as a last resort. Kevlar (considerably stronger than steel and used in the construction of Formula 1 cars), glassfibre laminate, carbon fibre and/or composites were used wherever possible, including the front apron, bonnet, front wings, centre and rear window members, roof, rear side panels, boot flat and rear apron. Some areas were reinforced with aluminium. Apart from a gain in strength, there was the all-important saving of weight – around 300kg less than the LWB quattro – a vital matter in a successful rally car.

## Engine and brakes

The engine was the DOHC, 20v cross-flow unit (a derivation of which was used in the 20v Ur quattro, and is still in use today in the Audi 100 S4) which, thanks to the huge KKK turbo and LH Jetronic injection, produced a hefty 306bhp. However, in rallying evolution guise, the same engine was good for 600bhp! The engine capacity changed from the usual 2144cc to 2133cc. This was so that Audi could start within the 3-litre rallying category. With a multiplication factor of 1.4 applied to balance out the effect of turbocharging, the Sport just sneaked in with a theoretical capacity of 2986cc.

Original performance figures were 0–60 in 4.9 seconds and a top speed of 155mph. All this 'go' required plenty of attention to the 'stop' department – ventilated and grooved discs were fitted all round, together with four-pot callipers. ABS was standard which, like the contemporary quattro, was automatically switched off when the differential locks were engaged, and could be switched off at any time by the driver, if required.

Additional track control arms were fitted to support the wishbones and, at the rear, a separate calliper was used for the handbrake. Because the rally drivers had complained about reflections from the Ur quattro windscreen, the Sport used the 'A' pillars and screen from the Audi 80 saloon, rather than the raked screen of the coupé.

## Inside

The interior of the car was sumptuous, with Recaro seats and full leather trim. From a driving point of view, the instrumentation was superb, with clear analogue dials (like the MKIII Audi 80/90 range) and ancillary gauges (water temperature, oil temperature, oil pressure) positioned almost alongside the main binnacle in the clear line of sight. The switchgear was a mish-mash, with some later model Audi parts bin switches (heated rear window, seat heater, etc) sitting alongside an original-style push/pull pneumatic differential locking knob and older Audi-style electric window control buttons. The driver and passenger were securely held in place by a pair of competition Sabelt harnesses. The Sport was described as a 2+2 but, in truth, you'd have to be Snow White to successfully carry your best friends in the back!

## Production and price

Production of the 214 Sport quattros began in 1984. However, not all escaped the confines of the factory, as chassis numbers SQ85EA905 006 to SQ85EA905 024 were used as 'in-house' experimental cars, and numbers SQ85EA905 101 to SQ85EA905 120 were commandeered by Audi Sport for 'test' purposes – many were written off in this way. Incredibly, the last Sport quattro produced didn't leave the factory until 1987 and, in fact, had previously been used for spares. As a homologation special, the price was also special. The original UK price ticket was £51,000, but selling them wasn't difficult, as rich enthusiasts around the world queued up clutching carrier-bags of currency, eager to buy such an exclusive and important automobile.

## Colours

Not surprisingly, most Sport quattros were red, with the final colour count being as follows:

| | |
|---|---|
| Red | 128 |
| White | 48 |
| Blue | 21 |
| Green | 15 |
| Black | 2 |

(Of the two black cars produced, one listed its first owner as one Walter Röhrl!)

## Technical specification

| | |
|---|---|
| Power | 306bhp at 6700rpm (225 kW) |
| Torque | 258lb/ft at 3700rpm (350Nm) |
| Capacity | 2133cc |
| Bore x stroke | 86.4mm x 79.3mm |
| Compression ratio | 8:1 |
| Fuel | 98 Ron (Premium) |
| Top speed | 155mph (250kph) |
| 0–50mph (80kph) | 3.6 seconds |
| 0–62mph (100kph) | 4.9 seconds |
| Climbing ability | 40 per cent |
| Kerb weight | 2862lb (1298kg) |
| Length | 163.8in (4160mm) |
| Width | 70in (1780mm) |
| Height | 53in (1345mm) |
| Wheelbase | 87.5in (2224mm) |
| Track (front/rear) | 58.5in/58.4in (1487mm/1485mm) |
| Wheels/tyres | 9J x 15in light alloy, 235/45 VR15 Michelin (or 225/50VR 15 Pirelli) |
| Winter use | 7J x 15in light alloy wheels with 185/65 HR 15 (87T) |

Like the Ur quattro, the Sport featured pneumatic centre and rear differential locks and a 5-speed gearbox. The Torsen diff appeared later in the quattro's history and was never fitted to the Sport. The ratios were different from the LWB car, as follows:

| | |
|---|---|
| 1st | 3.500:1 |
| 2nd | 2.083:1 |
| 3rd | 1.368:1 |
| 4th | 0.962:1 |
| 5th | 0.759:1 |

*The Sport quattro was truly a homologation special. The rally rules required a build-run of at least 200 cars, and Audi built 214, although only 175 escaped into public ownership. Short on inches but not on horsepower, the 2133cc 20v engine produced 306bhp, which gave performance figures of 0–60 in 4.5 seconds and a top speed of 155mph. It's every enthusiast's dream, though spares prices are a nightmare – how about £11,000 for that composite bonnet?!*

Above *The trademark flared arches were extended still further to cope with those huge 9J wheels and 235/45 section tyres. The extra flaring can be seen clearly here as an extension to the original line of the bodywork.*

Top right *As subtle as a charging bull, the Sport quattro was simply about going extremely fast. Cooling was even more of a problem than on the 10v cars, hence the extra cooling grilles and larger radiator and ...*

Above right *... bonnet cooling grilles at the front and at the side for the turbo, and under the bonnet ...*

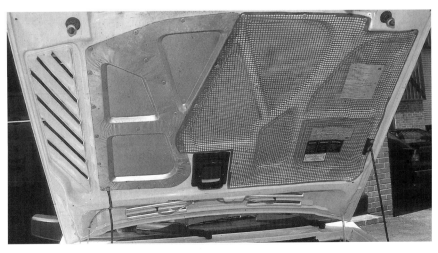

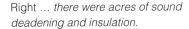

Right *... there were acres of sound deadening and insulation.*

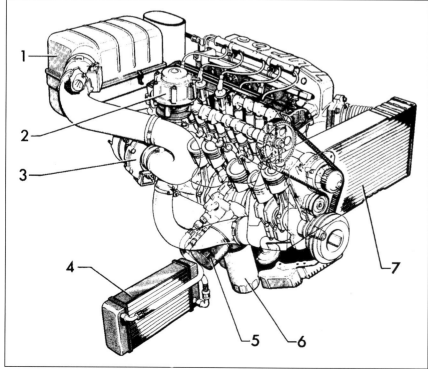

*But it was worth it – the hugely powerful engine looks, sounds and goes like no other. Check out the similarity with the later model quattro 20v.*

*The engine in detail. Compare the 10v and 20v LWB quattro units and spot the changes and similarities.*

*Key: 1. Air cleaner; 2. Wastegate; 3. Turbocharger; 4. Oil cooler; 5. Turbo oil filter; 6. Engine oil filter; 7. Charge air cooler.*

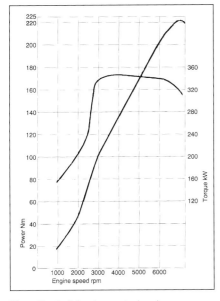

The effect of the larger turbocharger can be seen on this graph of power and torque production – all the 'go' is stacked at the top end of the rev range. Turbo lag is prominent, but it's worth the wait!

Inside, there was comprehensive instrumentation (and analogue dials), these being a mix and match collection of earlier and later Audi items. In fact, the hazard warning light switch had seen service in the MK1 VW Golf! Because of the better use of gauges, no computer was fitted. Luxury and leather were the order of the day with a specification which included ...

... top-notch, leather-covered Recaro seats. The stalk-mounted Blaupunkt stereo in this car is a non-standard addition.

## AN ENGLISHMAN IN INGOLSTADT

It comes as a bit of a shock to most quattro-istes to learn that the quattro's designer was Sheffield-born Englishman, Martin Smith. But what won't come as any surprise is that Martin is a true car enthusiast; in current jargon, a petrolhead of the first order and the sort of man who ran a Morgan 2-seater sports car and its antithesis, an Audi 200, and believed in them both.

After spending two years completing the post graduate car design course at the Royal College of Art, his sponsors (Ford) couldn't find him a job. So he joined Porsche for 2½ years before coming back to England and a job at Ogle Design. His talent shone through to the extent that he was 'head hunted' in 1977 by Audi to work as Project Manager on an interesting derivation of a new Audi Coupé – the Audi quattro.

The design brief, direct from Dr Piëch, stated that it should look technical and functional with an overall appearance to befit a supercar and, of course, it should be completed within the usual tight budget constraints.

It's interesting to note that while he was working on the angular, all-muscle fat-flared quattro, he was also part of the design team responsible for the super-smooth Audi 100. The latter, when launched, was the most aerodynamically efficient production saloon in the world, with a drag coefficient of just 0.30.

## CREATING THE QUATTRO

Hall N2 in Audi's huge manufacturing complex at Ingolstadt has a special place in Audi folklore, for this is where the Ur quattro was handbuilt for 11 years – an area then known throughout the factory as the 'exclusive boutique'. Compared to the hustle, bustle and noise in the rest of the plant, Hall N2 was a haven of relative quiet, since of the 1,700 cars Audi was producing each day during the late '80s only three were Ur quattros!

Whilst the main production line workers were each responsible for relatively few operations, all of the 20 plus personnel in Hall N2 would spend around two hours per vehicle and deal with an average of 100 components or sub-assemblies. With each car taking around 40 hours to complete, it follows that each man was responsible for some 5 per cent of the car. In essence, the building of each quattro was an assembly process, with components and sub-assemblies arriving from different parts of the factory throughout the day. Also some items came in from outside suppliers, notably those famous flared arches made by Baur (more commonly associated with BMW convertible conversions). Though the B2 quattro bodyshell pre-dated the later-style fully galvanized shells used on other models, some bits of the quattro *were* galvanized – the later the car, the more thorough the galvanization.

Roughly seven days after the painted bodyshell arrived in Hall N2, it left as a finished quattro, but not before it had completed some rigorous test procedures. The engine was started and run, and all electrical items were tested. The suspension geometry was checked (electronically) on the Polycontrol station and adjusted to the tolerances required. The car was then 'driven' on the rolling road for around five miles at speeds of up to 100mph. There followed a complete road test of around 40 miles over a mixture of roads in and around Ingolstadt. This was, and is, unique among production Audis.

The team of fortunate experts responsible for the testing were skilled in spotting any squeaks, rattles or other problems. According to Issay Popow, Chief Test Driver: 'We started with a cross-country section to assess the car's handling, and then we returned to the factory on the autobahn. We were restricted to 4000rpm, which meant in the quattro we were running in at about 115mph (185kph)! We always made two stops during the test to check fluid levels and look for leaks.'

Occasionally, particularly in winter, the test team would be involved in

minor mishaps but, according to Issay Popow, if a quattro was even slightly damaged, it would be scrapped and usable parts cannibalised for other cars.

Having survived the road test, it was then taken on the corrugated road section of the test track for the 'rattle' test – the surface, designed to put the steering and suspension through hell, made it impossible to travel at more than 10mph. After this, each quattro was driven into a huge 'shower cubicle' and drenched for ten minutes with some 3,500 litres of water. Other Audi models were actually only subjected to this test for 30 seconds! As well as checking for any leaks, the testers also took the opportunity to check the efficiency of the demister.

Unlike the rest of the factory, which worked a shift system to keep the lines going from 6 am to 11 pm, the quattro Hall was only open from 6 am to 2 pm – a single shift.

## SHOW AND GO

Although in 1991 the decision was made to discontinue the 20v quattro, that year saw Audi once again staggering the world's Press at the Frankfurt and Tokyo motor shows by introducing, respectively, the quattro Spyder and the Avus quattro. Neither of these has (yet) reached production, unlike the RS2 and TT series cars.

## TWO THAT GOT AWAY ...

### The quattro Spyder sports car study

At the Frankfurt Motor Show in September 1991, a bright orange, mid-engined sports car study wowed both Press and public. This was one of Audi's first forays into the world of non-steel bodywork, with the car being built of aluminium panels over a strong aluminium tubular spaceframe. The supplier was the Aluminium Company of America, and Audi was indeed Alcoa's first customer for aluminium spaceframe components from its £42m German plant at Soest. As well as being light and corrosion resistant, aluminium has an environmental advantage in that it is easily recyclable.

The engine was a 2.8 litre V6 unit producing 174bhp (as used in the then new Audi 100) and capable of touching 155mph. In the saloon cars it sat longitudinally at the front of the vehicle, but in the Spyder it was dropped into the centre of the car and turned through 90 degrees. The driveshafts that, in a FWD Audi, would turn the front wheels, became propshafts to the front and rear differentials (Torsen, of course) in the Spyder. It was a simple but effective set-up and one which allowed the choice of a 4-speed auto or 6-speed manual gearbox.

Just 4.22m long and 1.17m high, the Spyder ran on large 7J x 18in wheels (with 205/55 ZR 18 tyres) and featured a detachable roof which could be stored on top of the engine compartment when removed. The roof was, in fact, a solar panel which on sunny days could provide enough power to drive the blower, thus enabling ventilation of the interior to continue when the car was parked.

Sadly, the quattro Spyder did not reach the production line, largely because of the huge costs involved in developing a car which was essentially all-new.

## Engine specification

V6 petrol engine, OHC, multi-path intake manifold, mid-engine layout, transverse installation.

| | |
|---|---|
| Bore x stroke | 82.5mm x 86.4mm |
| Capacity | 2771cc |
| Compression ratio | 10.3:1 |
| Power | 174bhp at 5500rpm |
| Torque | 180lb/ft at 3000rpm |
| Fuel | Unleaded premium/95 RON |
| Transmission | Quattro permanent 4WD, variable torque split by self-locking Torsen centre differential, manual rear differential lock, 5-speed manual gearbox. |

## Avus quattro

Absolutely fabulous! Those without the soul to lust after Audi's greatest (to date) show car can only be pitied. Sleek as an Olympic athlete, its all-aluminium bodywork was left unpainted to show the whole car in appropriate polished silver. The overall length was 4.42m, the width 1.98m and the height a mere 1.17m. The bodywork weighed just 100kg and the tubular spaceframe tipped the scales at just 52kg. The chassis design and suspension set-up owed much to the experience Audi gained when racing in the American TransAm and IMSA series.

The mid-mounted engine was a revelation, being a 12 cylinder unit with three banks of four cylinders. Two banks of cylinders were arranged at an angle of 120 degrees with the third bank being positioned upright in the centre, between the other two banks. Apart from being highly efficient, it is also very little longer than a conventional 4-cylinder engine and thus suited for either front or mid-engined layouts. The 'W' formation set-up had a nominal capacity of 6 litres and produced a whopping 509bhp. Stopping the car required the use of huge ventilated discs at each corner.

As ever, the quattro drivetrain was used, this time with a 6-speed gearbox making the most of the Torsen set-up. The gearbox was positioned between the front wheels.

The name came from the Avus race track in Berlin, where many past racing records have been achieved. In startling silver, the Avus recalled the days of yore when teams went racing by colour; when the Auto Union 'Silver Arrows' went head-to-head with Italy's 'Red Devils', the blue Monoposti from France and cars from these shores in British Racing Green.

## ... AND TWO THAT DIDN'T!

### Avant RS2

Probably the fastest estate car in the world. The Avant RS2 was a collaboration between Audi and Porsche – or, rather, a more *overt* collaboration than

previously, as the two companies had often shared resources before, notably when Audi built the 924 and 944 series for Porsche. Clearly, much thought had been given to the naming of the beast, for though neither Audi nor Porsche is mentioned, Avant is Audi-speak for 'estate car' and RS is a long-established Porsche nomenclature for its sportiest motor cars. Both the Audi rings and the Porsche-script name appear on the car.

The original brief got the go-ahead early in 1993, and a team of designers (from both Audi and Porsche) worked around the clock to get the car ready for production in 1994. It was an impressive feat by any measure and Michael Holscher, project manager of the Porsche team, said: 'We are very proud of the achievement. The injection mouldings for the bumpers were our biggest headache and made in record time.'

Originally shown as a LHD-only car, response was such that a RHD version was produced, and the UK imported approximately 180.

The car was based on the Audi S2 estate car, itself no sluggard powered as it was by the 230bhp, 20v 5-cylinder engine (a derivative of the Sport quattro DOHC rally engine and used in 220bhp form in the last Ur quattros). The S2 engine was handed to Porsche, who breathed fire upon it to the point where it produced a staggering 315bhp – that's 143bhp per litre! Performance was suitably impressive, Audi claiming 5.4 seconds for the 0–62mph dash and an ungoverned maximum speed of 163mph. The special crank was protected by improved lubrication. Much of the credit for the extra 85bhp has to go to the huge KKK turbocharger, an obvious drawback of which is the turbo lag at low speeds. To some extent this was offset by the installation of a 6-speed Torsen transmission – quattro, of course. Another factor in its overall driveability was the production of a thumping great 302lb/ft of torque at just 3000rpm. There was also a lower-pressure exhaust system, re-profiled cam, re-tuned Bosch Motronic engine management system and enlarged injectors and intercooler.

Porsche 'Cup' 7J x 17in wheels were fitted, and they were shod with specially-made, ultra-low profile Dunlop 245/40 R17Z tyres. Visible through the large spokes were huge discs (ventilated at the front) with red Porsche callipers lifted directly from the company's 968 Sport. ABS was included, of course.

Inside, the driver was cosseted in hip-hugging, electrically adjustable sports Recaro seats while confronted by grey-backed dials with aluminium surrounds. Equipment was comprehensive, with virtually everything from the options list included as standard; and Martin Smith, designer of the Ur quattro, was responsible for the interior colour scheme.

The standard S2 shell was painted (but not trimmed) and then transported to Porsche's plant at Zuffenhausen, where it was deemed unnecessary to add any more reinforcement to take the extra power and torque – praise indeed, and reassuring to S2 owners. For two years up to the end of 1995, Porsche hand-assembled around 2,200 examples of the ultimate load-carrier in the plant where they were also making the E500 for Mercedes and where the fabulous Porsche 959 was made in the early 1980s.

Why make this fabulous, high performance vehicle an estate car? According to Audi's research, of all the 80 series S2 cars sold (that's the S2 and Audi 80 Avant S2), 46 per cent were Avants. According to the brochure, the RS2 was created '... in response to drivers of maturity and experience who want to express their individuality and to avoid the run-of-the-mill.'

## Avant RS2 technical specification

### Engine

Longitudinal, in-line 5-cylinder multivalve turbocharged unit, alloy cylinder head, iron block, water-cooled. Twin catalytic converters.

| | |
|---|---|
| Power | 315bhp at 6500rpm |
| Torque | 302lb/ft at 3000rpm |
| Capacity | 2226cc |
| Bore x stroke | 81.0mm x 86.4mm |
| Compression ratio | 9.3:1 |
| Fuel | Super premium/98 RON |
| Transmission | Permanent four-wheel drive with automatically locking Torsen differential, lockable rear axle differential, 6-speed close-ratio manual, hydraulic clutch, full synchromesh. |

### Official fuel consumption figures

| | |
|---|---|
| Urban cycle | 19.5mpg/14.5 litres per 100km |
| Constant 56mph | 37.2mpg/7.6 litres per 100 km |
| Constant 75mph | 31.0mpg/9.1 litres per 100 km |

### Gear ratios

| | |
|---|---|
| 1st | 3.500 |
| 2nd | 1.889 |
| 3rd | 1.320 |
| 4th | 1.034 |
| 5th | 0.857 |
| 6th | 0.711 |
| Reverse | 3.455 |
| Final drive | 4.111 |

## Audi TT and TTS

The Audi TT, in roadster and tin-top form, was shown at the Tokyo Motor Show in 1995 and, at the time of writing, has yet to reach production. Even so, according to several magazine reports, both versions had completely sold out their first two years production, despite the fact that no purchaser had seen them as anything but design studies!

As on so many occasions in the past, Audi had looked to create something different from the norm, but something workable in the real world, too.

Aiming for the minimalist look of the Porsche Speedster, it has detailing not a million miles away from that company's Boxster prototype (many of which had, sadly, been lost by the time the car was produced).

It would have been easy to dismiss the TT as a gimmicky show car which, like the Spyder before it, would never become reality. But, unlike the Spyder, the car was based on the floorpan and many mechanical parts of Audi's much-lauded 'small car', the A3. This massively reduced tooling up and other production costs and made producing such a relatively low-volume car much more viable.

The gorgeous lines of the TT were penned by Freeman Thomas, an American designer working in Audi's Californian studios who said: '... I wanted to create a car with the breadth of appeal of the original [Ford] Mustang which was offered with a wide range of engines to suit all tastes, from the secretary with the 6-cylinder automatic to the young blood with a Shelby V8.' To this end, the cars shown had different specifications; the TT Coupé had a 1.8 turbocharged engine (from the A4) which produced 150bhp. The TTS ('S' for sports) roadster on display used the same engine, but tuned to produce 210bhp. Estimated performance figures are a top speed of 140/150mph and 0–62mph figures of around 8 and 6 seconds, respectively. However, it is possible for the car to be equipped with the 1.6 litre normally aspirated engine, producing just 101bhp, or even the V6 unit. And the transmission? Four-wheel drive quattro, of course!

On the TTS roadster, the 225/40 ZR-rated tyres were wrapped around beautiful 18in alloy wheels which did little to hide the huge cross-drilled brake discs at each corner. Measuring just 13ft from stem to stern, the body was galvanized with aluminium doors, bonnet and boot lid. At the front there was MacPherson strut front suspension with triangulated lower links and double rear wishbones mounted on a subframe.

Audi took styling cues from the TT in designing the second generation A4, due for production in the year 2000. The inspiration for the TT's name came from the Tourist Trophy (the first motor race to be held on public roads in Britain) and the first sporty post-war Audi model, the 1965 NSU Prinz 1000 TT.

The Frankfurt Motor Show in 1991 saw Audi display their stunning Spyder quattro design study. It had too many unique parts to be a production possibility (despite the use of the Audi 100's V6 engine).

It was used to highlight Audi's increasing involvement with aluminium for chassis and bodywork. But the Spyder was just the bait for the Tokyo show where …

… the mind-blowing all-aluminium Avus quattro fairly leapt off the stand. We can only dream of driving the beast, with its mid-mounted, 6 litre, 12-cylinder, 'W' formation, 509bhp engine.

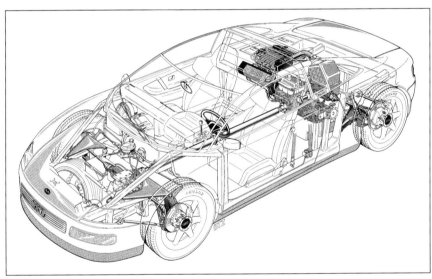

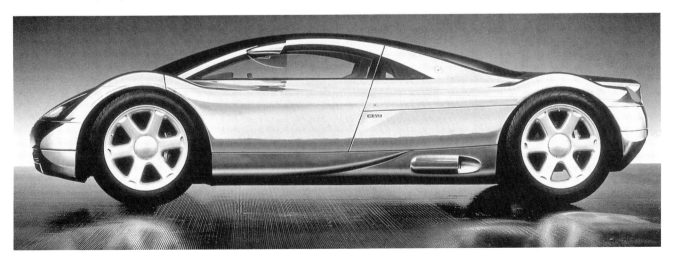

Not for the first time did Audi and Porsche collaborate, but surely this has to be the ultimate – a 315bhp, turbocharged, 4WD estate car. The engine was yet a further development of the 20v unit, first seen in the Sport quattro. The drive was Torsen diff quattro. Press cars were suitably painted eye-searing blue. Beautiful.

It was Tokyo again where the Audi wowed the world with their TT twins, a coupé and open-top version of a 2-seater sportscar, with quattro transmission and a TTS version with a 1.8 litre turbo engine producing 210bhp.

The interior was truly beautiful, mixing ancient and modern and getting it right. It echoes Porsche's Boxster prototype, with a combination of leather and aluminium much in evidence. According to newspaper reports, though not due until 1998, the first two years' production has been sold – to buyers who have only ever seen the cars in pre-production format!

## Audi Coupé and 80 quattro

Since the launch of the Ur quattro, Audi has applied its 4WD principle to every model in the range. However, the Audi 80 quattro was the first and, as such, it has gained its own niche in quattro history. Moreover, it had a very strong link with the Ur quattro, despite the fact that it was a 4-door saloon.

It was launched in Europe in 1982, with the first UK RHD cars seeing the light of day in July 1983 priced at £11,296.

Though it appeared to be just another 5-cylinder Audi 80, it used many parts from the Ur quattro, including the rear differential, propshaft, rear springs, suspension, rear sub-frame, gearbox and floor pan. In some sales areas it also featured the 6in Ronal alloy wheels but, despite its then relatively high price tag,

*Top Contrary to popular opinion, the non-turbo coupé on which the quattro was based, was launched in 1980 but after the turbo'd 4WD car and, ironically, did not receive 4WD (becoming the coupé quattro) until 1984. This is the 1.9 litre, carburettor-fed version complete with the 8-spoke alloy wheels also fitted to the Audi 80CD.*

*Middle Launched in 1982, the 80 quattro arrived in the UK a year later, minus its 6J Ronal alloy wheels – note the '80 quattro' script etched into the rear side glass. To a great extent, it was a 4-door version of the Ur quattro, with the same engine but without the turbo. A fine car, if somewhat understated, and set to become a classic in its own right, especially as Audi destroyed the formula in 1984 when it installed the underpowered 1.8 litre 'GTi' engine up front and changed the gear ratios. Though this formula worked well with the 80 Sport, the extra weight of the 4WD made the quattro far from the performance car it should have been.*

*Bottom In that year, Audi redesignated 5-cylinder '80' models as '90'. As such, the equivalent, facelifted model for 1984/85 became the Audi 90 quattro, complete with single lens headlamps, sloping grille and large under bumper spoiler.*

the UK models were fitted with 5½J steel wheels and 175/70 x 14 tyres.

The power unit for the first cars was a 5-cylinder, 2144cc, Bosch K-Jetronic fuel injected engine with a power output of 136bhp at 5900rpm, making the sub-dued saloon a real sleeper. (The later 2226cc engine was to produce exactly the same power.) Maximum torque was 130lb/ft at 4500rpm. The quoted performance figures were a top speed of 120mph and a 0–60 time of 9.1 seconds.

The very first models used a 215mm diameter clutch, though at the end of 1983 this was increased to 228mm.

The brakes were more than up to the job of stopping the first 4WD Audi saloon, with Ur quattro callipers and ventilated discs at the front and Audi 100 discs at the rear.

Inside the car it was very much as other 80s, though the centre console gave the game away as this is where the cable-operated diff locks were fitted, and there was 'Audi 80 quattro' script beneath the centre vents. There was power assisted steering, low-profile tyres, twin halogen headlamps, front fog lamps, metallic paint, rear boot spoiler, front electric windows, central locking and driver's seat height adjuster. The analogue dash featured an Econometer, a gauge fitted to other Audis of the era, but somewhat incongruous in such a high performance car.

## Technical specification

### Engine

5-cylinder in-line.

| | |
|---|---|
| Power | 136bhp at 5900rpm |
| Torque | 130lb/ft (176Nm) at 4,500rpm |
| Capacity | 2144cc |
| Bore x stroke | 79.5mm x 86.4mm |
| Compression ratio | 9.3:1 |

### Performance

| | |
|---|---|
| Max Speed | 120mph (193kph) |
| 0–50 | 6.2 secs |
| 0–60 | 9.1 secs |

### Fuel consumption

| | |
|---|---|
| Urban cycle | 20.6mpg/13.7 litres per 100km |
| Constant 56mph | 34.0mpg/8.3 litres per 100km |
| Constant 75mph | 27.7mpg/10.2 litres per 100km |

## AUDI S2 – PRETENDER TO THE CROWN

Enthusiasts mourned the passing of the Ur quattro, but Audi sought to placate them with the S2 – the quattro's successor, they said – a 2-door coupé body shell, with that 5-cylinder, 20v unit up front and quattro 4WD. The same but better? Not really. The S2 was undoubtedly extremely rapid and a competent car in its own right, but as a 'successor' to the mighty quattro it fell short, not least because its rounded, bulbous lines just didn't seem to gel. And, although it was entered for a number of rallies, it did little to commend itself in the field of motorsport.

### Will the real successor please stand up?

Aficionados all over the world have their own opinions, but the nearest we have to an Ur quattro successor has to be the amazing A4 quattro. It has 4WD, of course, and it looks simply beautiful. With 193bhp, it is pretty close to the original's power output and the V6 engine produces a howl to match the 'go'. But most important, perhaps, it has an unequalled competition history – in 1996 it competed in seven Touring Car championships and won the lot!

In road car terms, the ultimate version of this model (at the time of writing) has to be the S4 quattro, introduced in the UK in early 1998. In common with the 'S' badging throughout Audi's range, the S4 engine produces some serious horsepower – 265bhp at 5,800rpm, to be precise. The configuration is a first for the company, it being a 2.7 litre, 6-cylinder unit with 5-valve technology and not one, but two turbochargers. The peak torque is a staggering 295lb/ft (400Nm) which is even more impressive for being available in the rev band from 1850–3600rpm. Naturally enough, the suspension is of the sports variety and lowered by some 20mm compared with the standard A4 quattro.

For pulling away in extreme conditions, it features EDL – electronic differential lock – which regulates the action of the brakes at speeds of up to 50mph (80kph), and distributes more engine power to whichever wheels are momentarily producing greater traction.

More advanced specification comes from the Xenon headlamps with gas discharge bulbs for true 'night into day' lighting, as well as four airbags and automatic air conditioning with sunlight dependent control.

Technically the S2 was a fine car, being faster and cheaper than the quattro. Though it scored heavily in the wind tunnel, the third generation coupé lines gave it a bulbous, unbalanced look which led to disappointing sales. It lasted less than half the lifetime of the original. 'Nuff said!

Though not a coupé, the A4 quattro is much more suited to the title of 'quattro successor', with similar power output and performance and a staggering Touring Car Championship tally.

Better still, how about the bi-turbo, 265bhp S4 quattro? Form a queue, but make sure you've got £36,000 ready!

Left Having failed to kill off the quattro in 10v form, Audi succeeded with the 20v. In 1991 it was replaced by the S2. Cost was one of the major issues – the quattro was still being handbuilt, a factor which contributed to it costing around £5,000 more than the more modern counterpart. This photo shows clearly the effect of ten years development and the increasingly important role of the wind tunnel. Note the use of the new 'chunky' Audi grille (combined in the bonnet).

## UK QUATTRO SALES

### Ur quattros

| | '81 | '82 | '83 | '84 | '85 | '86 | '87 | | | | | | | | | Total |
|---|---|---|---|---|---|---|---|---|---|---|---|---|---|---|---|---|
| quattro 2.1 turbo 10v (WR) | 95 | 153 | 326 | 427 | 410 | 350 | 233 | | | | | | | | | 1,994 |

| | | | | | | | '87 | '88 | '89 | '90 | | | | | | Total |
|---|---|---|---|---|---|---|---|---|---|---|---|---|---|---|---|---|
| quattro 2.2 turbo 10v (MB) | | | | | | | 3 | 311 | 95 | 12 | | | | | | 421 |

| | | | | | | | | | '89 | '90 | '91 | '92 | '93 | | | Total |
|---|---|---|---|---|---|---|---|---|---|---|---|---|---|---|---|---|
| quattro 2.2 20V turbo (RR) | | | | | | | | | 45 | 174 | 64 | 10 | 2 | | | 295 |

**TOTAL – 2,710**

### 'Other' quattros

| | '83 | '84 | '85 | '86 | '87 | '88 | '89 | '90 | '91 | '92 | '93 | '94 | '95 | '96 | Total |
|---|---|---|---|---|---|---|---|---|---|---|---|---|---|---|---|
| 80 quattro 2.1 | 285 | 575 | 85 | 4 | 0 | 0 | 0 | 0 | 0 | 0 | 0 | 0 | 0 | 0 | 949 |
| 80 quattro 1.8 | 0 | 0 | 83 | 145 | 281 | 521 | 119 | 4 | 1 | 1 | 0 | 0 | 0 | 0 | 1,155 |
| 80 quattro 2.0 | 0 | 0 | 0 | 0 | 0 | 0 | 37 | 196 | 65 | 0 | 0 | 0 | 0 | 0 | 298 |
| 80 quattro SE | 0 | 0 | 0 | 0 | 0 | 0 | 0 | 0 | 14 | 1 | 0 | 0 | 0 | 2 | 17 |
| 80 2.0 16V quattro | 0 | 0 | 0 | 0 | 0 | 0 | 0 | 26 | 139 | 35 | 2 | 3 | 1 | 0 | 206 |
| 80 2.6 E quattro | 0 | 0 | 0 | 0 | 0 | 0 | 0 | 0 | 0 | 0 | 29 | 72 | 17 | 0 | 118 |
| 80 2.6 E quattro estate | 0 | 0 | 0 | 0 | 0 | 0 | 0 | 0 | 0 | 0 | 27 | 126 | 47 | 0 | 200 |
| 80 2.8 E quattro | 0 | 0 | 0 | 0 | 0 | 0 | 0 | 0 | 14 | 101 | 55 | 1 | 0 | 0 | 171 |
| 80 S2 estate | 0 | 0 | 0 | 0 | 0 | 0 | 0 | 0 | 0 | 0 | 101 | 136 | 82 | 1 | 320 |

**TOTAL – 3,434**

| | '85 | '86 | '87 | '88 | '89 | '90 | '91 | '92 | '93 | '94 | '95 | '96 | Total |
|---|---|---|---|---|---|---|---|---|---|---|---|---|---|
| 100 quattro 2.2 | 78 | 82 | 104 | 66 | 46 | 0 | 0 | 0 | 0 | 0 | 0 | 0 | 376 |
| 100 quattro turbo 2.2 | 0 | 0 | 0 | 0 | 10 | 66 | 6 | 0 | 0 | 0 | 0 | 0 | 82 |
| 100 Avant | 219 | 184 | 191 | 135 | 122 | 0 | 0 | 0 | 0 | 0 | 0 | 0 | 851 |
| 100 Avant turbo 2.2 | 0 | 0 | 0 | 0 | 1 | 2 | 2 | 0 | 0 | 0 | 0 | 0 | 5 |
| 100 quattro Avant 2.3 | 0 | 0 | 0 | 0 | 33 | 87 | 2 | 0 | 0 | 0 | 0 | 0 | 122 |
| 100 2.3 E quattro | 0 | 0 | 0 | 0 | 0 | 0 | 26 | 59 | 16 | 0 | 0 | 0 | 101 |
| 100 2.3 E quattro estate | 0 | 0 | 0 | 0 | 0 | 0 | 1 | 61 | 0 | 0 | 0 | 0 | 62 |
| 100 2.3 quattro | 0 | 0 | 0 | 0 | 0 | 1 | 1 | 0 | 0 | 0 | 0 | 0 | 2 |
| 100 2.8 E quattro | 0 | 0 | 0 | 0 | 0 | 0 | 65 | 38 | 35 | 33 | 0 | 0 | 171 |
| 100 2.8 E quattro auto | 0 | 0 | 0 | 0 | 0 | 0 | 0 | 12 | 23 | 11 | 1 | 0 | 47 |
| 100 2.8 E quattro estate | 0 | 0 | 0 | 0 | 0 | 0 | 12 | 189 | 109 | 49 | 0 | 0 | 359 |
| 100 2.8 E quattro est auto | 0 | 0 | 0 | 0 | 0 | 0 | 0 | 11 | 46 | 34 | 0 | 0 | 91 |
| 100 S4 | 0 | 0 | 0 | 0 | 0 | 0 | 1 | 0 | 1 | 22 | 0 | 0 | 24 |
| S4 auto sedan | 0 | 0 | 0 | 0 | 0 | 0 | 0 | 17 | 13 | 9 | 0 | 0 | 39 |
| S4 auto estate | 0 | 0 | 0 | 0 | 0 | 0 | 0 | 3 | 8 | 0 | 0 | 0 | 11 |
| 100 S4 5 speed | 0 | 0 | 0 | 0 | 0 | 0 | 22 | 24 | 0 | 0 | 0 | 0 | 46 |
| 100 S4 6 speed estate | 0 | 0 | 0 | 0 | 0 | 0 | 0 | 50 | 39 | 35 | 0 | 0 | 124 |
| 100 S4 6 speed sedan | 0 | 0 | 0 | 0 | 0 | 0 | 0 | 29 | 36 | 19 | 0 | 0 | 84 |
| 200 quattro | 115 | 77 | 41 | 12 | 34 | 0 | 0 | 0 | 0 | 0 | 0 | 0 | 279 |
| 200 Avant | 23 | 75 | 48 | 20 | 45 | 0 | 0 | 0 | 0 | 0 | 0 | 0 | 211 |

**TOTAL – 3,087**

| | '84 | '85 | '86 | '87 | '88 | '89 | '90 | '91 | '92 | '93 | '94 | '95 | '96 | Total |
|---|---|---|---|---|---|---|---|---|---|---|---|---|---|---|
| 90 quattro 2.2 | 6 | 433 | 434 | 206 | 504 | 341 | 1 | 0 | 0 | 0 | 0 | 0 | 0 | 1,925 |
| 90 quattro 2.3 | 0 | 0 | 0 | 0 | 0 | 22 | 122 | 46 | 0 | 0 | 0 | 0 | 0 | 190 |
| 90 20V quattro | 0 | 0 | 0 | 0 | 0 | 59 | 290 | 71 | 0 | 0 | 0 | 0 | 0 | 420 |
| 90 sport 20V quattro | 0 | 0 | 0 | 0 | 0 | 0 | 30 | 62 | 0 | 0 | 0 | 0 | 0 | 92 |

**TOTAL – 2,627**

| | '84 | '85 | '86 | '87 | '88 | '89 | '90 | '91 | '92 | '93 | '94 | '95 | '96 | Total |
|---|---|---|---|---|---|---|---|---|---|---|---|---|---|---|
| Coupé quattro 2.1 | 0 | 0 | 0 | 0 | 8 | 1 | 0 | 0 | 0 | 0 | 0 | 0 | 0 | 9 |
| Coupé quattro 2.2 | 1 | 405 | 705 | 486 | 64 | 0 | 0 | 0 | 0 | 0 | 0 | 0 | 0 | 1,661 |
| Coupé quattro 2.2 MK 3 | 0 | 0 | 0 | 0 | 41 | 422 | 48 | 0 | 0 | 0 | 0 | 0 | 0 | 511 |
| Coupé quattro 2.3 MK 3 | 0 | 0 | 0 | 0 | 0 | 28 | 105 | 37 | 2 | 1 | 0 | 0 | 0 | 173 |
| 2.8 E Coupé quattro | 0 | 0 | 0 | 0 | 0 | 0 | 0 | 0 | 62 | 61 | 68 | 65 | 16 | 272 |
| Coupé quattro 20V | 0 | 0 | 0 | 0 | 0 | 80 | 322 | 100 | 1 | 0 | 0 | 0 | 0 | 503 |

**TOTAL – 3,129**

| | '90 | '91 | '92 | '93 | '94 | '95 | '96 | Total |
|---|---|---|---|---|---|---|---|---|
| S2 Coupé | 23 | 226 | 136 | 118 | 109 | 114 | 56 | 782 |
| RS2 2.2 Avant | 0 | 0 | 0 | 0 | 46 | 126 | 1 | 173 |
| RS2 Avant | 0 | 0 | 0 | 0 | 0 | 0 | 1 | 1 |

**TOTAL – 956**

| | '90 | '91 | '92 | '93 | '94 | '95 | '96 | Total |
|---|---|---|---|---|---|---|---|---|
| V8 3.6 | 80 | 56 | 11 | 0 | 0 | 0 | 0 | 147 |
| V8 4.2 | 0 | 0 | 22 | 26 | 0 | 0 | 0 | 48 |
| A4 2.5 | 0 | 0 | 0 | 0 | 0 | 337 | 516 | 853 |
| A4 2.7 | 0 | 0 | 0 | 0 | 0 | 0 | 1 | 1 |
| A4 Tdi quattro Avant | 0 | 0 | 0 | 0 | 0 | 0 | 1 | 1 |

**TOTAL – 1,050**

| | '94 | '95 | '96 | Total |
|---|---|---|---|---|
| A6 2.5 TDI quattro | 0 | 4 | 0 | 4 |
| A6 2.5 TDI quattro estate | 0 | 5 | 102 | 107 |
| A6 2.5 TDI quattro 140 | 0 | 0 | 16 | 16 |
| A6 quattro auto | 17 | 52 | 16 | 85 |
| A6 quattro | 40 | 80 | 35 | 155 |
| A6 quattro estate auto | 23 | 46 | 27 | 96 |
| A6 quattro estate | 58 | 88 | 35 | 181 |
| A8 4.2 quattro | 33 | 274 | 166 | 473 |
| A8 sport quattro | 0 | 38 | 134 | 172 |

**TOTAL – 1,289**

| | '94 | '95 | '96 | Total |
|---|---|---|---|---|
| S6 | 0 | 0 | 30 | 30 |
| S6 auto | 0 | 0 | 7 | 7 |
| S6 2.2 turbo auto | 3 | 9 | 2 | 14 |
| S6 2.2 turbo | 11 | 23 | 3 | 37 |
| S6 estate auto | 8 | 23 | 24 | 55 |
| S6 estate | 19 | 43 | 55 | 117 |

**TOTAL – 260**

# Chapter 3

# The competition connection

In an interview with *Motoring News* in 1981 Hannu Mikkola, describing the quattro, said: 'It is the most terrifyingly effective way of covering loose surface at speed ever devised by man.'

## RALLYING AS IT WAS

Long before Audi launched it at Geneva in 1980, the plan was in place to use the quattro in the World Rally Championship, but at the time there was a problem – 4WD cars were banned! However, in 1979 a pair of Range Rovers were able to take part in the Ivory Coast Rally because, fortunately for Audi, FISA accepted the German Federation's suggestion that there was no real need to ban 4WD.

Prior to 1981 the world rallying scene was, it has to be said, fairly stale and predictable. The recipe for success was almost stereotyped: You should have a fairly light rear or mid-engined car with a powerful, normally aspirated power unit. This combination allowed the cars to be slung around with vigour by their drivers, who clearly enjoyed their work. Four-wheel drive had been considered before, of course, but had been rejected because it was too heavy, too complex and needed too much extra power to drag the extra weight around.

So, Audi bucked the established

trend by having a turbocharger* and 4WD, and they bucked it further by having three regular quattro crews for the WRC in which all six members were of different nationalities and included – whisper it not – two ladies!

## 1981

Right from the start the Audi quattro put its drivers on the winners podium. Its first competitive international event was a European Championship rally qualifier, the Janner Rally in Austria during January. Franz Wittermann drove it to a famous maiden victory – the first of many victories – romping home 21 minutes ahead of his nearest rival.

The Audi Sport drivers for 1981 were the Finn, Hannu Mikkola and Frenchwoman, Michèle Mouton, with their respective co-drivers Arne Hertz and Annie Arrii. Audi had being trying to get the 1980 world champion, Walter Röhrl, but he was already tied up with Mercedes. The first WRC event entered was the Monte Carlo Rally. To win such a famous rally is a dream for many and, indeed, that's the way it stayed for Audi. Mouton failed to complete the journey from Paris to Monaco because of dirt in the fuel, and Mikkola

---

*The quattro wasn't the first turbocharged car in WRC – Saab had entered its 99 Turbo in 1979, when Stig Blomqvist achieved the first ever WRC win for a turbo'd car in Sweden.

---

went out on the seventh stage because, apparently, his foot slipped off the brake pedal. But, up to this point, Mikkola had pulled out an average of a minute per stage and, despite the rest of the rally world's cynicism about the viability of this heavy and complex newcomer, the writing was most definitely on the wall.

In Sweden Mikkola made no such mistakes, leading home Arii Vatanen's Ford Escort by two minutes. In the third rally Mouton got herself into the points by finishing fourth. By one of those twists of fate, for this rally Italian woman Fabrizia Pons replaced Mouton's original co-driver Annie Arrii, who had rallying commitments elsewhere, and she thereafter stayed with Mouton during her successful career at Audi.

In the Greek Acropolis Rally Mikkola was again in the lead until a protest about the legality of the quattros' headlamp air vents resulted in his and Mouton's disqualification. Fellow driver Franz Witterman was also disqualified because of protests about an illegal cooling system. This was important because, just like the road cars, the rally cars always ran hot and the team knew that it was going to be a particular problem in the hot conditions in Greece. In the political wheeling and dealing that seems endemic in all forms of motorsport, team manager Walter Treser left and was replaced by another

Hannu Mikkola debuted the quattro as course car in the 1980 Algarve Rally in the European Championship. Had they been competing, he would have won by 20 minutes!

Audi produced plenty of cutaway drawings such as this to demonstrate to a disbelieving world just what was going on. Naturally, there were myriad detail changes to take the car rallying, but most immediately noticeable is the visibly larger turbocharger and the much bigger intercooler mounted centrally behind the radiator grille. As ever, the early quattros ran on Fuchs 7J alloy wheels on the loose surface stages.

Forever Audi – there were many Audi drivers, but these were the first and will be forever linked with the company. Hannu Mikkola was crucial to the initial development of the car and, with his co-driver Arne Hertz, scored many popular victories and won the World Rally Championship in 1983.

employee with a long-term quattro record, Roland Gumpert.

Nevertheless, overall reliability remained a real headache for all members of the team, especially the drivers who were becoming increasingly frustrated at the constant prospect of blowing away the opposition only to be beaten by mechanical gremlins beyond their control, such as camshaft and fuel injection problems.

The San Remo Rally was truly an historic event because Mouton won and became the first woman ever to win a World Championship rally. At the time of writing she remains the *only* woman to have done so! Mikkola took fourth place.

An emphatic victory on the Lombard RAC Rally, regarded by some as the worst/best there is, left no room for doubt that the quattro was going to be a tough cookie in 1982. Mikkola blasted home 11 minutes ahead of some serious opposition – despite having rolled the car during the event! This was not the last time the inherent structural integrity of the car was to be proved in the most extreme of circumstances. Mouton almost clinched third spot, but a slight error of judgement was punished harshly and she retired on her first Lombard event.

As to be expected with any new car, it was very much a time for proving the car and its components, but the results show that Audi was staggeringly near the mark first time out. A result of fifth in the World Championship for makes was an impressive debut performance and gave notice to the opposition that there was more to come.

## 1982

Applying the lessons learned in 1981 the quattro truly steamrollered the opposition in 1982. With Stig Blomqvist joining Mikkola and Mouton on the team it's hard to see how they could have lost! In the World Rally Championship the impressive array of drivers clinched seven wins from 11 entries. Blomqvist won the Swedish, Mouton the Portuguese, the Acropolis and the Brazilian. Mikkola won the 1000 Lakes

(with Blomqvist second), Blomqvist won the San Remo (with Mikkola second) and Mikkola finished the year with another win – his second – on the Lombard RAC, with Mouton second. Not surprisingly, Audi won the Manufacturers' World Championship by 12 points from its nearest rival, and Michèle Mouton almost became the first lady driver to win the Drivers' Championship, instead having to settle for second place. However, it wasn't all plain sailing for, although the quattro was becoming more reliable, there were still plenty of problems. Poor Mikkola ended up walking home on five consecutive rallies (effectively ruling him out of the World Championship running) and Mouton could conceivably have clinched the driver's title had her car not let her down in New Zealand.

It's interesting to note that tyres began to play an increasing part in the quattro's success during 1982. For example, when Blomqvist won the San Remo it was on Pirelli rubber, despite the fact that the sponsor's decals declared that Kleber tyres were being used.

## 1983

Audi's success in the UK during 1983 was matched by its success in the World Rally Championship arena. Eventual champion Hannu Mikkola won in Sweden, Portugal, Argentina and the 1000 Lakes in Finland. His points tally was topped off by second places on the RAC Rally and the Safari and was enough to see him crowned 1983 world rally champion – a deserving and popular winner. Though Mikkola didn't manage to win the Lombard RAC Rally for a third consecutive year, a quattro still made it first to the winner's ramp in the hands of Stig Blomqvist.

The Audi team, however, had to be content with second place in the World Championship for makes, handing over their 1982 crown to Lancia. The Italian team comprehensively outmanoeuvred them, using their many years of experience in the sport. Their expertise in getting the manufacturers' crown with a clearly out-moded 2WD car can only be admired.

## 1984

After just four full seasons of rallying, Audi managed the double – the World Rally Championship for makes *and* the driver's crown for Stig Blomqvist as he became the World Rally Champion. Blomqvist won in Sweden, Greece, New Zealand, Argentina and the Ivory Coast (see below), whilst Hannu Mikkola won in Portugal and Audi's latest recruit, German driver Walter Röhrl, won the Monte Carlo – the German impressively scoring a win on his first outing with the Audi. In the UK, Mikkola also won the National Breakdown (previously called the Mintex), the Welsh and the Scottish rallies.

Having started the super-powerful 4WD revolution in 1981, Audi faced some seriously stiff opposition during 1984. Moreover, the competition were taking to the rally tracks with what were effectively space-framed specials, designed to look fairly similar to a road-going car. Peugeot's T16 was the first up to the line and, on seeing it, Jorg Bensinger commented: 'Audi has used a production car to demonstrate the superiority of 4WD in motorsport. Now that our competitors are increasingly using out-and-out racing cars, we must also think about whether a basically different concept may promise more success.'

Something had to be done, and it was. Towards the end of the year the sizzling short-wheelbase Audi Sport quattro made its competition debut having been launched at the 1983 Frankfurt show. Though obviously a derivation of the famous blistered-arch quattro, it was instantly recognisable in its own right by the $12\frac{1}{2}$ inches that were missing from its middle!

In homologation road-going trim it produced a hefty 306bhp, but in rally form this was upped to some 450bhp – a figure that was to rise considerably by the time of Audi's retirement from rallying. The powerful 20v engine, with its crossflow, DOHC aluminium cylinder head was the forerunner to the quattro 20v road cars introduced in 1989.

The lighter and shorter Sport was

*Hannu Mikkola making a splash on his way to winning the 1982 Lombard RAC Rally – his second in a row for Audi, and his fourth all told. Mikkola was magnanimous in passing on the lessons he learned to his incredibly talented team-mate …*

*… Michèle Mouton, the girl from Grasse – to many pundits a surprise choice – who all but snapped up the 1982 Drivers' World Championship, losing to Walter Röhrl in his Opel by one breakdown too many. Her original quattro co-driver was Annie Arrii, but when she had double-booked the date of the third round of the '81 Championship in Portugal, Italian Fabrizia Pons stepped into the breach, producing the most successful ladies driver pairing ever.*

*Michèle Mouton made history at San Remo in 1981 by becoming the first woman to win a World Championship rally. To date, no other woman has done so.*

Left *In 1982, the fast French lady won in Portugal, Greece and Brazil, almost clinching the drivers' title in the process. In 1983, she split her time between the UK and World Championships and is seen here winning the Audi Sport Rally.*

Below left *Curiously, it was 1984 before Audi struck a major sponsorship deal, in this case the German HB cigarette company. It was obviously a good omen as, despite the increasingly difficult opposition, the quattro took victory in both Drivers' and Manufacturers' Championships in the hands of Stig Blomqvist.*

Bottom left *The short wheelbase Sport quattros proved unwieldy at first and took a while to develop. This is Walter Röhrl on a Tarmac section in the UK Ulster Rally.*

Below *The legend lives on – Audi had a strong presence at the 1996 and 1997 Goodwood Festival of Speed. Michèle Mouton appeared in both events and in '96 took the third fastest time of the day up the hill climb course – beaten only by Grand Prix cars!*

seen as a way of making the quattro more wieldy, but the S1 had its own handling problems. Walter Röhrl was especially critical of its wayward behaviour, particularly after a nasty off in the San Remo Rally, where he dubbed it dangerous. Throughout the year, the Audi Sport team chose not to rely solely on the Sport in World Rally Championship events, rather to run it in parallel with the lwb quattro A2.

It's a little ironic that the first rally it finished was a win in the Ivory Coast Rally and one which clinched the Drivers' Championship for Stig Blomqvist. Moreover, it was this victory that made Audi the most successful World Rally Championship team ever, with a total of 22 wins to outstrip Ford and Lancia, both of whom had many, many more years of experience. Michèle Mouton brought her Sport home in fourth place in the Lombard RAC.

## 1985

This was the first full year of rallying for the Sport quattro and, though it performed well in the circumstances, the scales had tipped against Audi. The purpose-made rally cars of the opposition were far too much for the Sport which, despite all its add-ons, was still basically a souped-up road car.

Though the Sport was still a bit of a handful, Audi's engineers were not to take defeat lying down. Exploiting the rules to the full, they attached wings and spoilers to virtually all aspects of the car and called it the Evolution 2. These endowed it with some much-needed high speed and cornering downforce (even more necessary as the power had been uprated to 500+ bhp) which made it more popular with the drivers when it debuted in the 1000 Lakes Rally where it took Stig Blomqvist to second place. Walter Röhrl used it to score its only win at San Remo.

## 1986

The Monte Carlo Rally was the last World Championship event for the Sport quattro prior to an unprecedented change in the international rallying rule book designed to bring to an end

the Group B supercar era, and it acted as a prelude to concentration on a Group A production car class. The power produced by the rallying supercars was growing out of proportion, and controlling them was getting ever more difficult, even with the world's top rally stars driving. In many rallies the enthusiasts could not be restrained from wandering on to the track, leaving it ever later before leaping back to safety. During the very first stage of the ill-fated San Remo Rally, Joaquim Santos' Ford RS200 left the road and killed four spectators. This tragedy struck at the heart of rallying and was still in everyone's mind when there was a similar accident during the Safari Rally. This time a Group A Golf, driven by Kenneth Eriksson, killed a spectator. It took yet another tragic accident before the governing bodies finally cried enough.

On the rally of Corsica, Henri Toivonen and his co-driver, American Sergio Cresto, were killed when their Lancia S4 left the forest track and exploded. There was a sad irony in this terrible fiery accident, in that safety fuel tanks had made fuel leakage, let alone explosion, virtually unheard of. Hannu Mikkola said: 'There have been very few fires since they introduced safety tanks. I remember a huge testing accident with Audi, but not a drop of fuel was spilled, even after we rolled eight or ten times.'

Audi Sport retired from rallying after the first fatal incident in Portugal, a move followed within a few days by Audi Sport UK. In five and a half seasons of rallying Audi had stuck to the rules, but broken convention, to turn the established rally world on its head. The rightness of the car from the start was incredible and the basic premise was clearly right, as even as the '90s draw to a close, most World Championship rally cars feature 4WD and turbocharged engines. Sounds familiar, doesn't it?

## 1987

With revised rules and less powerful categories, Audi entered a 200 quattro for the 1987 season, albeit somewhat

half-heartedly. Most of the rallies were not contested at all, although the team did score an unexpected first and second in the Safari Rally, with Mikkola and Röhrl leading home the rest of the field. Clearly, the well of rallying success was drying up, with little chance of repeating the earlier winning ways without investing lots of D-Marks. So, why not look for other fields to conquer? Why not, indeed?

## WORLD RALLY CHAMPIONSHIP RESULTS

### 1981

**Monte Carlo (Round 1) 24–30 Jan.**
**Total 3,930km, 32 special stages**

| 1. Ragnotti/ | | |
| Thimonier | Renault 5 Turbo | 9.55.55 |
| 2. Frequelin/ | | |
| Todt | Talbot Sunbeam | 9.58.49 |
| 3. Kleint/ | | |
| Wanger | Opel Ascona 400 | 10.02.54 |
| 4. Kulläng/ | | |
| Berglund | Opel Ascona 400 | 10.08.44 |
| 5. Toivonen/ | | |
| Gallagher | Talbot Sunbeam | 10.11.42 |
| 6. Darniche/ | | |
| Mahe | Lancia Stratos | 10.13.02 |
| Retirements: | Mouton/Arrii dirt in fuel; Mikkola/Hertz went off. | |

**Sweden (Round 2) 13–15 Feb.**
**Total 1,368km, 25 special stages**

| 1. *Mikkola/* | | |
| *Hertz* | *Audi quattro* | 3.48.07 |
| 2. Vatanen/ | | |
| Richards | Ford Escort RS | 3.50.00 |
| 3. Airikkala/ | | |
| Virtanen | Ford Escort RS | 3.51.47 |
| 4. Kulläng/ | | |
| Berglund | Opel Ascona 400 | 3.53.12 |
| 5. Blomqvist/ | | |
| Cederberg | Saab 99 Turbo | 3.53.37 |
| 6. Johansson/ | | |
| Andersen | Opel Ascona 400 | 3.54.38 |

**Portugal (Round 3) 4–7 Mar.**
**Total 2,571km, 46 special stages**

| 1. Alen/ | | |
| Kivimäki | Fiat Abarth 131 | 8.27.26 |

2. Toivonen/
Gallagher — Talbot Sunbeam — 8.36.37

3. Waldegard/
Thorszelius — Toyota Celica — 8.43.47

4. *Mouton/
Pons* — *Audi quattro* — 8.49.57

5. Pond/
Grindrod — Datsun 160J — 8.57.39

6. Frequelin/
Todt — Talbot Sunbeam — 9.17.22

Retirements: Mikkola/Hertz went off.

## Safari (Round 4) 16–20 Apr.
## Total 4,718km

1. Mehta/
Doughty — Datsun Violet GT — *3.39

2. Aaltonen/
Drews — Datsun Violet GT — 3.42

3. Kirkland/
Haworth — Datsun 160J — 4.51

4. Salonen/
Harjanne — Datsun Silvia — 7.28

5. Kleint/
Wanger — Opel Ascona 400 — 8.06

6. Lefebvre/
Delferrier — Peugeot 504 — 9.12

*No Audi works entry.*
* penalties

## Corsica (Round 5) 30 Apr–2 May.
## Total 1,144km, 24 special stages

1. Darniche/
Mahe — Lancia Stratos — 14.26.23

2. Frequelin/
Todt — Talbot Sunbeam — 14.42.25

3. Pond/
Grindrod — Datsun Violet GT — 14.45.29

4. Ballet/
Guinchard — Porsche 911 SC — 15.17.09

5. Kaby/
Arthur — Datsun 160J — 15.22.06

6. Eklund/
Bohlin — Toyota Celica — 15.43.33

Retirements: Mikkola/Hertz engine;
Mouton/Pons engine.

## Acropolis (Round 6) 1–4 Jun.
## Total 2,504km, 46 special stages

1. Vatanen/
Richards — Ford Escort RS — 13.17.25

2. Alen/
Kivimäki — Fiat Abarth 131 — 13.22.00

3. Bettega/
Perissinot — Fiat Abarth 131 — 13.25.19

4. Frequelin/
Todt — Talbot Sunbeam — 13.50.44

5. Mehta/
Mehta — Datsun 160 J — 13.54.40

6. Moschous/
Konstantakos — Datsun Violet GT — 13.57.22

Retirements: Mikkola/Hertz, Wittmann/
Nestlinger, Mouton/Pons
disqualified.

## Argentina (Round 7) 18–23 Jul.
## Total 3,639km, 16 special stages

1. Frequelin/
Todt — Talbot Sunbeam — 14.22.52

2. Mehta/
Mehta — Datsun Violet GT — 15.07.44

3. Recalde/
del Buono — Datsun 160J — 16.01.19

4. Soto/
Silva — Renault 12 — 17.12.50

5. Albertengo/
Alberto — Peugeot 504 — 17.37.35

6. Echegoyen/
Horovitz — Ford Escort RS — 17.45.30

*No Audi works entry.*

## Brazil (Round 8) 6–8 Aug.
## Total 1,669km, 21 special stages

1. Vatanen/
Richards — Ford Escort RS — 9.39.40

2. Frequelin/
Todt — Talbot Sunbeam — 9.48.11

3. de Vitta/
Muzio — Ford Escort RS — 10.20.26

4. Recalde/
del Buono — Datsun160J — 10.46.50

5. Torres/
Morais — Ford Escort RS — 11.10.45

6. Trelles/
Caulim — Fiat 147 — 12.06.35

*No Audi works entry.*

## 1000 Lakes (Round 9) 28–30 Aug.
## Total 1,419km, 46 special stages

1. Vatanen/
Richards — Ford Escort RS — 4.07.27

2. Alen/
KivimIki — Fiat Abarth 131 — 4.08.26

3. *Mikkola/
Hertz* — *Audi quattro* — 4.10.19

4. Salonen/
Harjanne — Datsun Violet GT — 4.13.26

5 Airikkala/
Nirtanen — Ford Escort RS — 4.15.40

6. Johansson/
Andersson — Opel Ascona 400 — 4.16.18

Retirements: Wittmann/Nestlinger
stopped after accident.

## San Remo (Round 10) 5–11 Oct.
## Total 2,874km, 59 special stages

1. *Mouton/
Pons* — *Audi quattro* — 8.05.50

2. Toivonen/
Gallagher — Talbot Sunbeam — 8.09.15

3. Tony/
Rudy — Opel Ascona 400 — 8.12.08

4. *Mikkola/
Hertz* — *Audi quattro* — 8.18.20

5. Lucky/
Penariol — Opel Ascona 400 — 8.19.51

6. Biasion/
Siviero — Opel Ascona 400 — 8.21.44

Retirements: Cinotto/Radaelli went off.

## Ivory Coast (Round 11) 26–31 Oct.
## Total 5,087km

1. Salonen/
Harjanne — Datsun 160 Violet — *9.57

2. Eklund/
Spujth — Toyota Celica — 11.09

3. Mehta/
Doughty — Datsun 160 Violet — 11.22

4. Mitri/
Copetti — Datsun 160 Violet — 12.29

5. Frequelin/
Todt — Peugeot 504 — 13.15

6. Ambrosino/
Le Saux — Peugeot 504 — 13.16

*No Audi works entry.*
*penalties.

## Lombard RAC (Round 12) 22–25 Nov.
## Total 2,780km, 65 special stages

1. *Mikkola/
Hertz* — *Audi quattro* — 8.30.00

2 Vatanen/
Richards — Ford Escort RS — 8.41.05

3. Blomqvist/
Cederberg — Talbot Sunbeam — 8.43.36

4. Airikkala/
Short — Ford Escort RS — 8.48.43

| 5. Ragnotti/ | | | |
|---|---|---|---|
| Holmes | Renault 5 Turbo | 8.53.55 | |
| 6. Eklund/ | | | |
| Spujth | Toyota Celica | 8.54.54 | |

Retirements: Mouton/Pons went off.

**Drivers' Championship**:
1. Vatanen 96; 2. Frequelin 89;
3. Mikkola 62; 4. Alen 56; 5. Mehta 55;
6. Salonen 40; 8. Mouton 30.

**Manufacturers' Championship**:
1. Talbot 117; 2. Datsun 106; 3. Ford 90;
4. Opel 69; 5. Audi 63; 6. Fiat 63.

# 1982

**Monte Carlo (Round 1) 16–22 Jan.**
**Total 4,155km, 32 special stages**

| 1. Röhrl/ | | | |
|---|---|---|---|
| Geistdörfer | Opel Ascona 400 | 8.20.33 | |
| 2. Mikkola/ | | | |
| Hertz | Audi quattro | 8.24.22 | |
| 3. Therier/ | | | |
| Vial | Porsche 911 SC | 8.32.38 | |
| 4. Frequelin/ | | | |
| Fauchille | Porsche 911 SC | 8.37.40 | |
| 5. Saby/ | | | |
| Sappey | Renault 5 Turbo | 8.43.34 | |
| 6. Snobeck/ | | | |
| Emanuelli | Renault 5 Turbo | 8.50.28 | |

Retirements: Mouton/Pons went off;
Cinotto/Radaelli went off.

**Sweden (Round 2) 12–14 Feb.**
**Total 1,390km, 25 special stages**

| 1. Blomqvist/ | | | |
|---|---|---|---|
| Cederberg | Audi quattro | 3.40.15 | |
| 2. Vatanen/ | | | |
| Harryman | Ford Escort RS | 3.42.15 | |
| 3. Röhrl/ | | | |
| Geistdörfer | Opel Ascona 400 | 3.44.29 | |
| 4. Eklund/ | | | |
| Spjuth | Saab 99 Turbo | 3.45.20 | |
| 5. Mouton/ | | | |
| Pons | Audi quattro | 3.46.08 | |
| 6. Lampi/ | | | |
| Kuukkala | Ford Escort RS | 3.46.14 | |

Retirements: Mikkola/Hertz went off.

**Portugal (Round 3) 3–6 Mar.**
**Total 2,312km, 40 special stages**

| 1. Mouton/ | | | |
|---|---|---|---|
| Pons | Audi quattro | 7.39.36 | |

| 2. Eklund/ | | | |
|---|---|---|---|
| Spjuth | Toyota Celica | 7.52.43 | |
| 3. Wittmann/ | | | |
| Diekmann | Audi quattro | 8.07.25 | |
| 4. Torres/ | | | |
| Lopes | Ford Escort RS | 8.30.58 | |
| 5. Cuppier/ | | | |
| Laloz | Citroen Visa | 8.54.11 | |
| 6. Silva/ | | | |
| Bavilacqua | Ford Escort RS | 9.01.12 | |

Retirements: Mikkola/Hertz went off.

**Safari (Round 4) 8–12 Apr.**
**Total 5,120km**

| 1. Mehta/ | | | |
|---|---|---|---|
| Doughty | Datsun Violet GT | *4.26 | |
| 2. Röhrl/ | | | |
| Geistdörfer | Opel Ascona 400 | 5.07 | |
| 3. Kirkland/ | | | |
| Levitan | Datsun Violet GTS | 6.16 | |
| 4. Pond/ | | | |
| Harryman | Datsun Violet GTS | 7.00 | |
| 5. Shah/ | | | |
| Khan | Datsun 160J | 8.15 | |
| 6. Collinge/ | | | |
| Fraser | Range Rover | 8.54 | |

No Audi works entries.
* penalties.

**Corsica (Round 5) 6–8 May.**
**Total 1,616km, 27 special stages**

| 1. Ragnotti/ | | | |
|---|---|---|---|
| Andrie | Renault 5 Turbo | 14.11.19 | |
| 2. Andruet/ | | | |
| Biche | Ferrari 308 GTB | 14 16 57 | |
| 3. Beguin/ | | | |
| Lenne | Porsche 911SC | 14:20:11 | |
| 4. Röhrl/ | | | |
| Geistdörfer | Opel Ascona 400 | 14.20.41 | |
| 5. Saby/ | | | |
| Sappey | Renault 5 Turbo | 14.27.31 | |
| 6. Frequelin/ | | | |
| Fauchille | Porsche 911 SC | 14.35.16 | |

Retirements: Mikkola/Hertz gearbox;
Wittmann/Diekmann engine.

**Acropolis (Round 6) 31 May–3 Jun.**
**Total 2,603km, 56 special stages**

| 1. Mouton/ | | | |
|---|---|---|---|
| Pons | Audi quattro | 12.54.44 | |
| 2. Röhrl/ | | | |
| Geistdörfer | Opel Ascona 400 | 13.08.23 | |

| 3. Toivonen/ | | | |
|---|---|---|---|
| Gallagher | Opel Ascona 400 | 13.17.21 | |
| 4. Mehta/ | | | |
| Mehta | Datsun Violet GT | 13.27.28 | |
| 5. Moschous/ | | | |
| Konstantin | Datsun Violet GTS | 13.36.44 | |
| 6. McRae/ | | | |
| Grindrod | Opel Ascona 400 | 13.40.16 | |

Retirements: Mikkola/Hertz suspension;
Wittmann/Diekmann steering;
Cinotto/Radaelli electrics.

**New Zealand (Round 7) 26–29 Jun.**
**Total 2,216km, 38 special stages**

| 1. Waldegard/ | | | |
|---|---|---|---|
| Thorszelius | Toyota Celica | 10.28.09 | |
| 2. Eklund/ | | | |
| Spjuth | Toyota Celica | 10.37.21 | |
| 3. Röhrl/ | | | |
| Geistdörfer | Opel Ascona 400 | 10.33.37 | |
| 4. Salonen/ | | | |
| Harjanne | Datsun Violet GTS | 10.41.25 | |
| 5. Millen/ | | | |
| Bellefleur | Mazda RX7 | 10.54.55 | |
| 6. Teesdale/ | | | |
| Smith | Ford Escort RS | 11.30.17 | |

Retirements: Mikkola/Hertz steering;
Mouton/Pons oil pipe.

**Brazil (Round 8) 11–14 Aug.**
**Total 2,295km, 29 special stages**

| 1. Mouton/ | | | |
|---|---|---|---|
| Pons | Audi quattro | 8.16.24 | |
| 2. Röhrl/ | | | |
| Geistdörfer | Opel Ascona 400 | 8.51.49 | |
| 3. de Vitta/ | | | |
| Muzio | Ford Escort RS | 10.15.30 | |
| 4. Rodrigues/ | | | |
| Mattos | VW Passat 1600 | 11.41.08 | |

Retirements: Mikkola/Hertz went off.

**1000 Lakes (Round 9) 27–29 Aug.**
**Total 1,432km, 47 special stages**

| 1. Mikkola/ | | | |
|---|---|---|---|
| Hertz | Audi quattro | 4.19.05 | |
| 2. Blomqvist/ | | | |
| Cederberg | Audi quattro | 4.19.33 | |
| 3. Airikkala/ | | | |
| Piironen | Mitsubishi Lancer | 4.23.22 | |
| 4. Salonen/ | | | |
| Harjanne | Datsun Silvia | 4.25.02 | |
| 5. Laine/ | | | |
| Virtanen | Talbot Sunbeam | 4.31.54 | |

6. Brookes/
Morgan          Vauxhall Chevette   4.37.10

Retirements:    Mouton/Pons went off.

## San Remo (Round 10) 3–8 Oct.
## Total 2,663km, 56 special stages

| 1. *Blomqvist/* | | |
|---|---|---|
| *Cederberg* | *Audi quattro* | 8.37.47 |
| 2. *Mikkola/* | | |
| *Hertz* | *Audi quattro* | 8.40.03 |
| 3. Röhrl/ | | |
| Geistdörfer | Opel Ascona 400 | 8.40.14 |
| 4. *Mouton/* | | |
| *Pons* | *Audi quattro* | 8.40.59 |
| 5. Toivonen/ | | |
| Gallagher | Opel Ascona 400 | 8.41.43 |
| 6. *Cinotto/* | | |
| *Radaelli* | *Audi quattro* | 8.55.51 |

Retirements:    Wittmann/Diekmann went
off; Demuth/Fischer engine.

## Ivory Coast (Round 11) 27 Oct–1 Nov.
## Total 4,995km

| 1. Röhrl/ | | |
|---|---|---|
| Geistdörfer | Opel Ascona 400 | *8.43 |
| 2. Eklund/ | | |
| Spjuth | Toyota Celica | 10.17 |
| 3. Waldegard/ | | |
| Thorszelius | Toyota Celica | 11.00 |
| 4. Saby/ | | |
| Le Saux | Renault 5 Turbo | 17.51 |
| 5. Ambrosino/ | | |
| Fauchille | Peugeot 505 | 19.43 |
| 6. Salim/ | | |
| Konan | Mitsubishi Lancer | 23.48 |

Retirements:    Mouton/Pons went off.
* penalties.

## Lombard RAC (Round 12) 20–25 Nov.
## Total 2,970km, 68 special stages

| 1. *Mikkola/* | | |
|---|---|---|
| *Hertz* | *Audi quattro* | 8.01.46 |
| 2. *Mouton/* | | |
| *Pons* | *Audi quattro* | 8.06.03 |
| 3. Toivonen/ | | |
| Gallagher | Opel Ascona 400 | 8.06.12 |
| 4. Alen/ | | |
| Kivimäki | Lancia Rally | 8.11.43 |
| 5. *Demuth/* | | |
| *Daniels* | *Audi quattro* | 8.14.10 |
| 6. Brookes/ | | |
| Broad | Vauxhall Chevette | 8.14.50 |

## Drivers' Championship:
1. Rohrl 109; 2. Mouton 97; 3. Mikkola 70;
4. Blomqvist 58; 5. Eklund 57;
6. Waldegard 36.
## Manufacturers' Championship:
1. Audi 116; 2. Opel 104; 3. Datsun 57;
4. Ford 55; 5. Toyota 41; 6. Renault 34.

# 1983

## Monte Carlo (Round 1) 22–28 Jan.
## Total 4,197km, 31 special stages

| 1. Röhrl/ | | |
|---|---|---|
| Geistdörfer | Lancia Rally 7 | 7.58.57 |
| 2. Alen/ | | |
| Kivimäki | Lancia Rally | 8.05.49 |
| 3. *Blomqvist/* | | |
| *Cederberg* | *Audi quattro* | 8.10.15 |
| 4. *Mikkola/* | | |
| *Hertz* | *Audi quattro* | 8.13.02 |
| 5. Vatanen/ | | |
| Harryman | Opel Ascona 400 | 8.14.03 |
| 6. Toivonen/ | | |
| Gallagher | Opel Ascona 400 | 8.15.54 |

Retirements:    Mouton/Pons went off.

## Sweden (Round 2) 11–13 Feb.
## Total 1,390km, 24 special stages

| 1. *Mikkola/* | | |
|---|---|---|
| *Hertz* | *Audi quattro* | 4.28.47 |
| 2. *Blomqvist/* | | |
| *Cederberg* | *Audi 80 quattro* | 4.29.34 |
| 3. *Lampi/* | | |
| *Kuukkala* | *Audi quattro* | 4.32.51 |
| 4. *Mouton/* | | |
| *Pons* | *Audi quattro* | 4.33.56 |
| 5. Grundel/ | | |
| Melleroth | VW Golf GTI | 4.38.33 |
| 6. Vatanen/ | | |
| Harryman | Opel Ascona 400 | 4.40.38 |

## Portugal (Round 3) 2–5 Mar.
## Total 2,325km, 40 special stages

| 1. *Mikkola/* | | |
|---|---|---|
| *Hertz* | *Audi quattro* | 7.17.24 |
| 2. *Mouton/* | | |
| *Pons* | *Audi quattro* | 7.18.19 |
| 3. Röhrl/ | | |
| Geistdörfer | Lancia Rally | 7.19.14 |
| 4. Alen/ | | |
| Kivimäki | Lancia Rally | 7.24.29 |
| 5. Vudafieri/ | | |
| Perissinot | Lancia Rally | 7.41.49 |

6. Zanini/
Sabater        Talbot Lotus        7.50.29

Retirements:    Blomqvist/Cederberg
differential.

## Safari (Round 4) 30 Mar–4 Apr.
## Total 5,034km

| 1. Vatanen/ | | |
|---|---|---|
| Harryman | Opel Ascona 400 | *6.36 |
| 2. *Mikkola/* | | |
| *Hertz* | *Audi quattro* | 6.42 |
| 3. *Mouton/* | | |
| *Pons* | *Audi quattro* | 7.35 |
| 4. Shah/ | | |
| Khan | Nissan 240 RS | 7.58 |
| 5. Takaoko/ | | |
| Sunahara | Subaru 1800 Sedan | 13.51 |
| 6. Iwase/ | | |
| Vinayak | Nissan 160J | 14.03 |

Retirements:    Preston/Lyall went off.
* penalties.

## Corsica (Round 5) 5–7 May.
## Total 1,715km, 28 special stages

| 1. Alen/ | | |
|---|---|---|
| Kivimäki | Lancia Rally | 12.43.38 |
| 2. Röhrl/ | | |
| Geistdörfer | Lancia Rally | 12.45.27 |
| 3. Vudafieri/ | | |
| Pirollo | Lancia Rally | 12.50.08 |
| 4. Bettega/ | | |
| Perissinot | Lancia Rally | 12.57.27 |
| 5. Saby/ | | |
| Williams | Renault 5 Turbo | 13.25.27 |
| 6. Pond/ | | |
| Arthur | Nissan 240 RS | 13.44.51 |

Retirements:    Mikkola/Hertz went off;
Mouton/Pons fire.

## Acropolis (Round 6) 30 May–2 Jun.
## Total 2,263km, 45 special stages

| 1. Röhrl/ | | |
|---|---|---|
| Geistdörfer | Lancia Rally | 11.12.22 |
| 2. Alen/ | | |
| Kivimäki | Lancia Rally | 11.18.42 |
| 3. *Blomqvist/* | | |
| *Cederberg* | *Audi quattro* | 11.26.18 |
| 4. Vatanen/ | | |
| Harryman | Opel Ascona 400 | 11.35.11 |
| 5. Bettega/ | | |
| Perissinot | Lancia Rally | 11.36.38 |

6. Mehta/
Mehta          Nissan 240 RS        11.49.41

Retirements:    Mouton/Pons went off;
                Mikkola/Hertz engine.

## New Zealand (Round 7) 25–28 Jun.
## Total 2,622km, 33 special stages

| 1. Röhrl/ | | |
|---|---|---|
| Geistdörfer | Lancia Rally | 12.10.13 |
| 2. Salonen/ | | |
| Harjanne | Nissan 240 RS | 12.26.11 |
| 3. Bettega/ | | |
| Perissinot | Lancia Rally | 12.41.42 |
| 4. Mehta/ | | |
| Mehta | Nissan 240 RS | 13.10.35 |
| 5. Donald/ | | |
| Porter | Datsun Bluebird | 13.20.50 |
| 6. Stewart/ | | |
| Parkhill | Ford Escort RS | 13.30.58 |

Retirements:    Mikkola/Hertz injection;
                Blomqvist/Cederberg
                disqualified;
                Mouton/Pons engine.

## Argentina (Round 8) 2–6 Aug.
## Total 3,244km, 18 special stages

| 1 *Mikkola/* | | |
|---|---|---|
| *Hertz* | *Audi quattro* | 10.18.54 |
| 2: *Blomqvist/* | | |
| *Cederberg* | *Audi quattro* | 10.27.28 |
| 3. *Mouton/* | | |
| *Pons* | *Audi quattro* | 10.25.35 |
| 4. *Mehta/* | | |
| *Mehta* | *Audi quattro* | 10.40.02 |
| 5. Alen/ | | |
| Kivimäki | Lancia Rally | 10.50.12 |
| 6. *Wurz/* | | |
| *Stohl* | *Audi 80 quattro* | 12.09.37 |

## 1000 Lakes (Round 9) 26–28 Aug.
## Total 1,460km, 50 special stages

| 1. *Mikkola/* | | |
|---|---|---|
| *Hertz* | *Audi quattro* | 4.23.44 |
| 2. *Blomqvist/* | | |
| *Cederberg* | *Audi quattro* | 4.24.05 |
| 3. Alenl | | |
| Kivimäki | Lancia Rally | 4.24.33 |
| 4. *Eklund/* | | |
| *Spjuth* | *Audi quattro* | 4.26.03 |
| 5. Airikkala/ | | |
| Piironen | Lancia Rally | 4.32.09 |
| 6. Kankkunen/ | | |
| Pettersson | Toyota Celica | 4.34.49 |

## San Remo (Round 10) 2–10 Oct.
## Total 2,663km, 58 special stages

| 1. Alen/ | | |
|---|---|---|
| Kivimäki | Lancia Rally | 8.50.17 |
| 2. Röhrl/ | | |
| Geistdörfer | Lancia Rally | 8.52.26 |
| 3. Bettega/ | | |
| Perissinot | Lancia Rally | 8.55.27 |
| 4. Toivonen/ | | |
| Gallagher | Opel Manta 400 | 8.59.49 |
| 5. Biasion/ | | |
| Siviero | Lancia Rally | 9.00.42 |
| 6. Cerrato/ | | |
| Cerri | Opel Manta 400 | 9.08.04 |

Retirements:    Blomqvist/Cederberg went
                off; Mikkola/Hertz fire.

## Ivory Coast (Round 11) 25–30 Oct.
## Total 4,498km

| 1. Waldegard/ | | |
|---|---|---|
| Thorszelius | Toyota Celica Turbo | *5.18 |
| 2. *Mikkola/* | | |
| *Hertz* | *Audi quattro* | 5.29 |
| 3. Eklund/ | | |
| Spjuth | Toyota Celica Turbo | 6.58 |
| 4. Assef/ | | |
| Barrault | Toyota Celica | 12.09 |
| 5. Ambrosino/ | | |
| Le Saux | Peugeot 505 | 14.22 |
| 6. Salim/ | | |
| Konan | Mitsubishi Lancer | 16.08 |

*penalties.

## Lombard RAC (Round 12) 19–24 Nov.
## Total 2,243km, 57 special stages

| 1. *Blomqvist/* | | |
|---|---|---|
| *Cederberg* | *Audi quattro* | 8.50.28 |
| 2. *Mikkola/* | | |
| *Hertz* | *Audi quattro* | 9.00.21 |
| 3. McRae/ | | |
| Grindrod | Opel Manta 400 | 9.12.79 |
| 4. *Lampi/* | | |
| *Kuukkala* | *Audi quattro* | 9.16.57 |
| 5. Brookes/ | | |
| Broad | Vauxhall Chevette | 9.19.01 |
| 6. *Buffum/* | | |
| *Wilson* | *Audi quattro* | 9.21.16 |

Retirements:    Mouton/Pons went off.

## Drivers' Championship:
1. Mikkola 125; 2. Röhrl 102; 3. Alen 100;
4. Blomqvist 89; 5. Mouton 53; 6. Vatanen 54.

## Manufacturers' Championship:
1. Lancia 118; 2. Audi 116; 3. Opel 87;
4. Nissan 52; 5. Renault 27;
6. Toyota 24.

# 1984

## Monte Carlo (Round 1) 22–27 Jan.
## Total 3,499km, 26 special stages

| 1. *Röhrl/* | | |
|---|---|---|
| *Geistdörfer* | *Audi quattro* | 8.52.29 |
| 2. *Blomqvist/* | | |
| *Cederberg* | *Audi quattro* | 8.53.42 |
| 3. *Mikkola/* | | |
| *Hertz* | *Audi quattro* | 9.05.09 |
| 4. Therier/ | | |
| Vial | Renault 5 Turbo | 9.16 53 |
| 5. Bettega/ | | |
| Perissinot | Lancia Rally | 9.21.41 |
| 6. Biasion/ | | |
| Siviero | Lancia Rally | 9.29.49 |

## Sweden (Round 2) 10–13 Feb.
## Total 1,703km, 27 special stages

| 1. *Blomqvist/* | | |
|---|---|---|
| *Cederberg* | *Audi quattro* | 4.16.45 |
| 2. *Mouton/* | | |
| *Pons* | *Audi quattro* | 4.24.12 |
| 3. *Eklund/* | | |
| *Whittock* | *Audi quattro* | 4.33.27 |
| 4. Jonsson/ | | |
| Gustavsson | Opel Ascona 400 | 4.35.25 |
| 5. Torph/ | | |
| Svanstrom | Opel Ascona | 4.36.46 |
| 6. Johansson/ | | |
| Olsson | Opel Ascona | 4.37.10 |

## Portugal (Round 3) 7–10 Mar.
## Total 2,400km, 45 special stages

| 1. *Mikkola/* | | |
|---|---|---|
| *Hertz* | *Audi quattro* | 7.35.32 |
| 2. Alen/ | | |
| Kivimäki | Lancia Rally | 7.35.59 |
| 3. Bettega/ | | |
| Perissinot | Lancia Rally | 7.58.21 |
| 4. Biasion/ | | |
| Siviero | Lancia Rally | 7.59.22 |
| 5. Ragnotti/ | | |
| Thimonier | Renault 5 Turbo | 8.13.42 |
| 6. *Röhrl/* | | |
| *Geistdörfer* | *Audi quattro* | 8.21.22 |

Retirements:    Blomqvist/Cederberg went
                off.

## Safari (Round 4) 19–23 Apr.
## Total 5,264km

| | | |
|---|---|---|
| 1. Waldegard/ Thorszelius | Toyota Celica Turbo | *2.02 |
| 2. Aaltonen/ Drews | Opel Manta 400 | 2.11 |
| 3. *Mikkola/ Hertz* | *Audi quattro* | 2.25 |
| 4. Alen/ Kivimdki | Lancia Rally | 3.08 |
| 5. Mehta/ Combes | Nissan 240 RS | 3.35 |
| 6. Preston/ Lyall | Lancia Rally | 4.14 |

Retirements: Mouton/Pons turbocharger; Blomqvist/Cederberg engine.
\* penalties.

## Corsica (Round 5) May.
## Total 1,617km, 30 special stages

| | | |
|---|---|---|
| 1. Alen/ Kivimäki | Lancia Rally | 13.24.56 |
| 2. Biasion/ Siviero | Lancia Rally | 13.29.11 |
| 3. Ragnotti/ Thimonier | Renault 5 Turbo | 13.33.16 |
| 4. Nicolas/ Pasquier | Peugeot 205T16 | 13.44.50 |
| 5. *Blomqvist/ Cederberg* | *Audi quattro* | 13.45.55 |
| 6. Andruet/ Rick | Lancia Rally | 13.48.07 |

Retirements: Röhrl/Geistdörfer engine (*Audi Sport quattro*).

## Acropolis (Round 6) 28–31 May.
## Total 2,265km, 47 special stages

| | | |
|---|---|---|
| 1. *Blomqvist/ Cederberg* | *Audi quattro* | 1 0.41.51 |
| 2. *Mikkola/ Hertz* | *Audi quattro* | 10.44.58 |
| 3. Alen/ Kivimäki | Lancia Rally | 10.56.01 |
| 4. Bettega/ Cresto | Lancia Rally | 11.03.49 |
| 5. *Buffum/ Gallagher* | *Audi quattro* | 11.22.10 |
| 6. Salonen/ Harjanne | Nissan 240 RS | 11.26.29 |

Retirements: Röhrl/Geistdörfer (*Audi Sport quattro*) electrics;

Mouton/Pons (*Audi Sport quattro*) engine.

## New Zealand (Round 7) 23–26 Jun.
## Total 2,626km, 45 special stages

| | | |
|---|---|---|
| 1. *Blomqvist/ Cederberg* | *Audi quattro* | 10.40.41 |
| 2. Alen/ Kivimäki | Lancia Rally | 10.45.28 |
| 3. *Mikkola/ Hertz* | *Audi quattro* | 10.48.10 |
| 4. Salonen/ Harjanne | Nissan 240 RS | 11.05.29 |
| 5. Waldegard/ Thorszelius | Toyota Celica Turbo | 11.35.58 |
| 6. Cook/ Jones | Nissan 240 RS | 11.44.20 |

Retirements: Röhrl/Geistdörfer engine.

## Argentina (Round 8) 27 Jul–1 Aug.
## Total 2,619km, 23 special stages

| | | |
|---|---|---|
| 1. *Blomqvist/ Cederberg* | *Audi quattro* | 10.33.38 |
| 2. *Mikkola/ Hertz* | *Audi quattro* | 10.36.54 |
| 3. *Recalde/ del Buono* | *Audi quattro* | 10.38.48 |
| 4. Stillo/ Stillo | Renault 12 | 12.12. 20 |
| 5. Iwase/ Thatti | Opel Ascona 400 | 12.18.24 |
| 6. Torras/ Stella | Renault 12 | 12.20.57 |

## 1000 Lakes (Round 9) 26–28 Aug.
## Total 1,420km, 50 special stages

| | | |
|---|---|---|
| 1. Vatanen/ Harryman | Peugeot 205 T16 | 4.08.49 |
| 2. Alen/ Kivimäki | Lancia Rally | 4.10.49 |
| 3. Toivonen/ Piironen | Lancia Rally | 4.12.57 |
| 4. *Blomqvist/ Cederberg* | *Audi quattro* | 4.14.01 |
| 5. Kankkunen/ Gallagher | Toyota Celica Turbo | 4.19.39 |
| 6. *Eklund/ Whittock* | *Audi quattro* | 4.20.18 |

Retirements: Mikkola/Hertz (*Audi Sport quattro*) steering; Mouton/Pons (*Audi Sport quattro*) went off.

## San Remo (Round 10) 30 Sep–5 Oct.
## Total 2,576km, 54 special stages

| | | |
|---|---|---|
| 1. Vatanen/ Harryman | Peugeot 205 T16 | 8.44.34 |
| 2. Bettega/ Perissinot | Lancia Rally | 8.50.01 |
| 3. Biasion/ Siviero | Lancia Rally | 8.53.58 |
| 4. Tabaton/ Tedeschini | Lancia Rally | 9.07.53 |
| 5. Nicolas/ Pasqier | Peugeot 205 T16 | 9.13.16 |
| 6. Grundel/ Diekmann | VW Golf GTI | 9.43.30 |

Retirements: Blomqvist/Cederberg (*Audi quattro*) engine; Röhrl/Geistdörfer (*Audi quattro* ) went off.

## Ivory Coast (Round 11) 31 Oct–4 Nov.
## Total 4,112km

| | | |
|---|---|---|
| 1. *Blomqvist/ Cederberg* | *Audi Sport quattro* | *7.05 |
| 2. *Mikkola/ Hertz* | *Audi quattro* | 7.23 |
| 3. Mehta/ Combes | Nissan 240 RS | 8.05 |
| 4. Ambrosino/ Le Saux | Opel Manta 400 | 8.44 |
| 5. Horsey/ Williamson | Peugeot 504 | 13.58 |
| 6. Tauziac/ Cournil | Mitsubishi Colt | 24.13 |

\*penalties.

## Lombard RAC (Round 12) 25–29 Nov.
## Total 3,205km, 56 special stages

| | | |
|---|---|---|
| 1. Vatanen/ Harryman | Peugeot 205 T16 | 9.19.48 |
| 2. *Mikkola/ Hertz* | *Audi Sport quattro* | 9.20.29 |
| 3. Eklund/ Whittock | Toyota Celica Turbo | 9.37.07 |
| 4. *Mouton/ Pons* | *Audi Sport quattro* | 9.37.28 |
| 5. Brookes/ Broad | Opel Manta 400 | 9.48.06 |
| 6. Salonen/ Harjanne | Nissan 240 RS | 9.49.37 |

## Drivers' Championship:
1. Blomqvist 125; 2. Mikkola 104;
3. Alen 90; 4. Vatenen 60; 5. Bettega 49;

6. Biasion 43; 11. Röhrl 26; 12. Mouton 25.
**Manufacturers' Championship**:
1. Audi 120; 2. Lancia 108; 3. Peugeot 74;
4. Toyota 62; 5. Renault 55; 6. Opel 48.

# 1985

### Monte Carlo (Round 1) 26 Jan–2 Feb.
### Total 3,999km, 33 special stages

| | | |
|---|---|---|
| 1. Vatanen/ Harryman | Peugeot 205 TI6 | 10.20.49 |
| 2. *Röhrl/ Geistdörfer* | *Audi Sport quattro* | 10.26.06 |
| 3. Salonen/ Harjanne | Peugeot 205 T16 | 10.30.54 |
| 4. *Blomqvist/ Cederberg* | *Audi Sport quattro* | 10.40.11 |
| 5. Saby/ Fauchille | Peugeot 205 T16 | 10.40.45 |
| 6. Toivonen/ Piironen | Lancia Rally | 10.43.16 |

### Sweden (Round 2) 15–17 Feb.
### Total 1,640km, 29 special stages

| | | |
|---|---|---|
| 1. Vatanen/ Harryman | Peugeot 205 TI 6 | 4.38.49 |
| 2. *Blomqvist/ Cederberg* | *Audi Sport quattro* | 4.40.38 |
| 3. Salonen/ Harjanne | Peugeot 205 T16 | 4.42.15 |
| 4. *Mikkola/ Hertz* | *Audi Sport quattro* | 4.50.32 |
| 5. *Eklund/ Whittock* | *Audi quattro* | 4.55.50 |
| 6. *Pettersson/ Pettersson* | *Audi 80 quattro* | 5.02.03 |

Retirements: Röhrl/Geistdörfer (*Audi Sport quattro*) engine.

### Portugal (Round 3) 5–10 Mar.
### Total 2,455km, 47 special stages

| | | |
|---|---|---|
| 1. Salonen/ Harjanne | Peugeot 205 T16 | 8.07.25 |
| 2. Biasion/ Siviero | Lancia Rally | 8.12.12 |
| 3. *Röhrl/ Geistdörfer* | *Audi Sport quattro* | 8.13.23 |
| 4. *Blomqvist/ Cederberg* | *Audi Sport quattro* | 8.31.17 |
| 5. *Grissmann/ Pattermann* | *Audi quattro* | 9.13.20 |
| 6. Faria/ Nascimento | Ford Escort RS | 9.28.42 |

### Safari (Round 4) 4–8 Apr.
### Total 5,167km

| | | |
|---|---|---|
| 1. Kankkunen/ Gallagher | Toyota Celica Turbo | *5.78 |
| 2. Waldegard/ Thorszelius | Toyota Celica Turbo | 5.52 |
| 3. Kirkland/ Levitan | Nissan 240 RS | 6.07 |
| 4. Aaltonen/ Drews | Opel Manta 400 | 6.12 |
| 5. Weber/ Wanger | Opel Manta 400 | 6.56 |
| 6. Ambrosino/ Le Saux | Nissan 240 RS | 7.58 |

Retirements: Mikkola/Hertz (*Audi Sport quattro*) engine; Blomqvist/Cederberg (*Audi Sport quattro*) gearbox.
* penalties.

### Corsica (Round 5) 1–5 May.
### Total 1,603km, 29 special stages

| | | |
|---|---|---|
| 1. Ragnotti/ Thimonier | Renault 5 Turbo | 12.54.15 |
| 2. Saby/ Fauchille | Peugeot 205 T16 | 13.06.47 |
| 3. Beguin/ Lenne | Porsche 911 SC | 13.20.04 |
| 4. Coleman/ Morgan | Porsche 911 SC | 13.51.22 |
| 5. Loubet/ Vieu | Alfa Romeo GTV | 14.03.53 |
| 6. Ballas/ Laine | Alfa Romeo GTV | 14.16.53 |

Retirements: Röhrl/Geistdörfer (*Audi Sport quattro*) brakes.

### Acropolis (Round 6) 25–31 May.
### Total 2,295km, 47 special stages

| | | |
|---|---|---|
| 1. Salonen/ Harjanne | Peugeot 205 T16 | 10.20.19 |
| 2. *Blomqvist/ Cederberg* | *Audi Sport quattro* | 10.24.34 |
| 3. Carlsson/ Melander | Mazda RX7 | 11.08.15 |
| 4. Mehta/ Mehta | Nissan 240 RS | 11.10.46 |
| 5. Al Hajri/ Spiller | Porsche 91 1 SC | 11.21.50 |
| 6. Warmbold/ Biche | Mazda RX7 | 11.25.16 |

### New Zealand (Round 7) 29 Jun–2 Jul.
### Total 2,486km, 46 special stages

| | | |
|---|---|---|
| 1. Salonen/ Harjanne | Peugeot 205 TI6 | 8.29.16 |
| 2. Vatanen/ Harryman | Peugeot 205 TI6 | 8.30.33 |
| 3. *Röhrl/ Geistdörfer* | *Audi Sport quattro* | 8.31.42 |
| 4. *Blomqvist/ Cederberg* | *Audi Sport quattro* | 8.35.22 |
| 5. *Stewart/ Parkhill* | *Audi quattro* | 9.29.04 |
| 6. Cook/ Jones | Nissan 240 RS | 9.46.53 |

### Argentina (Round 8) 30 Jul–4 Aug.
### Total 2,615km, 23 special stages

| | | |
|---|---|---|
| 1. Salonen/ Harjanne | Peugeot 205 T16 | 10.04.33 |
| 2. *Wiedner/ Zehetner* | *Audi quattro* | 10.18.29 |
| 3. Reutemann/ Fauchille | Peugeot 205 T16 | 10.35.47 |
| 4. Mehta/ Mehta | Nissan 240 RS | 11.04.46 |
| 5. Soto/ Christie | Renault 18 GTX | 11.10.58 |
| 6. Stillo/ Stillo | Renault 12 | 11.49.42 |

Retirements: Blomqvist/Cederberg (*Audi Sport quattro*) engine.

### 1000 Lakes (Round 9) 23–25 Aug.
### Total 1,417km, 51 special stages

| | | |
|---|---|---|
| 1. Salonen/ Harjanne | Peugeot 205 TI6 | 4.10.35 |
| 2. *Blomqvist/ Cederberg* | *Audi Sport quattro* | 4.11.23 |
| 3. Alen/ Kivimäki | Lancia Rally | 4.14.14 |
| 4. Toivonen/ Piironen | Lancia Rally | 4.22.01 |
| 5. Grundel/ Diekmann | Peugeot 205 T16 | 4.22.03 |
| 6. *Eklund/ Berglund* | *Audi quattro* | 4.23.08 |

Retirements: Mikkola/Hertz (*Audi Sport quattro SI*) loss of oil.

### San Remo (Round 10) 29 Sep–4 Oct.
### Total 2,300km, 43 special stages

| | | |
|---|---|---|
| 1. *Röhrl/ Geistdörfer* | *Audi Sport quattro S1* | 7.10.10 |

| 2. Salonen/ | | |
|---|---|---|
| Harjanne | Peugeot 205 T16 | 7.16.39 |
| 3. Toivonen/ | | |
| Piironen | Lancia Rally | 7.18.02 |
| 4. Alen/ | | |
| Kivimäki | Lancia Rally | 7.18.43 |
| 5. Cerrato/ | | |
| Cerri | Lancia Rally | 7.25.35 |
| 6. Biasion/ | | |
| Siviero | Lancia Rally | 7.33.33 |

## Ivory Coast (Round 11) 29 Oct–3 Nov.
### Total 4,200km

| 1. Kankkunen/ | | |
|---|---|---|
| Gallagher | Toyota Celica Turbo | *4.46 |
| 2. Waldegard/ | | |
| Thorszelius | Toyota Celica Turbo | 4.46 |
| 3. Ambrosino/ | | |
| Le Saux | Nissan 240 RS | 6.19 |
| 4. Kirkland/ | | |
| Combes | Nissan 240 RS | 8.36 |
| 5. Salim/ | | |
| Konan | Mitsubishi Lancer | 13.33 |
| 6. Molino/ | | |
| Massela | Subaru Leone | 19.53 |

Retirements: Mouton/Hertz (*Audi Sport quattro*) gave up
* penalties.

## Lombard RAC (Round 12) 23–28 Nov.
### Total 3,528km, 63 special stages

| 1. Toivonen/ | | |
|---|---|---|
| Wilson | Lancia Delta S4 | 9.32.05 |
| 2 Alen/ | | |
| Kivimäki | Lancia Delta S4 | 9.33.01 |
| 3. Pond/ | | |
| Arthur | MG Metro 6R4 | 9.34.32 |
| 4. Eklund/ | | |
| Cederberg | *Audi quattro* | 10.00.35 |
| 5. Kankkunen/ | Toyota Celica | |
| Gallagher | Turbo | 10.10.53 |
| 6. McRae/ | | |
| Grindrod | Opel Manta 400 | 10.16.01 |

Retirements: Röhrl/Short (*Audi Sport quattro S1*) went off;
Mikkola/Hertz (*Audi Sport quattro*) electrics.

## Drivers' Championship:
1. Salonen 127; 2. Blomqvist 75;
3. Röhrl 59; 4.Vatanen 55; 5. Kankkunen 48;
6. Toivonen 48.
## Manufacturers' Championship:

1. Peugeot 142; 2. Audi 126; 3. Lancia 70;
4. Nissan 56; 5. Toyota 44; 6. Renault 38.

## Hongkong–Beijing 15–19 Sep.
### Total 3,412km, 23 special stages

| 1. *Mikkola/* | | |
|---|---|---|
| *Hertz* | *Audi quattro* | 4.01.08 |
| 2 Torph/ | | |
| Thorszelius | Nissan 240RS | 4.07.53 |
| 3. Weber/ | | |
| Wanger | Opel Manta 400 | 4.12.15 |
| 4. *Dawson/* | | |
| *Pegg* | *Audi quattro* | 4.14.13 |
| 5. Mehta/ | | |
| Mehta | Nissan 240RS | 4.14.23 |
| 6. Kirkland/ | | |
| Nixon | Nissan 240RS | 4.16.06 |

# 1986

## Monte Carlo (Round 1) 18–24 Jan.
### Total 3,984km, 36 special stages

| 1. Toivonen/ | | |
|---|---|---|
| Cresto | Lancia Delta S4 | 10.11.24 |
| 2. Salonen/ | | |
| Harjanne | Peugeot 205 TI6 | 10.15.28 |
| 3. *Mikkola/* | *Audi Sport* | |
| *Hertz* | *quattro SI* | 10.18.46 |
| 4 *Röhrl/* | *Audi Sport* | |
| *Geistdorfer* | *quattro SI* | 10.20.59 |
| 5. Kankkunen/ | | |
| Piironen | Peugeot 205 T16 | 10.39.47 |
| 6. Saby/ | | |
| Fauchille | Peugeot 205 T16 | 10.45.54 |

## Sweden (Round 2) 14–16 Feb.
### Total 1,670km, 30 special stages

| 1 Kankkunen/ | | |
|---|---|---|
| Piironen | Peugeot 205 T16 | 5.09.19 |
| 2. Alen/ | | |
| Kivimäki | Lancia Delta S4 | 5.11.13 |
| 3. Grundel/ | | |
| Melander | Ford RS 200 | 5.15.35 |
| 4. *Ericsson/* | | |
| *Michel* | *Audi 90 quattro* | 5.24.39 |
| 5. *Pettersson/* | *Audi Coupé* | |
| *Pettersson* | *quattro* | 5.24.57 |
| 6. Andruet/ | | |
| Peuvergne | Citroën BX4TC | 5.33.05 |

## Portugal (Round 3) 4–9 Mar.
### Total 2,368km, 42 special stages

| 1. Moutinho/ | | |
|---|---|---|
| Fortes | Renault 5 Turbo | 7.50.44 |

| 2. Bica/ | | |
|---|---|---|
| Junior | Lancia Rally | 8.04.11 |
| 3. del Zoppo/ | | |
| Roggia | Fiat Uno Turbo | 8.07.36 |
| 4. Ortigao/ | | |
| Perez | Toyota Corolla GT | 8.10.26 |
| 5. Tchine/ | | |
| Thimonier | Opel Manta 400 | 8.13.04 |
| 6. Couloumies/ | | |
| Causse | Peugeot 205 GTi | 8.36.27 |

The top drivers withdrew after a serious accident, when Portuguese driver Joaquim Santos lost control of his Ford and careered into the spectators. Audi withdrew from the World Rally Championship.

## Hong Kong–Beijing 14–19 Sep.
### Total 3,864km, 19 special stages

| 1. *Blomqvist/* | | |
|---|---|---|
| *Berglund* | *Audi quattro* | 8.19.58 |
| 2. Ning/ | Mitsubishi Starion | |
| Xiang | Turbo | 9.53.37 |
| 3. Satoh/ | | |
| Abe | Toyota Corolla | 10.03.42 |
| 4. Himeji/ | | |
| Omoto | Toyota Corolla GT | 10.06.05 |
| 5. Nishiyama/ | | |
| Nagayama | Toyota Supra | 10.13.13 |
| 6. Noda/ | | |
| Hashizume | Mazda RX7 | 10.20.06 |

# 1987

## Monte Carlo (Round 1) 17–22 Jan.
### Total 3,160km, 25 special stages

| 1. Biasion/ | | |
|---|---|---|
| Siviero | Lancia Delta HF | 7.39.50 |
| 2. Kankkunen/ | | |
| Piironen | Lancia Delta HF | 7.40.49 |
| 3. *Röhrl/* | | |
| *Geistdorfer* | *Audi 200 quattro* | 7.44.00 |
| 4. Carlsson/ | | |
| Carlsson | Mazda 323 | 7.55.45 |
| 5. Eriksson/ | | |
| Diekmann | VW Golf GTI 16V | 8.08.09 |
| 6. Ragnotti/ | | |
| Thimonier | Renault 1 1 Turbo | 8.13.26 |

## Sweden
No Audi works entry.

## Portugal
No Audi works entry.

## Safari (Round 4) 16–20 Apr.
## Total 4,017km

| | | |
|---|---|---|
| 1. *Mikkola/* | | |
| *Hertz* | *Audi 200 quattro* | *3.39.44 |
| 2. *Röhrl/* | | |
| *Geistdorfer* | *Audi 200 quattro* | 3.56.59 |
| 3. Torph/ | | |
| Melander | Toyota Supra | 4.31.09 |
| 4. Weber/ | | |
| Feltz | VW Golf GTI 16V | 5.47.27 |
| 5. Eklund/ | | |
| Whittock | Subaru Coupé | 6.00.42 |
| 6. Ulyate/ | | |
| Street | Toyota Supra | 6.33.07 |

\* penalties.

## Corsica
No Audi works entry.

## Acropolis (Round 6) 31 May–3 Jun.
## Total 1,911km, 33 special stages

| | | |
|---|---|---|
| 1. Alen/ | | |
| Kivimäki | Lancia Delta HF | 7.25.57 |
| 2. Kankkunen/ | | |
| Piironen | Lancia Delta HF | 7.26.45 |
| 3. *Mikkola/* | | |
| *Hertz* | *Audi 200 quattro* | 7.31.21 |
| 4. *Recalde/* | *Audi Coupé* | |
| *del Buono* | *quattro* | 7.32.29 |
| 5. Ragnotti/ | | |
| Thimonier | Renault 11 Turbo | 7.34.27 |
| 6. Weber/ | | |
| Feltz | VW Golf GTI 16V | 7.36.53 |
| Retired: | Röhrl/Geistdorfer (*Audi 200 quattro*) engine. | |

## Olympus
No Audi works entry.

## New Zealand
No Audi works entry.

## Argentina
No Audi works entry.

## 1000 Lakes (Round 10) 27–30 Aug.
## Total 1,701km, 51 special stages

| | | |
|---|---|---|
| 1. Alen/ | | |
| Kivimäki | Lancia Delta HF | 5.12.22 |

| | | | |
|---|---|---|---|
| 2. Vatanen/ | | | |
| Harryman | Ford Sierra RS | 5.17.54 | |
| 3. Blomqvist/ | | | |
| Berglund | Ford Sierra RS | 5.18.51 | |
| 4. *Eklund/* | *Audi Coupé* | | |
| *Whittock* | *quattro* | 5.21.00 | |
| 5. Kankkunen/ | | | |
| Piironen | Lancia Delta HF | 5.21.34 | |
| 6. Edling/ | | | |
| Andersson | Mazda 323 | 5.23.47 | |
| Retired: | Mikkola/Hertz (*Audi 200 quattro*) went off. | | |

## Ivory Coast
No Audi works entry.

## San Remo
No Audi works entry.

## Lombard RAC
No Audi works entry.

## Drivers' Championship:
1. Kankkunen 100; 2. Biasion 94; 3. Alen 88
4; Eriksson 70; 5. Ragnotti 51; 6. Weber 44;
8. Mikkola 32; 11. Röhrl 27.

## Manufacturers' Championship:
1. Lancia 140; 2. Audi 82; 3. Renault 71;
4. Volkswagen 64; 5. Ford 62; 6. Mazda 52.

# TO AMERICA

## 1988 – TransAm
Having achieved all that could reasonably be achieved in the European rallying arena, Audi set off across the Atlantic to show how tarmac racing should be tackled. The first traditional stronghold to be breached was TransAm NASCAR in the 1988 season. By then the turbocharged quattro was outmoded by the new breed of slippery shaped aerodynamic cars from the era heralded by the arrival of the world-beating (0.30 Cd) Audi 100 in 1983. The car chosen for the USA invasion was actually the 100's bigger, plusher brother, the Audi 200 – quattro, of course. This choice allowed Audi two bites at the PR cherry – to push their new baby and reinforce the quattro principle. However, by the time the car hit the tracks, it bore only scant resemblance to the road car.

One can imagine the smirks of dyed-in-the-wool enthusiasts as they heard of this 5-cylinder (Not a V8? Whatever next?) luxury limousine that was coming over to race. One can also imagine how quickly they turned to frowns of consternation when the car was not only competitive straight away, but by the second race was a winner! Audi entered three cars for Hans-Joachim Stuck, Walter Röhrl and American Hurley Haywood. Audi strode to victory in eight races, winning them the manufacturers' title ahead of Chevrolet, Oldsmobile and Mercury.

Haywood won two of those races and scored consistently well enough in the rest to give him the Drivers' Championship.

## Drivers' Championship:
1. Haywood 152; 2. Huerr 141;
3. Pruett 117; 4. Derhaag 104;
5. Brassfield 100; 6. Stuck 99.
## Manufacturers' Championship:
1. Audi 92; 2. Chevrolet 63;
3. Oldsmobile 51; 4. Mercury 48.

## Audi 200 quattro TransAm – basic specification

| | |
|---|---|
| Engine | 5-cylinder in line, 10v, 2110cc producing 510bhp at 7500rpm. |
| Transmission | Permanent 4WD, 6 gears. |
| Length | 4897mm |
| Width | 2033mm |
| Weight | 1115kg |

## 1989 – Imsa GTO
In 1989 Audi, ever seeking new challenges, contested the North American Imsa GTO championship. This time the car chosen for battle was the smaller and more wieldy Audi 90. It was a silhouette championship, where the race car must use the original pillars and roof of the production model but the rest of the bodywork can be adapted to suit. As the photos show, it certainly was! Apart from these items, it was a space frame of steel tubes with a carbon-fibre floor and rear-mounted rubber fuel tank (encased in alloy for safety). The cockpit area was surrounded by aluminium to improve the stiff-

Left *Taking a 510bhp, 4WD luxury limousine tarmac racing was almost laughable – until the end of the year when Hurley Haywood all-wheel drove into the history books, with the drivers' and manufacturers' titles under his belt.*

Below left *It says Audi quattro on the front, but would you recognise it as such? The fearsome Audi 90-based Imsa car was more familiar …*

Bottom left *… from the rear, where the boot lid and line of lights were straight from the road car. Not that huge wing, though!*

ness of the car, and the bodywork was carbon-fibre.

Engines could be based on any block from the manufacturer's range, and Audi selected a 5-cylinder unit based on the 20v engines originally used in the Sport quattros. Bosch Motronic engine management was used along with Nicasil-coated aluminium bores (rather than iron cylinder liners), new cams more suited to going-round-in-circles tarmac racing, and a redesigned cylinder head for more efficient cooling and rigidity.

The driveline was essentially that used in the 200 quattro (itself descended from the rally cars) with six gears. Weight penalties were applied on a sliding scale, the 90 quattro picking up 10 per cent because of the 4WD advantage.

Because the 4WD system requires the same size tyres at front and rear, it is believed that they were the largest steered wheels ever used in motor racing at the time – 25.5in diameter by 14in width on 17in diameter rims.

At the start of the season the power output was officially declared to be 'around 620bhp'. Walter Röhrl smiled when he said: 'No, the engine has, today, 700 horsepower. And in two or three months, when we have got the Motronic working perfectly, I think that figure will rise by ten per cent.' The final officially listed figure was 720bhp.

Hurley Haywood and Hans-Joachim Stuck drove the cars, the latter taking victory at Summit Point, Mid-Ohio,

Topeka, Sears Point, Watkins Glen, Lime Rock and Laguna Seca. Though the most successful individual driver of the year, both he and Audi failed to clinch the championship, largely because of a decision not to compete in the long-distance races in Daytona and Sebring at the start of the season. Nevertheless, in two years of tarmac racing in the USA, Audi had proved conclusively that 4WD is not solely the preserve of loose-surface racing.

**Drivers' championship**:

1. Halsmer 203; 2. Dallenbach 201;
3. Stuck 170; 4. Haywood 130;
5. Millen 103; 6. Morton 79.

**Manufacturers' championship**:

1. Mercury 236; 2. Audi 195; 3. Nissan 122;
4. Chevrolet 81; 5. Mazda 61; 6. Porsche 15.

## Audi 90 quattro Imsa GTO – basic specification

| | |
|---|---|
| Engine | 5-cylinder in-line, 20v, 2190cc producing 720bhp at 7500rpm. |
| Transmission | Permanent 4WD, 6 gears. |
| Length | 4480mm |
| Width | 2000mm |
| Weight | 1206kg |

## Pikes Peak

Still in the States but a world away from racing on smooth tarmac, the Pikes Peak Hillclimb in Colorado has to be, in anyone's book, one of the most hair-raising motorsport events ever devised. The competitors charge around the side of a mountain, with terrifying drops awaiting those who put so much as a wheel wrong. Those with vertigo need not apply!

Audi went there for three years, winning each time. In 1985 Michèle Mouton took a Sport quattro from bottom to top in 11.25.39 minutes, beating Rod Millen's Mazda RX7 into second place by 47 seconds. In 1986 Rod was second again, improving his time by four seconds, but it was still an Audi which won, this time a Sport quattro S1 with American racing legend Bobby Unser Snr at the wheel with a

time of 11.09.22 minutes. In 1987 it looked almost like a European rally event, with Malcolm Wilson's Ford RS200 in fifth place and the next three places taken by Peugeot 205 T16s. However, still at the top was Audi with Walter Röhrl blasting through the lights in his Sport quattro S1 at 10.47.85.

## THE TARMAC TERRORS

### 1990

Nothing is wasted in motorsport, least of all experience. Audi took its experience of tarmac racing in the USA and applied it to Touring Cars. Audi started in 1990 in its homeland with, incredibly, the top-of-the-range V8 quattro as the basis for its honours contender. As ever, critics found Audi's strategy hard to believe; after all, it was a fat cat up-market luxury saloon – surely the Audi 80, 90 or coupé would be more appropriate? Maybe so, but none of them could have done any better than Hans-Joachim Stuck, who drove his luxury liner to crush the opposition and win the Championship, with occasional driver Walter Röhrl taking 11th place. This was in the face of massive opposition from the experienced teams of Mercedes, BMW and Opel, the latter appearing to have everything sewn up with their Omega, one of the lightest cars using one of the most powerful engines.

The 1990 V8 quattro saloon racer was an impressive motor car by any

*Walter Röhrl powers the 600bhp Audi Sport quattro S1 up the tortuous 12.4-mile 156-corner gravel road of Colorado's Pikes Peak in July 1987. He reached the 14,100ft summit in a record-breaking 10 minutes 47.85 seconds, smashing the previous record – also held by an Audi – by over 20 seconds.*

standards. The basic profile of the 4-door saloon was kept, with carbon/Kevlar composite used for the bonnet, boot and rear bumper. The 24v 3561.8cc engine had DOHC per 90 degree vee bank, with standard 81mm bore and 86.4mm stroke, and wet sump lubrication. The exhaust system was full length, lightweight and featured twin catalytic converters with a tuned-length induction system. Bosch Motronic MP 1.8 engine management replaced the standard Motronic system. The power output was quoted at 420bhp at 8200rpm (250bhp at 5800rpm), and the torque was 380Nm at 6000rpm (340Nm at 4000rpm).

The transmission was 6-speed permanent 4WD (a derivative of the 6-speed box previously used in rallying) with the alternative of Torsen/ZF limited-slip rear differentials and viscous coupling or Torsen central power split/viscous coupling front differential. Discs were ventilated all round, being 330x32mm and 335x36mm at front and rear respectively. Cockpit braking bias adjustment was possible, but ABS was not fitted. BBS 11J x 18in wheels were used, as opposed to the road cars 7.5J x 15in Tyres depended on circuit and conditions – typically 255/645 x 18 Dunlop slicks.

Hans-Joachim Stuck won the Championship, taking 189 points against the 177 of second placed man, Johnny Cecotto in his BMW M3.

## 1991/92

Frank Biela began a long and happy Audi touring car points tally when he repeated Stuck's success in 1991 (Stuck himself finished third that year). But in 1992 Audi didn't finish an acrimonious season, which saw the ruling body declaring the V8's crank illegal, even though Audi had taken great pains to check its legality earlier in the season.

From then on Audi worked at making its mid-range 80 model a winner on the Touring Car circuits of the world, the 80 Competition and quattro being very impressive – check the results in this chapter. But the A4 quattro was to eclipse everything else in a staggering 1996 season, which saw the Audis sweep all before them all over the world.

## A4 crosses the channel

The British Touring Car Championship (BTTC) is recognised by most as the biggest challenge in touring car racing. Those who know were of the opinion that the established front and rear-wheel drive cars would eat the Audis for breakfast. After all, with all that weight and complexity ... OK, *maybe* they'd have an advantage if it rained, and *maybe* on twisty circuits, but on

faster tracks they'd be outclassed.

The Buckingham-based Audi Sport Team was headed by John Wickham (who had previous experience at March Formula 2, Arrows Grand Prix and Nissan Touring Cars) with Richard Lloyd, ex-Audi and VW Golf racer, and one of the original partners (with Brian Ricketts) in GTi Engineering.

Frank Biela was the Number One driver, but the choice of John Bintcliffe was a surprise as he had no experience of driving at this level – though he had entered and won the British one-make Ford Fiesta and Renault Clio challenges.

The cars themselves were all factory machines, built in Germany at the Ingolstadt plant, using engines which were developed at Neckarsulm.

Ford and Nissan both experimented with 4WD for their touring cars during 1995, but couldn't make it work. Not surprising, really, as Audi have been hard at work developing their 4WD cars since 1977 – you can't catch-up almost 20 years of experience in a single season!

At the start of the season the Audis were handicapped by having to carry an extra 65kg of weight to offset the advantage of 4WD. After winning so convincingly in the early part of the season, TOCA (the ruling body) decided that, in the interests of good racing, a further 30kg should be added, which meant that Frank and John effectively drove with a 15 stone passenger on board!

Despite this, Biela hammered home enough wins and places to clinch the Championship by over 100 points. This

success was repeated all over the world, with the A4 quattro winning all seven race series it entered.

One wag commented that for 1997 all German cars with 4WD would have to tow a caravan! The truth was worryingly close!

## 1997

The outcry from the 2WD brigade was constant, and the reaction from the powers-that-be was that 4WD was banned for 1998, a ridiculous situation in a sport where technical supremacy is almost always a leapfrog situation; the Formula 1 McLarens, all-conquering during the '80s, weren't banned because the Williams or Ferrari teams weren't winning. Nor were the Williams cars banned in the early '90s when they came to rule the racing roost.

Nevertheless, the rule was passed, which put Audi in a dilemma. Normally, the current year's car is a great deal better than the previous year's, with many technical features being replaced or improved. But investing so much time, effort and money just for one season made no sense, thus much of the R & D work during 1997 went on the 1998 progenitor – a 2WD version of the A4. The effects of this were two-fold; first it put Audi behind in overall development compared with their 2WD rivals, and second, it combined with a massive 90kg weight penalty imposed right from the word go. As such, we had the incredible scenario of the Silver Arrows struggling to get into the top half of the grid. You don't have to be overly cynical to question the ruling body's reasoning through the year, though. Audi were,

## EUROPEAN TOURING CAR SPECIFICATIONS

| | V8 quattro – DTM | V8 quattro – DTM | 80 quattro 16v | 80 Competition | A4 quattro Supertouring |
|---|---|---|---|---|---|
| First race | Zolder 1990 | Zolder 1992 | Nogaro 1993 | Monza 1994 | Misano 1995 |
| Cylinders | V8 | V8 | 4 in-line | 4 in-line | 4 in-line |
| Displacement | 3561.8cc | 3561.8cc | 1988cc | 1998cc | 1998cc |
| Bore x stroke | 81 x 86.4mm | 81 x 86.4mm | 84 x 89.7mm | 85 x 88.1mm | 85 x 88.1mm |
| Torque | 280lb/ft at 6000rpm | 280lb/ft at 7000rpm | 177lb/ft at 7000rpm | 184lb/ft at 7000rpm | 166lb/ft at 7000rpm |
| Power | 420bhp at 8200rpm | 470bhp at 9500rpm | 272bhp at 8500rpm | 285bhp at 8250rpm | 296bhp at 8250rpm |
| No. of gears | 6 | 6 | 6 | 6 | 6 |
| Weight | 1220kg | 1250kg | 1050kg | 1050kg | 1040kg |

apparently, penalised the previous year for being too successful, and the organisers said they wanted more even racing and more competition. However, when Alain Menu's Williams Renault simply ran away with the Championship, winning races almost as a matter of course, and winning the Championship by a country mile, no weight penalty was even considered.

Eventually the organisers relented (slightly) on the Audi weight penalty, and instantly they were more competitive. At the double-header race at Scotland's twisty Knockhill course, the status quo was resumed. More important, perhaps, it was a landmark event, for in race one John Bintcliffe put his car on pole and led from flag to flag – two firsts before a frustrated but impressed Biela. In race two the grid and race positions were reversed, though a full tally of points for the Manufacturers' Championship put a smile on Audi's corporate face. Two more wins followed at Snetterton – again one each for the two drivers. However, the points situation was such that Audi simply could not accumulate the points required to beat Menu.

Top *For many, Audi's return to UK tarmac in 1996 was a first, though enthusiasts will remember the Audi 80s raced by Stirling Moss, Richard Lloyd and GP ace, Martin Brundle (seen here at Silverstone) in the late 1970s. However, British motorsport fans got their first sight of a silver Audi in 1936 at the Shelsley Walsh hill climb. It was then that Hans Stuck (father of Hans-Joachim Stuck) drove a twin rear-wheeled, 5.3 litre V16. In 1937 Bernd Rosemeyer won the Donington Grand Prix in a V16 C type, and a year later Tazio Nuvolari repeated the win at the same circuit, this time driving a 3-litre V12 D type.*

Middle *Fresh from their success in America, Hans-Joachim Stuck drove the V8 quattro luxury liner to victory in the German Touring Car Championship, a feat that was rounded off neatly …*

Right *… by a 1-2-3 win at Hockenheim by himself, Frank Jelinski and Walter Röhrl.*

Left *All-conquering car – the A4 quattro scooped no fewer than seven Touring Car Championships world-wide during 1996. The opposition reacted in true racing fashion, arguing (and succeeding) for the banning of 4WD in 1998.*

Below left *The low-down, mean look of the quattro's rear-end, complete with huge wing. It's a view familiar to most of the '96 competition.*

Below *All-conquering hero – Frank Biela, having previously been German, French and Italian Touring Car Champion, came to the UK in 1996 and cleaned up in his A4 quattro Supertouring – this despite a vicious weight penalty applied during the second part of the season.*

## AUDI EUROPEAN TOURING CAR RESULTS

Below are the important results of Audi's European Tarmac attack since its first foray in Germany in 1990.

### 1990
**German Touring Car Championship**

| | | |
|---|---|---|
| 1st | Hans-Joachim Stuck | Audi V8 quattro |
| 11th | Walter Röhrl | Audi V8 quattro |

### 1991
**German Touring Car Championship**

| | | |
|---|---|---|
| 1st | Frank Biela | Audi V8 quattro |
| 3rd | Hans-Joachim Stuck | Audi V8 quattro |
| 10th | Frank Jelinski | Audi V8 quattro |

### 1992
**German Touring Car Championship**

Audi withdrew from the DTM after the crankshaft used in the V8 quattro was outlawed by the ONS, even though it had originally been expressly accepted as legal.

### 1993
**French Touring Car Championship**

| | | |
|---|---|---|
| 1st | Frank Biela | Audi 80 quattro |
| 3rd | Marc Sourd | Audi 80 quattro |

### 1994
**D1 ADAC Touring Car Cup**

| | | |
|---|---|---|
| 2nd | Frank Biela | Audi 80 Competition |
| 3rd | Emanuele Pirro | Audi 80 Competition |
| 8th | Hans-Joachim Stuck | Audi 80 Competition |

**Italian Touring Car Championship**

| | | |
|---|---|---|
| 1st | Emanuele Pirro | Audi 80 Competition |
| 10th | Frank Biela | Audi 80 Competition |

### 1995
**D1 ADAC Super Touring Car Cup**

| | | |
|---|---|---|
| 3rd | Frank Biela | Audi A4 Supertouring |
| 4th | Hans-Joachim Stuck | Audi A4 Supertouring |

**Italian Touring Car Championship**

| | | |
|---|---|---|
| 1st | Emanuele Pirro | Audi A4 Supertouring |
| 2nd | Rinaldo Capello | Audi A4 Supertouring |

**FIA Touring Car World Cup**

| | | |
|---|---|---|
| 1st | Frank Biela | Audi A4 Supertouring |
| 2nd | Emanuele Pirro | Audi A4 Supertouring |

**South African Touring Car Championship**

| | | |
|---|---|---|
| 4th | Terry Moss | Audi 80 Competition |

### 1996
**D1 ADAC Super Touring Car Cup**

| | | |
|---|---|---|
| 1st | Emanuele Pirro | Audi A4 quattro |
| 4th | Christian Abt | Audi A4 quattro |
| 5th | Karl Wendlinger | Audi A4 quattro |
| 7th | Tamara Vidali | Audi A4 quattro |

**British Touring Car Championship**

| | | |
|---|---|---|
| 1st | Frank Biela | Audi A4 quattro |
| 7th | John Bintcliffe | Audi A4 quattro |

**Italian Touring Car Championship**

| | | |
|---|---|---|
| 1st | Rinaldo Capello | Audi A4 quattro |
| 4th | Yvan Muller | Audi A4 quattro |

**South African Touring Car Championship**

| | | |
|---|---|---|
| 1st | Terry Moss | Audi A4 quattro |
| 2nd | Chris Aberdein | Audi A4 quattro |

**Australian Touring Car Championship**

| | | |
|---|---|---|
| 1st | Brad Jones | Audi A4 quattro |
| 3rd | Greg Murphy | Audi A4 quattro |

**Belgian Procar Championship**

| | | |
|---|---|---|
| 1st | Jean-Francois Hermroulle | Audi A4 quattro |

**Spanish Touring Car Championship**

| | | |
|---|---|---|
| 1st | Jordi Gene | Audi A4 quattro |
| 4th | Joan Vinyes | |

**Central Europe Cup**

| | | |
|---|---|---|
| 1st | Josef Venc | Audi A4 quattro |

**Macao Grand Prix**

| | | |
|---|---|---|
| 1st | Frank Biela | Audi A4 quattro |
| 2nd | Brad Jones | Audi A4 quattro |

# Chapter 4

# The quattro in detail

## THE 10v ENGINE

With just a few modifications, the most notable of which was the addition of an air-to-air intercooler, the quattro engine was based on the Audi 200T unit, and the strength and reliability of the 5-cylinder concept has been proved by Audi for more than 20 years. Parts are available from many sources and, equally important, there is a great deal of expertise to draw on.

Two types of 10v engines have been used throughout the quattro's life and are referred to by their prefixes of WR 2144cc and MB 2226cc. In essence, refinement distinguishes them through the years, with very early WR engines having plenty of power but turbo lag measured in aeons. It doesn't make them bad cars, but getting the best from them demands more effort – you pays your money …

### Basic specifications

|  | 10v 1980–1988 |
|---|---|
| **Engine** | SOHC |
| Prefix | WR |
| Capacity | 2144cc |
| Bore x stroke | 79.5 x 86.4mm |
| Power | 200bhp at 5500rpm |
| Torque | 210lb/ft at 3500rpm |
| Compression ratio | 7.0:1 |
| Oil pressure (idle) | 5.3 bar |
| Oil temperature | 80°C |
| Valve clearances: inlet | 0.20–0.30 |
| exhaust | 0.40–0.50 |
| Firing order | 1 – 2 – 4 – 5 – 3 |

### Cooling system

| | |
|---|---|
| Thermostat opening temp | 87°C |
| Radiator cap pressure | 1.2–1.4 bar |

### Fuel system

| | |
|---|---|
| Idle speed | 800rpm +/-50 |
| CO at idle speed | 1.0% +/-0.2 |
| Fuel injection system | Bosch K-Jetronic plus turbo |
| Injection pressure | 3.6–4.0 bar |

### Ignition system

| | |
|---|---|
| Coil type | Bosch |
| Primary resistance | 0.61–0.83 ohms |
| Rotation | Anti-clockwise |
| Spark plug type | Bosch W4DP |
| Electrode gap | 0.80–0.90mm |

### Electrical system

| | |
|---|---|
| Battery (volts/cold cranking/amp hour) | 12/300/63 |

### Capacities

| | |
|---|---|
| Engine oil & filter | 4.0 litres |
| Gearbox | 3.2 litres |
| Final drive | Rear 2.2 litres |
| Cooling system | 9.3 litres |
| Fuel tank | 90 litres |

### Torque wrench settings

| Cylinder head: | |
|---|---|
| Stage 1 | 40Nm |
| Stage 2 | 60Nm |
| Stage 3 | + 90° |
| Stage 4 | + 90° |
| Big end bearings | 50Nm |
| Main bearings | 25Nm |
| Front/rear hubs | 280Nm |
| Road wheel bolts | 110Nm |
| Spark plugs | 30Nm |

|  | 10v 1988–1989 |
|---|---|
| **Engine** | SOHC |
| Prefix | MB |
| Capacity | 2226cc |
| Bore x stroke | 81 x 86.4mm |
| Power | 200bhp at 5500rpm |
| Torque | 210lb/ft at 3500rpm |
| Compression ratio | 8.6:1 |
| Oil pressure (idle) | 5.3 bar |
| Oil temperature | 80°C |
| Valve clearances: inlet | N/A (hydraulic) |
| exhaust | N/A (hydraulic) |
| Firing order | 1 – 2 – 4 – 5 – 3 |

### Cooling system

| | |
|---|---|
| Thermostat opening temp | 87°C |
| Radiator cap pressure | 1.2–1.5 bar |

### Fuel system

| | |
|---|---|
| Idle speed | 800rpm +/-50 |
| CO at idle speed | 1.5% +/-0.5 |

| | |
|---|---|
| Fuel injection system | Bosch K-Jetronic plus turbo |
| Injection pressure | 3.0–4.1 bar |

### Ignition system
| | |
|---|---|
| Coil type | Bosch |
| Primary resistance | 0.5–0.7 ohms |
| Rotation | Anti-clockwise |
| Spark plug type | Bosch W7DTC |
| Electrode gap | 0.80–0.90mm |

### Electrical system
| | |
|---|---|
| Battery (volts/cold cranking/amp hour) | 12/300/63 |

### Capacities
| | |
|---|---|
| Engine oil & filter | 4.0 litres |
| Gearbox | 3.2 litres |
| Final drive | Rear 2.2 litres |
| Cooling system | 9.3 litres |
| Fuel tank | 90 litres |

### Torque wrench settings
| | |
|---|---|
| Cylinder head: | |
| Stage 1 | 40Nm |
| Stage 2 | 60Nm |
| Stage 3 | + 90° |
| Stage 4 | + 90° |
| Big end bearings | 50Nm |
| Main bearings | 25Nm |
| Front/rear hubs | 280Nm |
| Road wheel bolts | 110Nm |
| Spark plugs | 20Nm |

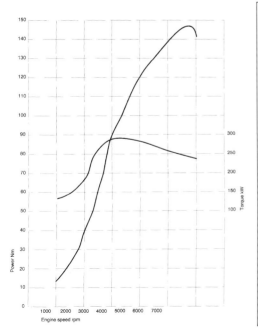

Below left *The quattro was all about power and torque, and lots of it. This graph shows the effect of the turbo as both power and torque come rushing in with a bang as the rev counter gets towards the 3000rpm mark. The often-quoted statistic reveals the true effect: From 20–60mph in fifth the quattro was slower than a 900cc Volkswagen Polo. However, from 60–100mph it was quicker than a Porsche 911SC!*

Above *The 5-cylinder unit was canted to one side (to fit under the bonnet) and the turbocharger/wastegate were sited on the right. Heat was always a quattro problem, as can be seen by the fitment of a slave radiator (at extreme front) and a thermo-fan to cool the injectors. The quattro was given an extra 30bhp over the 200 version largely through fitting the intercooler, seen almost off the bottom of this photo but …*

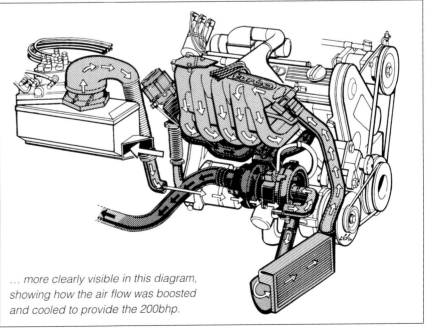

*… more clearly visible in this diagram, showing how the air flow was boosted and cooled to provide the 200bhp.*

This cutaway diagram shows the engine in detail from the rear left-hand side.

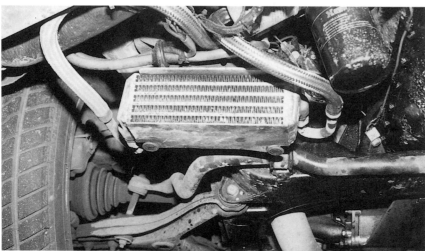

The oil cooler is quite vulnerable and there are many stories of it being damaged by flying stones, etc.

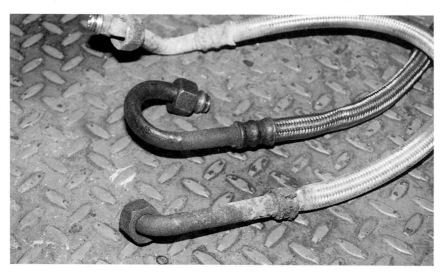

A more common occurrence is corrosion of the hose connections to the oil cooler. They are very much out of sight and out of mind, until they let go and deposit all your oil on the M1. Check them regularly and replace if you've even half a doubt – a new engine may be necessary if you get it wrong.

*The turbocharger on all models lives on the lower RH side of the engine, where it gets very hot – not least because the impeller blade spins at speeds over 100,000rpm! From the MB engine onwards, the turbos were water-cooled and thus less prone to wearing out so quickly. On WR cars it is vital to let the engine tickover for a short while after a journey (particularly after hard driving) in order to let it cool down. If this is not done the oil bakes hard and the turbo life is reduced. In this photo a WR turbo is at left, while on the right is an MB version. Look hard and spot the extra holes for the water cooling pipe. Note the wastegate at top left.*

## Servicing

The quattro always had an official service interval of 10,000 miles. However, this assumed two things: First, that the car would be doing an average mileage, ie between 10–12,000 miles per year, and second, that the car would get the correct servicing every time it was required. Almost without exception an older quattro will have suffered many years of average (or even non-existent) servicing. It follows that your first job on getting your newly acquired car home is to give it a complete major service.

Many quattros are now run as second, third or even high-days-and-holidays cars, meaning that it would take years for the official service interval to arrive. It is a fact, though, that cars doing low mileages need more servicing, not less. If this is the case it would be best to service your car on a time interval. As a rough guide, 5,000 miles a year should equate to six-monthly service intervals.

## DIY servicing

Though not as tricky to work on as the 20v unit, the 10v quattro engine has plenty of traps for the unwary. Very basic work is possible, but things very soon get complicated – the water pump, for example, would be a relatively simple fix on a non-turbo 5-cylinder car, but it's extremely hard work on a quattro and requires several special tools.

## Oil

This turbocharged supercar needs the best quality oil – regardless of whether or not you can afford it! The general thinking is that it benefits from fully synthetic oil which can, in the case of the 20v (and USA cars), actually help preserve the catalytic converters. It is also vital that pukka Audi oil filters are used. Remember that there are two – one for the engine and one for the turbocharger.

*Care of your engine starts and ends with oil; good quality synthetic oil is reckoned to be best, complete with two filters at every change.*

## Air today

The engine is meant to be 'totally sealed' in that there should be no air leaks. A typical problem area is the cloth reinforced pipe between the metering head and the turbo. This can fail over the years, resulting in the engine running lean, which can lead to serious engine problems if left unattended. A leaking injector 'O' ring can cause the same problem.

After an oil change, the author's car was difficult to start and reluctant to idle or pull properly. On checking everything it was noticed that the oil filler cap was not seating exactly as it should. Half a turn of the cap restored the *status quo*! An experiment showed the same effect if the oil dipstick was not pushed fully home.

## Exhaust manifold

The quattro manifold is an expensive item, and because so much of the engine and its ancillaries have to be dismantled for it to be replaced, the fitting of a new one is also an expensive job. A manifold can be welded, though the results are not always good, and if

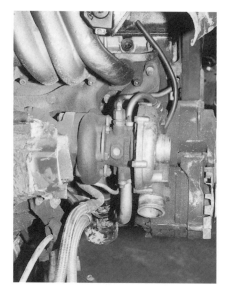

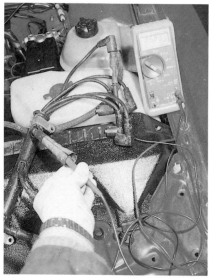

Far left *In this unusual picture, you can see how the exhaust manifold is really buried and how difficult it would be to remove it. In this case, a heavy impact accident has removed the wing altogether! Note that the extra water cooling pipe leading to the turbo denotes this model an MB engined-car.*

Left *You can test the resistance of plug leads with a decent multimeter, although ...*

Below left *... replacement on older cars is usually worthwhile – these are Beru leads from Hella.*

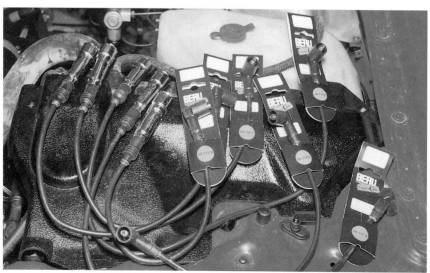

Bottom left *Access to the 3rd and 4th plugs is tricky, not just because of the pipes and wires going across the head, but also because of the injector cooling motor. It's a simple job to remove it. Take out the two screws holding the securing brackets and the single screw holding the flexible hose. This done, you'll be able to pull the whole assembly away. These plugs may stick, as many owners don't carry out this procedure. Don't force anything – remember, that alloy head is both soft and expensive!*

Below *It's a good move to chase the plug threads through regularly with an S-P tool.*

you plan keeping the car for any length of time it's best to bite the bullet and go for a new one. Brian Ricketts advises:

'When replacing the manifold it is important to change all the head-to-manifold studs and nuts, as these harden with continual heating and cooling. If they don't break when they are re-torqued on the new manifold, then they will when the heat expands them. Use the correct nuts and studs when refitting the turbo to the manifold and the downpipe to the turbo. The heat escaping from a cracked manifold can cause excessive underbonnet heat which normally causes the RH engine mount to fail. Also, it has been known to damage the wiring on the O/S wing.'

Though it's no fun, you have to keep things in perspective. Most manifolds last upwards of 80,000 miles handling massive temperature extremes. It's not really that bad, is it?

## Spark plugs

Many cars will run happily on just about any type of plug, but the quattro isn't one of them, and it's generally reckoned that Bosch's original specification items work best (see table). Whichever you choose, quattro plugs are expensive (compared to lesser cars) simply because of the extra hammering they take.

Removing the spark plugs on most cars is one of the simplest DIY tasks to undertake, but on a 10v quattro it can be a harrowing experience. This is largely because the 3rd and 4th plugs (from the front of the vehicle) are tricky to get at, being baulked by the injector cooling motor. Though anyone servicing the car on a professional basis will simply move the motor, private owners are generally less inclined to do so, and thus it's likely that these plugs have been in situ for some time. So, take care when removing all plugs – it's an aluminium cylinder head and a replacement is mortgage money – but especially so with plugs 3 and 4. (Removing 20v plugs is a much easier task

because their central position, right on top of the engine, is ideal.)

## Compression checking

Having removed the plugs for routine maintenance or replacement, it's advisable to run a thread cleaner into the holes. After that, a compression test will give you an update on the general condition and, if you're unlucky, a portent of bad things to come. The details are covered in Chapter 5. Where a cylinder gives a particularly lower reading than the rest, pour a teaspoon of light oil into the bore and repeat the compression test. If the reading is the same, it points to valve guide wear problems. If it increases, it indicates bore wear, piston ring trouble, etc.

When replacing the spark plugs, remember that they do not need a million lb/ft of torque. Half a turn more than *tight* is ample – after all, they're hardly going to fall out, are they? Trouble caused by spark plugs not being tightened enough is unheard of. Trouble (notably stripped threads and broken ceramics) caused by over-tightened plugs is common, tricky to sort out and often expensive to solve.

## THE 20v ENGINE

Although Audi had considered deleting the quattro from its range in 1989, public demand (not least in the UK – the quattro's best export market) convinced them that they should not do so. Instead they uprated it and brought it more into line with the rest of their cars, and the most obvious benefit to the new model was the change to the already-lauded 5-cylinder 20v engine. As with the 10v engines, the 20v engine is often referred to by its prefix – it being RR in this case.

## Basic specifications

| Engine | 1989–1991 |
|---|---|
| | DOHC |
| Prefix | RR |
| Capacity | 2226cc |
| Bore x stroke | 81 x 86.4mm |
| Power | 220bhp at 5900rpm |

| Torque | 228lb/ft at 1950rpm |
|---|---|
| Compression ratio | 9.3:1 |
| Oil pressure (idle) | 5.3 bar |
| Oil temperature | 80°C |
| Valve clearances: inlet | N/A (hydraulic) |
| exhaust | N/A (hydraulic) |
| Firing order | 1 – 2 – 4 – 5 – 3 |

### Cooling system
| | |
|---|---|
| Thermostat opening temp | 87°C |
| Radiator cap pressure | 1.2–1.5 bar |

### Fuel system
| | |
|---|---|
| Idle speed | 740/860rpm |
| CO at idle speed | < 0.5% |
| Fuel injection system | Bosch Motronic plus turbo |
| Injection pressure | 3.0–3.2 bar |

### Ignition system
| | |
|---|---|
| Coil type | Bosch |
| Primary resistance | 0.5–0.7 ohms |
| Rotation | Anti-clockwise |
| Spark plug type | Bosch F5DPOR |
| Electrode gap | 0.60–0.70mm |

### Electrical system
| | |
|---|---|
| Battery | 12 volts/300 cold cranking/63 amp hour |

### Capacities
| | |
|---|---|
| Engine oil & filter | 4.5 litres |
| Gearbox | 3.2 litres |
| Final drive | Rear 2.2 litres |
| Cooling system | 9.3 litres |
| Fuel tank | 90 litres |

### Torque wrench settings
| Cylinder head: | |
|---|---|
| Stage 1 | 40Nm |
| Stage 2 | 60Nm |
| Stage 3 | +90° |
| Stage 4 | +90° |
| Big end bearings | 30 +90° |
| Main bearings | 25Nm |
| Front/rear hubs | 280Nm |
| Road wheel bolts | 110Nm |
| Spark plugs | 30Nm |

This impressive unit was based on the 4-valve-per-cylinder engine used to such good effect in the fearsome rally Sport quattros (which gave up to

600bhp) and the homologation special road-going versions which produced 'just' 306bhp.

The Ur quattro's power output was 220bhp at a screaming 5900rpm, but the most important aspect for a road car was that the impressive torque figure of 228lb/ft came in at an even more impressive 1950rpm.

Compared to its predecessors the DOHC unit featured a newly developed, low inertia, liquid-cooled turbocharger installation, a charge-air intercooler, sequential fuel injection into the intake pipes and twin regulated catalytic converters. And, despite its 'sports car' performance (100bhp per litre of power and 103lb/ft per litre of torque) it was well suited for day-to-day motoring in a way that many more specialised competitors could only dream of.

Like its SOHC forebears, the engine remained at a nominal capacity of 2.2 litres (2226cc) with a bore and stroke of 81mm x 86.4mm, figures that are well-suited to producing high-torque at low engine speeds. The compression ratio of 9.3:1 was unusually high for a turbocharged engine but, of course, was ideal for producing large amounts of power. Moreover, it was one of the key factors in ensuring immediate accelerator response.

The rigid cylinder block, crankshaft and connecting rods – as well as many other components – were taken from the 165bhp 5-cylinder units, since they proved more than suitable for the intended torque level.

The two camshafts in the aluminium cylinder head operated the 20 valves via hydraulic tappets. The valve diameters were the same as in the Sport quattro (28mm exhaust/32mm intake) but with less valve overlap and more moderate valve timing, in order to make the car more tractable and 'user friendly'. Both intake and exhaust valves were specially strengthened, with the exhaust valves being sodium cooled. In fact, having double the usual number of valves wasn't something entered into in order to achieve more power, but more to offer minimum resistance to the air

delivered from the turbocharger at all engine speeds.

The camshafts were linked by a short single roller chain running in oil, and the exhaust camshaft was driven from the crankshaft by means of a toothed belt. (This set-up was common to all Audi 20v engines.) Uniform engine temperatures were almost guaranteed with the crossflow cooling principles being employed; the water entered on the exhaust side and left the cylinder head on the intake side.

The liquid-cooled turbocharger, driven as ever by the exhaust gasses, operated in conjunction with a charge air intercooler and electronic boost pressure control for optimum pressure characteristics throughout the operating range.

Lower pressures ahead of the throttle butterfly, lower exhaust system back-pressure and reduced air and exhaust temperatures helped cut fuel consumption significantly in the part-load area.

## Intercooler

The charge air intercooler brought the air temperature from the turbocharger down by around 60 degrees centigrade before it reached the cylinders. Boost pressure at full throttle in the peak torque range (1950rpm) was 1.83 bar and was electronically regulated by the Motronic system.

## Bosch Motronic engine management

The Bosch Motronic adaptive engine management system was used, having been developed jointly by the company and Audi, and came with a collection of basic parameters within which it could work. 'Adaptive' in this case meant that the system 'learned' to change various settings depending on the input received from the many sensors; ignition timing, fuel-air mixture and idle speed were checked many times per second and adjusted by the Motronic 'black box' accordingly. It was no longer possible, or necessary, to adjust the engine idle speed, for example. As with most catalytic exhausts a Lambda sensor, placed

early in the exhaust system, was used to ensure that the mixture remained constantly correct. The 20v engine has to be fuelled only with *unleaded* petrol – to use leaded with the catalysts in place will ruin them, and they're expensive. It was designed to run on 95 octane unleaded fuel but, if necessary, can be run on 91 octane. The fuel tank capacity was 19.8 gallons (approximately 90 litres).

## Fuel injection

Electronic fuel injection was used (unlike the 10v engines), employing a hot-wire air mass sensor in the air cleaner housing. This measured the amount of air drawn into the engine and related it to the input from other sensors enabling just the right fuel mixture and spark to be provided at just the right time. Two sensors were fitted to detect any sign of 'knocking' from the engine, in which case the ignition timing was automatically retarded. If this proved insufficient to stop the knocking, the boost pressure at the turbocharger was reduced as well.

The fuel injection was electronic sequential, meaning that it was accurately metered for each cylinder and injected at precisely the right moment. As such, all cylinders received the same mixture with obvious benefits in terms of smooth running, fuel consumption and combustion noise.

The 'brain' had 40 kilobytes of memory which meant that it could check the various ignition and fuel settings many times every second, to make sure they were spot-on. Such things as manually setting the idle speed were not necessary or possible with this system. It was more complex than the previous K-Jetronic system which, on the one hand made it very difficult for the DIY enthusiast and more expensive when things went wrong – a Bosch specialist is best consulted when problems occur. On the other hand, it offered better performance, fuel economy and emissions, and could be 'chipped' very easily for substantial power uprates.

The heart of the matter is under the bonnet, with the installation of the glorious 20v, 5-cylinder motor, based on the Sport quattro unit. Note, among other things, that although the turbo stays more or less where it was, the wastegate has moved forward slightly.

A full, hi-tech Bosch Motronic engine management system was fitted and so were twin 3-way catalysts in the exhaust system. These necessitated one of the few real in-the-metal changes to the Ur quattro ...

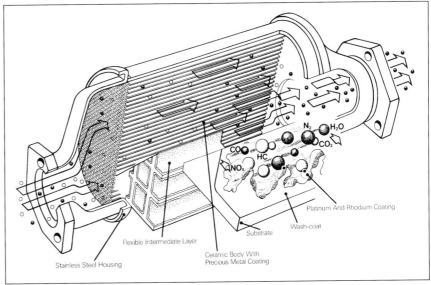

... because the floorpan had to be modified to suit. Look closely to see the bulge in the transmission tunnel to the right of the passenger seat.

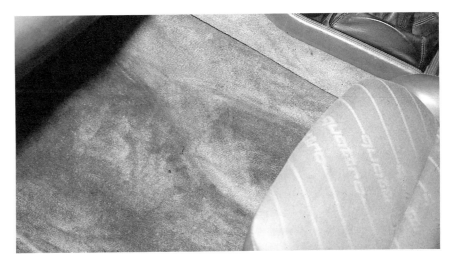

*If you ever wondered what the inside of a turbocharger looked like, well now you know! With some ten years development over the original engines, it's not surprising the 20v unit got such rave reviews. Its great strength wasn't so much its 20bhp power increase …*

*… but its massive spread of torque, as shown on this graph, with a whopping 228lb/ft at just 1950rpm. Though not totally eradicated, turbo lag had been reduced drastically compared with the first 10v cars.*

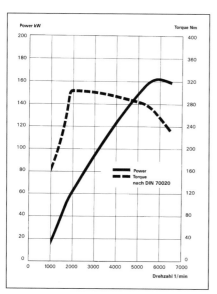

## MORE ABOUT FUEL SYSTEMS

With 4-star fuel becoming ever more difficult to find, a common question is whether or not unleaded fuel can be used in the quattro. In answer to this the official line is that '… all Audi quattros can run on 98 RON Super Plus/Super Unleaded green fuel …' The 20v quattros, of course, are catalyst-equipped and you MUST use unleaded fuel all the time with these.

**SAFETY**: Do not attempt to deal with any aspects of your quattro's fuel supply unless you are suitably qualified to do so. Never work on your fuel system when the engine is hot and always remember that both types of fuel injection (Bosch K-Jetronic and Bosch Motronic) work under pressure – removing a connection or pipe will result in fuel spraying around.

## Bosch K-Jetronic fuel injection system

The K-Jetronic is a mechanically and hydraulically controlled fuel-injection system which needs no form of drive and which meters the fuel as a function of the intake air quantity and injects it continuously on to the engine intake valves. It was fitted to both types of 10v engine (WR and MB) and, compared to modern systems and the Motronic system fitted to the 20v, is fairly simple. Though it has an electronic control unit (ECU) fitted into the right-hand side lower dash panel, it is little more than a complex switching unit, acting on information received from the various sensors around the car. The ECU fitted to MB engines is different from that in the WR engines. Given here is a basic overview of the system.

Remember the truism that although the 'black box' is almost always blamed, most fuel injection troubles relate to the sensors themselves or their connections.

*This K-Jetronic schematic gives a simple illustration of how the system works.*

*Key: 1. Fuel tank; 2. Electric fuel pump; 3. Fuel accumulator; 4. Fuel filter; 5. Warm-up regulator; 6. Injectors; 7. Intake manifold; 8. Cold-start valve; 9. Fuel distributor; 10. Air-flow sensor; 11. Timing valve; 13. Thermo-time switch; 14. Ignition distributor; 15. Auxiliary air device; 16. Throttle valve switch; 17. ECU; 18. Ignition and starting switch; 19. Battery.*

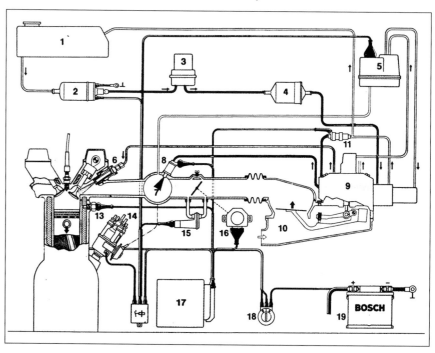

Right *To prove a point, the author's car went through a period of non-starting cold, then not starting hot, then being OK – totally at random. After exhaustive and patient testing, it was found that the plug on the cold start sensor at the back of the engine block had been damaged internally. A cursory check revealed that the plug was in place, but the truth was that the electrical connection was not being made.*

Below right *The full relationship can be seen in this flow chart.*

Bottom right *The K-Jetronic and Motronic systems are as different as chalk and cheese. These are the respective 'brains', with the Motronic on the right.*

Below *When push comes to shove, it's best to seek the attention of a Bosch specialist – if you can find one with an Audi background, all the better. Performance Car Services of Milton Keynes is one such, operated by Dave Abbott, who is a fully-trained VAG mechanic. Like all dealers, he has the full computerised works that enable him to plot exactly what is happening and what isn't. Though you will have to pay for his time, a dealer will probably discover in an hour what would take you all day – or maybe you wouldn't find it even then!*

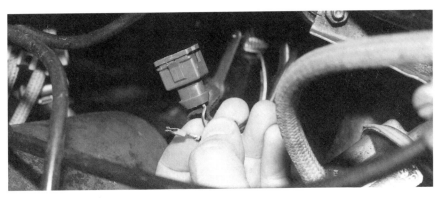

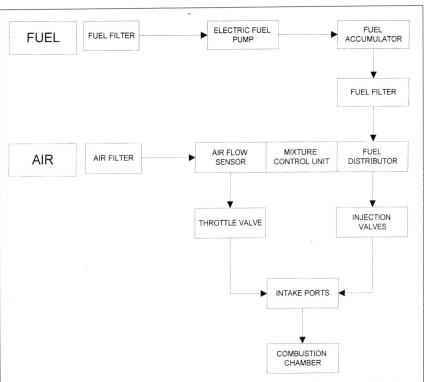

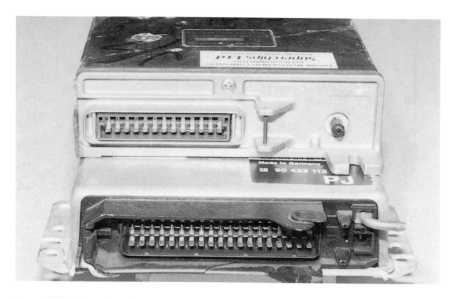

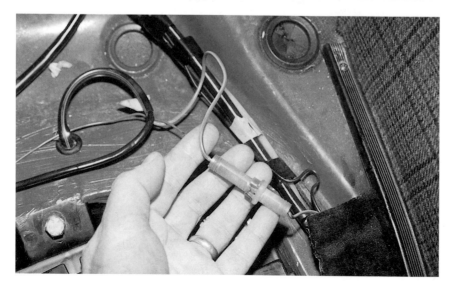

Left *As you can see, the Motronic box (below) has far more pin connections than its predecessor.*

Below left *Many of the fuel hardware components are situated under the car where they can be battered by stones and covered in water and road dirt. Under the rear left-hand side passenger seat is the fuel pump mounted on a small bracket. In the pipe leading to it from the fuel tank is the fuel pump filter which can, of course, get blocked on occasion. Replacement is simple, but make sure that the arrow on the filter faces the flow of the fuel, ie towards the front of the car. As with many fasteners under the car, you may have trouble undoing them. Apply patience and lots of Plus Gas, etc.*

Bottom left *A common problem is that the connection under the rear seat alongside the battery has either come adrift or has corroded to the point of non-conductivity. This is it, despite the fact that it looks like an in-line fuse. It goes directly through a hole in the bodywork to the fuel pump beneath it. The terminals on the pump itself are prone to corrosion.*

## Fuel pump

The fuel pump sends fuel to the metering distributor at a pressure of around 100 psi, with excess fuel being returned to the tank. This has several advantages, in that the pump is cooled and lubricated by the fuel, the fuel delivered to the metering distributor is always cool and there is always enough fuel available to meet the demands of the engine.

If the pump doesn't work, the car won't start and if it stops whilst the engine is running, the engine will stop. However, pump failure is rare and usually only occurs at a very high mileage. A pump becoming increasingly noisy is an early warning of impending failure. It cannot be repaired and must be replaced.

Never allow your quattro to run totally out of fuel because if air is sucked into the pump, the internal rollers may be damaged. This will make the pump noisy and may wreck it altogether.

*Slightly to the right and forward of the fuel pump is the fuel accumulator, which holds some fuel pressure when the engine is not running so it is ready for cold starting. Like the pump, it is very reliable – a 'clanging' noise is usually the spring pushing on the internal diaphragm – quite normal.*

Check a non-functioning pump with your meter to make sure power is getting there – two terminals on the end of the pump (ignition on).

Listen for the fuel pump relay (in the box in the plenum chamber) cutting in correctly. With ignition off, disconnect the fuel pump relay and bridge the earth and power terminals (30 and 87). With the ignition on, the pump should operate – DO NOT start the engine! No pump means either it's failed or there is a wiring fault.

*This large metal canister, fitted under the RH rear passenger seat is the fuel filter which contains a paper element. It must be fitted the right way round, with the arrow pointing in the direction of fuel flow, otherwise the engine will not fire. You can expect around 24,000 miles of useful life from your filter. Dealers will change it automatically, but in DIY servicing, it often gets forgotten. When clogged, fuel flow is restricted, the rate of flow is reduced and this can cause starting problems and erratic running. It also puts more strain on the fuel pump.*

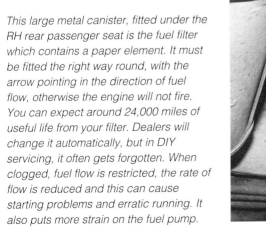
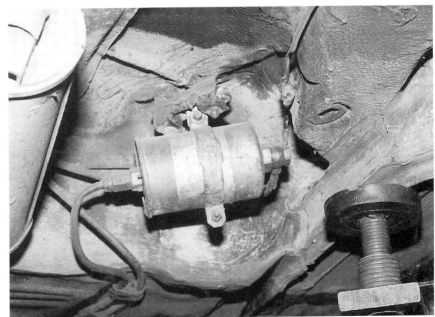

## Fuel injectors

K-Jetronic injectors are simple pressure-operated valves which atomise the fuel supplied to them, and perform absolutely no metering function. When the injector operating pressure is exceeded (around 3.5 bar), the injector opens and fuel is injected into the combustion chamber. Once it opens, the pressure drops and almost instantly the injector closes – at which point the pressure builds again, causing it to open. This on/off action causes the vaporisation of the fuel, and it happens very quickly indeed. The chattering action of the needle valves is some-times referred to as 'singing'.

Make sure all injector connections are sound and check for leaks on a regular basis – use two spanners to avoid damaging the pipe and/or injector. A leak will cause low fuel pressure which will not open the injector correctly and cause poor starting and misfires. A common problem is deterioration of the rubber sealing 'O' ring. Remove the injector and examine it. Replace if required.

## Fuel distributor

Fuel comes into the fuel distributor from the pressure accumulator, and from there it goes to the five injectors. The two pipes in the centre of the distributor lead to the control pressure regulator and the two large pipes running from the side of the unit are the petrol feed in and the excess fuel return pipe.

Most problems occur in old age when they tend to get gummed up by the resins in the fuel build up inside. It operates within fine tolerances, so the plunger can stick, usually in the open position, hence over-rich fuelling. It's possible to dismantle and clean the unit and plunger, but DO NOT use any abrasive materials. Make sure everything is spotlessly clean before reassembly. You should, however, be aware that getting a good seal is extremely difficult and even the experts baulk at splitting the distributor in this way.

## Air sensor

A throttle butterfly controls air into the engine. It passes the sensor plate which is fitted to the pivot arm below the fuel distributor. As the plate lifts to allow air to pass, it acts on the arm and allows more fuel. Over time, dirt and dust can jam the plate slightly open, or adjustment may be required. Dismantle and clean, and adjust as necessary.

*A specialist centre will be able to test your injectors. As a rule of thumb, the cost of renovating a mechanical injector isn't far off the cost of a new one. But renovating an electronic injector (where possible) is around half the cost of a new one. In older/high mileage engines the injectors can become partially clogged with carbon from exhaust gasses and/or gum and resins from the petrol. This affects the spray pattern which can become offset and results in poor atomisation. The spray pattern should be perfectly round and cone shaped. Having removed the injectors, the rubber seals should be replaced.*

*To test your injection system pressure yourself (only work on a cold engine) you will need special testing equipment, such as this S-P 314800 kit from Sykes-Pickavant which conforms to BS1780 (1985) and reads from 0–150 psi (0–10 bar).*

# Quattros in colour

## SPORTING

*WET . . .*
*1982 and Hannu Mikkola repeated his victory of the previous year on the arduous Lombard RAC Rally. Michèle Mouton followed him home in second place with Harald Demuth in fifth – three out of the top five ain't bad!*

*. . . AND DRY!*
*No bull-bar debate here – those huge lumps of tubing on the front of the quattro were a real necessity to handle the 4-legged dangers on the African Safari rally. It's a curious fact that the quattro never won a Safari rally, the only scores being second and third places for Mikkola and Mouton in 1983, and a third place for Mikkola the following year.*
*(Courtesy Audi Sport)*

# Audi quattro

*The fearsome Sport quattro was introduced in 1984 and, with its shortened (by 12in) wheelbase and more powerful 20v engine, it was hoped to tip the scales against the purpose-built off-road racers proffered by the opposition. (Courtesy Audi Sport)*

*However, despite its muscle-bound appearance and undoubtedly powerful engine, the shorter car was decidedly twitchy on the limit, and Walter Röhrl in particular made no bones about his dislike of the car. Audi wisely ran it alongside the original lwb car. The Sport won only one World Championship rally in 1984, with Blomqvist at the wheel on the Ivory Coast. (Courtesy Audi Sport)*

*In 1985 even more power was available to the Sport pilots (500bhp plus) and so Audi fitted all those wings and spoilers to keep it on the ground through the corners.*

The Sport was more popular with the drivers when it debuted in the 1000 Lakes rally where it took Stig Blomqvist to second place. Walter Röhrl used it to score its only win at San Remo.

Despite what it looks like, the myriad aerodynamic appendages fitted to the staggeringly powerful Sport quattro Evolution 2 were to hold the car down, not make it fly!

Walter Röhrl again, this time hammering around the side of a mountain from top to bottom! The American Pikes Peak event has all the danger of world class rallying with the added bonus that the car might get a little more airborne than usual! Having won in 1985 and 1986, Audi completed the hat-trick in 1987 when Röhrl conquered the hill in his Evolution 2 Sport. (Courtesy Audi Sport)

The 1987 Audi 200 quattro rally programme lacked the impetus of the original. The 238bhp car is seen here on the Monte Carlo, where Walter Röhrl came third but, the real surprise . . . (Courtesy Audi Sport)

. . . to everyone (not least Audi) was when Mikkola and Röhrl came home first and second in the Safari rally, taking the rough dry conditions . . . (Courtesy Audi Sport)

. . . with the rough wet ones! Despite these encouraging results, the season was lacking in interest for many spectators, not least because of the massive reduction in power outputs called for by the new rules. (Courtesy Audi Sport)

Having won first time out with the 200 quattro in the American TransAm series in 1988, Audi contested the American IMSA GTO tarmac racing series the following year with what was loosely referred to as an Audi 90 – form a queue here! Power output was quoted as 720bhp, but by the end of the season, it was producing much more. (Courtesy Audi Sport)

## DEVELOPMENT

*Designed in the late '70s, early quattros had the twin headlamps which were all the rage. Note that the radiator grille and lights are perpendicular. In keeping with its (hefty) price tag, items like auxiliary lamps and headlamp washers were standard equipment right from the start. This is one of the earliest LHD imports around and is currently owned by AM Cars.*

*By 1986 the engine was the same basic unit, though more refined, and the exterior had several minor changes: Cibié single piece headlamps replaced the originals and the radiator grille was now sloping. The removable sunroof was not made standard until the following year. This particularly stunning press car was finished in pearlescent white, the icing on this superb slice of motoring cake.*

*The quattro's rear view had always been impressive and was even more so following the introduction of the hefty 8J Ronal (R8) alloy wheels and 215/50 VR tyres in 1984.*

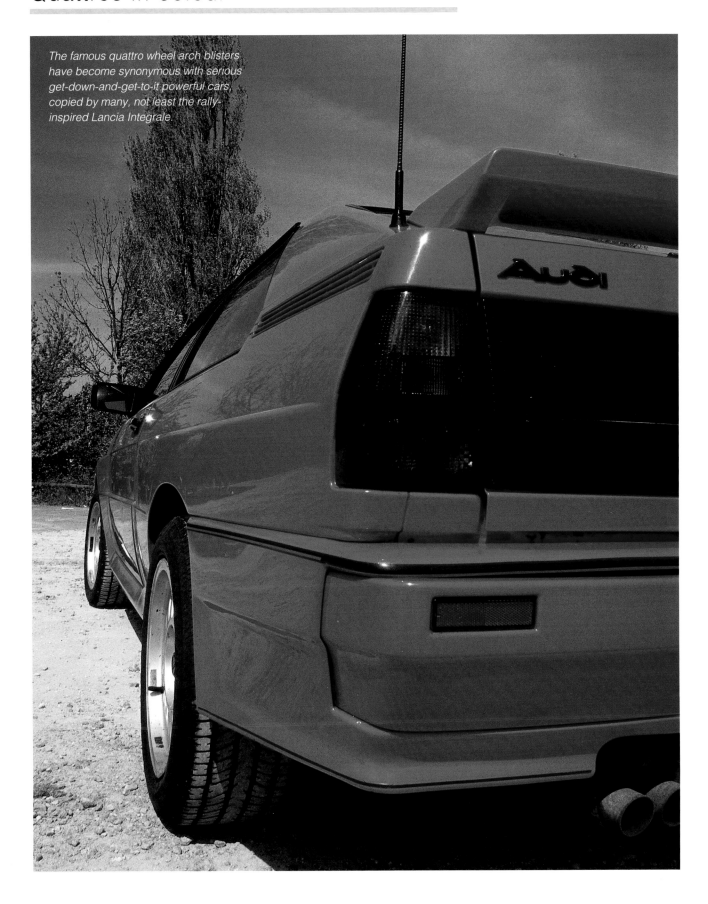

The famous quattro wheel arch blisters have become synonymous with serious get-down-and-get-to-it powerful cars, copied by many, not least the rally-inspired Lancia Integrale.

*Bringing a new car to the World Championship rally stage is always a big event … but one with turbocharging and four-wheel drive! The impact of the quattro's arrival cannot be overemphasised, and Audi found the best way to explain its new baby was by such superb cut-away diagrams as this one by Bruno Bell. Note the wing-mounted oil cooler, huge turbocharger and relocation of the intercooler to the opposite side of the engine bay. Fuchs 7J alloy wheels were favoured for the rough stages and offered on the road cars as factory options to the (original) 6J Ronal alloy wheels.*

*Quattro is all it says, for it need say no more. In fact, by the time of the 20v cars (1989–91) the boot lid merely reminded onlookers that the car was an Audi.*

A sunny day, open (but winding) roads and a quattro. Who could ask for more?

Early interiors were never a quattro strong point, with garish '70s colours attacking the eyes. By the time serious production got under way, the design department had veered wildly the other way, offering brown plastic with brown seats and light brown check inserts, more suited to an Allegro!

Quattro 20v owners fared much better, a leather-trimmed interior and part leather seats with Jacquard quattro logo inserts.

The King is dead, long live . . . the S2? Taken on its own, the S2 coupé, complete with 20v engine from the last model quattro, was a fine car. But, as a direct successor, it really couldn't cut the mustard. Its mainstream, even dumpy looks and distinct lack of sporting heritage led to its demise in a mere five years.

## THE SPORT QUATTRO

*Good things come in small packages. The road-going Sport quattro was truly a homologation special. Its shorter wheelbase was achieved by the simple expedient of hacking some 12in from the centre of the car!*

*Technically this made it a 2+2, although that second pair would have to be either very small, or very easily pleased. You can almost smell the leather which was used . . .*

*. . . throughout the car, including the lovely Recaro seats. The Sport was only available in lhd.*

*From the rear, there's little to give the game away – until you look closely. Huge wheel arch flares were required for the 9J wheels and 235/45VR tyres, resulting in an obvious lip around the lamp clusters.*

The Sport quattro's boot lid logo was quite restrained, consisting of stick-on vinyl lettering in a contrasting colour to the bodywork.

The massive turbo sucked in air, birds and small boys! The vents on the bonnet were definitely not just for show.

Under the bonnet was a real monster of an engine, designed for going extremely quickly. The 20v alloy head, electronic engine management and massive turbo all contributed to a power output of 306bhp. Adequate, as they say at Rolls Royce. Derivatives of this superb unit went on to power the 20v quattro and other top-notch Audis well into the '90s.

## SHOW AND GO

*Made to make your mouth water. The Spyder was a 1991 quattro Spyder Sportscar Study. It was technically adept, with easily recyclable aluminium panels over an aluminium spaceframe. It was designed to take the alloy V6 engine from the (then) current Audi 100 range.*

*On paper the Spyder was an engineer's dream. In the flesh it chilled the blood and fired the soul. A mid-engined firecracker to rival Ferrari. Weighty production costs meant that it stayed a dream.*

*Incredibly, the TT series was always meant for production. Initially, it looks a world away from the 1980 original quattro, but the permanent 4wd principles are still being adhered to. This is the open-top TTS car, with the Audi A4, turbocharged 4-cylinder motor tuned to produce a healthy 210bhp.*

## Cold start valve

This is the extra valve on top of the manifold which serves the same function as a carburettor choke, increasing the amount of fuel into a cold engine. It's controlled by a thermo switch which triggers the valve when the engine is cold. To prevent excessive over-fuelling when the engine is cranking (and not firing) it cuts out after about ten seconds. The CSV either works or it doesn't – if the latter, a replacement is required.

## Thermo-time switch

This is screwed into the back on the engine (nearest the bulkhead) so that it is always immersed in coolant. With a cold engine it allows the cold start valve to operate. With a hot engine it doesn't. As with most sensors it cannot be repaired and must be replaced.

## Control pressure (warm-up) regulator

This regulator is mounted on to the left-hand side of the engine (ie, opposite the turbo) and gets hot as the engine warms up. Inside the regulator is a bi-metal strip which reacts to the heat (or cold) from the engine. Quite simply, it allows more fuel to get to the fuel distributor when the engine is cold than when it is hot.

If the bi-metal strip fails, you'll get over-fuelling with a warm engine and this could lead to hot-starting problems.

## System pressure regulator and shut-off valve

Fuel returning to the tank from the control pressure regulator passes through a 'shut valve'. When the engine is running, this is held open by the regulator plunger. With the engine off, the plunger shuts and prevents further fuel from passing through, thus maintaining the fuel pressure.

The rubber valve 'O' ring is prone to deterioration which means the holding pressure will not be as high as it should be and will lead to troublesome hot-starting. Check this physically and, if necessary, dismantle the valve to check the condition of the 'O' ring. It is vital that no dirt gets into the valve or the fuel system.

## Auxiliary air valve (extra air valve)

This lets more air past the sensor plate (thus increasing fuelling) to increase the idle speed when the engine is cold.

## Mechanical fuel injection basic fault-finding guide

This guide is aimed at pointing you in the right direction when you suspect fuel injection problems. However, despite its relative simplicity, there are still a lot of parts to the K-Jetronic system and it can't possibly cover every eventuality.

**Engine will not start when cold.**
No ignition pulse to main relay.
Main relay faulty.
Fuel pump relay faulty.
Fuel pump faulty.
No fuel pressure.
Cold start injector faulty.
Thermo time switch faulty.
Fuel distributor faulty.

**Engine runs OK, but is difficult to start.**
Cold start injector.
Thermo-time switch.

**Engine starts but has poor cold-running characteristics.**
Cold control pressure too high.
Extra air system faulty.
System pressure incorrect.
Sensor plate out of adjustment.
Fuel distributor plunger sticking.
Faulty injectors.
Idle speed and CO incorrectly set when hot.

**Engine has flat-spot or hesitation on acceleration.**
System pressure incorrect.
Hot control pressure incorrect.
Warm-up regulator faulty.
Sensor plate out of adjustment.
Fuel distributor plunger sticking.
Fuel distributor faulty.

**Idle rough when engine warm; occasional stalling.**
Fuel distributor plunger sticking.
Fuel distributor faulty.
High system pressure.

**Poor engine performance when hot.**
System pressure incorrect.
Control pressure incorrect.
Faulty fuel distributor.
Engine will not start when warm.
Not holding fuel pressure.

## THE COOLING SYSTEM

The quattro cooling system is fairly conventional. It is pressurised (to raise the boiling point of the coolant) with a radiator mounted to the side of the engine – simply because there is no room for it at the front of the engine bay, as on 4-cylinder Audis. There is also a small auxiliary radiator which is mounted behind the centre grille panel, directly in front of the inlet manifold. A water pump is driven by the timing belt, and the thermostat is mounted in the inlet on the left-hand side of the cylinder block. A remote expansion tank is fitted to the nearside inner front wing.

Operation is typical, in that when the engine is cold the thermostat is closed and the water pump pushes the coolant around the internal engine passages (and the heater circuit, if it is switched on). As the coolant temperature increases, the thermostat opens and water flows from the cylinder head top hose into the radiator where it travels from top to bottom through a long series of tubes cooled by fins. When it eventually reaches the bottom of the radiator it is much cooler and it then passes into the water pump via the bottom hose and over the open thermostat for recirculation around the engine. The coolant in the radiator is usually kept cool by the rush of air from the forward motion of the vehicle. When the car is stationary or moving very slowly, an electric thermostatically-controlled fan, mounted behind the radiator, cuts in to keep the temperature down.

Thermostat opening temp 87°C
Radiator cap pressure:

| | |
|---|---|
| WR | 1.2–1.4 bar |
| MB | 1.2–1.5 bar |
| RR | 1.2–1.5 bar |

| | |
|---|---|
| Coolant capacity | 8 litres (7.4 US quarts) |

Radiator thermoswitch:

| | |
|---|---|
| cut in temperature | 90–95°C |
| cut off temperature | 85–90°C |

FOR CARS WITH AIR CONDITIONING
Radiator thermoswitch:

| | |
|---|---|
| cut in temp | 106–111°C |
| cut off temp | 118–123°C |

The highly stressed and powerful 5-cylinder quattro turbo engine needs more efficient cooling than most. That the engine is prone to getting extremely hot is shown by the addition of the thermostatically-controlled fan for the injectors. Unfortunately, the cooling system rarely comes in for much attention until a hose blows. Even then, it is likely to be just a simple hose replacement.

## Radiator removal

Removing the radiator is a relatively simple matter of undoing the securing nuts and bolts and taking off the various hoses. ALWAYS do this with a cold engine, for obvious reasons and make sure you collect all the coolant in a suitably large container. DON'T throw it down the drain – it's poisonous and it's illegal to dispose of it like that. See Appendix 1 for safe fluid disposal. Don't reuse coolant but replace with a 50/50 mix of water and anti-freeze.

## Anti-freeze

This is something of a misnomer, as it serves two main purposes; not only does it reduce the risk of frozen waterways in cold winter weather, but it also helps prevent boiling-up in summer. A good anti-freeze will also contain rust inhibitors. It should be mixed with water in a 50:50 ratio and changed at least every two years. When the engine is cold, the coolant must be at least up to minimum mark – with a warm engine, the level should be *above* the minimum mark.

## Bleeding the coolant

When you have had a leak, or have drained off the coolant in order to change it, you must remember to bleed the system. There is a bleed screw on top of the main radiator which should be used to prevent air locks in the system, which in turn will lead to overheating, especially in heavy slow-moving traffic. Remove the bleed screw (engine cold) and check that the coolant level is right up to the top of the radiator. If not, add more coolant via the expansion tank until it overflows from the bleed screw. Replace the bleed screw and the expansion tank cap.

**SAFETY.** *Remember that coolant stays hot for a long while after the engine is turned off and that the fan can operate even when the ignition is off. The system is under pressure, so take extreme care if you remove the expansion tank cap. The cap often fails, but not completely, which means that you're unlikely to notice the effects of it until much later, when serious engine overheating problems occur. If you don't know when it was last replaced (quite possibly, never!) then for £10 it's best to replace it anyway.*

## Radiator replacement

*Replacing or re-coring a radiator is a distress purchase and often a last resort. Because the quattro has a thermostatic fan, radiator problems can go unnoticed for a long while, during which time the engine will not be running as efficiently as it should. With the quattro running so hot all the time, cooling is an area not to be ignored. Serck Marston carry quattro radiators in stock, including the small auxiliary radiator. The part numbers are: Main radiator for a 10v engine – 271–0251 (metal); and for a 20v engine – 271–9504 (plastic). The auxiliary radiator for both 10v and 20v engines – 271–3481. The 10v engine metal radiators were made by AKG, and the 20v (and some very late 10v engines) plastic tanks were made by Beher.*

*I watched while Tony Clarke of Serck Marston's Aylesbury branch removed the original worn-out cores from a pair of quattro radiators and re-cored them. The first job was to pressure test them at 15 psi, slightly less than the typical in-car pressure. In this case, the main radiator was 'breathing' – ie, pushing out against the sides. The core is the centre section of any radiator and is a collection of thin tubes running back and forth, surrounded by metal 'fins' which cool the water inside the tubes. The pieces at the top and bottom of the radiator (whether plastic or metal) are called tanks. He made a careful note of where the various fittings went, and which way up – not immediately obvious. He wire-brushed the tanks and used a blow torch to melt the solder …*

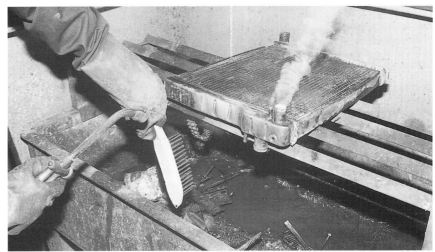

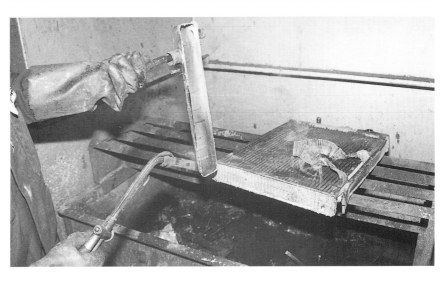

*… allowing the tanks to be pulled free of the original core – note how part of the original finning has started to fall away with age.*

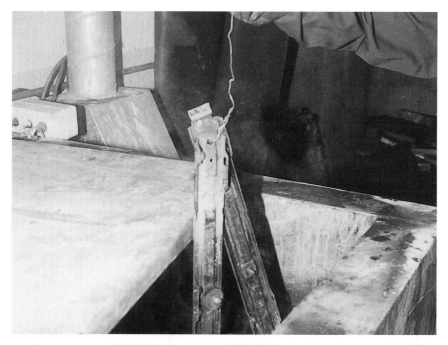

The sides were removed and cleaned by putting them in a bath of caustic soda, which does the job without causing harm to the rubber fittings.

This is a view looking down the ends of some of the tubes. As you can see, the radiator tends to 'fur up' like a kettle. The more obstructions there are, the less efficiently it will cool.

The two tanks were placed in a bead blaster and looked like new when they came out.

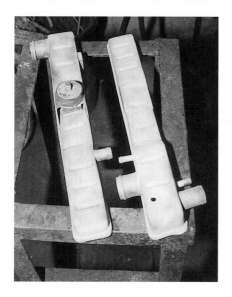

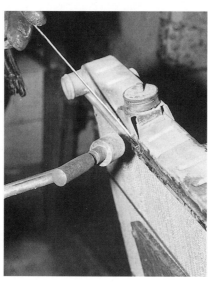

Tony then skilfully soldered the cleaned tanks on to the new core after applying spirit flux, which also acts as a cooling agent. The ends of the tanks were soldered first, to prevent the possibility of warping along their length. The sides were refitted and Tony added extra bracing pieces.

*The final job was also pressure tested again, just in case.*

*The tank was then placed in an oven where it was baked at 190°C – hot enough to get rid of the moisture but not enough to melt the solder. After 45 minutes it was dry enough to be sprayed. Serck Marston's neat touch is to attach a brass identification plate to every radiator.*

*Back in situ and with plenty of work to do!*

*It's common to find that the lower two mounting pegs on the auxiliary radiator have corroded over the years and that the securing nuts have sheared off. It's not the end of the world, as the rad should still be held at the top. This was one owner's method of fixing it – a cable tie! Not pretty, but usually hidden by the grille, and it worked.*

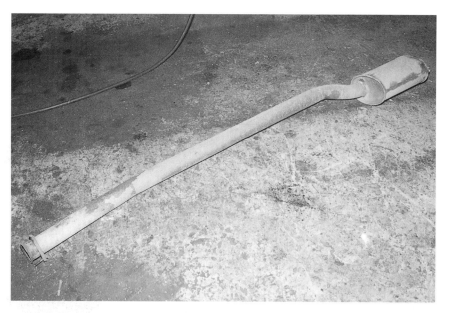

## THE EXHAUST SYSTEM

It is often said that the quattro's exhaust system was made from stainless steel. Sounds good (literally!) but it isn't quite accurate. It's true that the pipes were made from T304 stainless, but the centre and rear boxes and the tail pipes were fashioned out of good old rot-prone mild steel. The standard bore size was 75mm (just under 3in). A quattro needs to 'breathe' efficiently, so leaks in the pipe joins or from the boxes should be attended to straightaway. Quattro exhaust replacement is required as often as you'd expect on any other Audi.

*This is the long section of pipe leading from the rear of the car to the front box.*

*You can buy a system from Audi, but you'll end up with the same problems again. Probably the best bet is to fit a stainless exhaust, such as the Scorpion system available from Demon Tweeks. The Scorpion system is literally hand-made from high quality T304 aircraft spec stainless steel and, as you can see here, comes in three pieces rather than the original two.*

*It's TIG and MIG welded construction with full-bore mandrel bending, and this close-up shows the high quality of workmanship.*

With the back box removed, it's an opportunity to check out the condition of the boot heat shield. This is quite a thin piece of aluminium held on by large washers. After a while, the reaction between the aluminium and steel causes the former to rot and fall over the washers. It's unlikely to fall off, but it will rest on the back box and rattle annoyingly. As can be seen in this photo, one of the original washers is in place at front left, but at back right and left, two sections of aluminium have been used as makeshift 'washers' to keep the shield in place.

Fitting requires attention to detail, as quattro exhausts run very close to the floorpan, prop shaft, subframe, etc. The golden rule is simple – fit the system in its entirety but tighten nothing. That way you can ease the system up and round until it's exactly right, especially …

… around the rear subframe and differential. It's important to get this just right, otherwise the constant rattling will drive you crazy!

*Close-up, those large stainless pipes look great, but it's not just for appearance; it has been designed to enhance gas flow and reduce back pressure. The sound when driving 'normally' is suitably subdued (unlike some, which become deafening after a few miles) but open her up and it barks like a rally car. Better yet, it has a lifetime written guarantee. Great stuff!*

*The final result. From a distance it's hard to tell it's non-standard – and you won't be able to read the 'Scorpion' logo once there's a little road dirt on it.*

## Catalytic converter

The only UK quattro to be fitted with a catalytic exhaust system was the DOHC 20v model, produced from 1989.

A full replacement system, only available from Audi, costs serious money, and many owners 'cheat' by taking the option of removing the twin cats and replacing them with a straight piece of stainless steel exhaust pipe. AM Cars can supply this. Though initially this may appear to be eco-unfriendly, it is by no means certain that the catalyst and unleaded fuel are the pollution saviours they were originally thought to be.

**SAFETY**: In order to work at its best, the catalyst has to be very hot. Consequently you should take great care when parking. Do not leave the car over dry grass or any other inflammable material. The catalytic converter can be destroyed or seriously damaged by using leaded fuel; by an engine backfire; physically bumping it (say, on sleeping policemen); faulty engine management sensors.

## TRANSMISSION

Vehicles with all four wheels driven have been around for some considerable time, but before the Audi quattro they were almost always designed for use over rugged terrain and, despite the traction advantages, the technical complexity, additional space requirements, poor efficiency, high cost and unsatisfactory handling behaviour made 4WD an unattractive proposition for road cars – especially those of the high-performance variety. .

Also, in those vehicles with it, the

4WD facility was largely selectable, and for much of the time they would run with only two driven wheels. Audi's groundbreaking idea – the quattro principle – was to develop a transmission system which could deliver power to all four wheels, all of the time. It seemed logical that if the optimum suspension set-up were designed for one drive configuration, it would not be at its optimum should the configuration be changed. It was asserted that if the 4WD transmission unit and suspension was designed and fitted correctly, there simply would be no reason to chop and change.

## The quattro transmission

To turn their idea into reality, Audi had to overcome the disadvantages of the cumbersome traditional 4WD systems. A solution would have been to continue the drive rearward from a FWD transaxle installed lengthways. However, in very tight corners where the front wheels follow a larger radius than the rear wheels, there would be considerable 'wind-up' between the front and rear. Apart from an annoying (and embarrassing) tyre squeal, it would also lead to extra tyre wear and fuel consumption. Audi considered this problem and devised an ingenious way of fitting an inter-axle differential within the gearbox.

The primary shaft, as an extension of the crankshaft, drives the secondary or output shaft. This was made hollow and it drives the differential cage. The gears in this differential drive the pinions on the inner part of the secondary shaft going to the front differential and to the propeller shaft going to the rear wheels.

Thus, with the car driving in a straight line, the internal shaft to the front final drive revolves at the same speed as the hollow shaft. But when negotiating a corner, the internal shaft can turn rather faster, hence wind-up between front and rear is prevented. In this way additional friction losses from bearings, gears, seals and oil churning is kept to a minimum.

The gearbox, front and centre differentials require SAE 80 or 80/90 weight lubricant, and the rear differential needs SAE 80 lubricant.

## Gear ratios

One criticism of the first quattros was that the gear ratios were adrift. The five forward ratios were:

| | |
|---|---|
| 1st | 3.6:1 |
| 2nd | 2.125:1 |
| 3rd | 1.360:1 |
| 4th | 0.967:1 |
| 5th | 0.778:1 |

In December 1983 ('84 model year) modified 3rd and 4th gear ratios were used as follows, the object being to improve driveability and mid-range performance;

| | |
|---|---|
| 1st | 3.6:1 |
| 2nd | 2.125:1 |
| 3rd | 1.458:1 |
| 4th | 1.071:1 |
| 5th | 0.778:1 |

## Differentials

In order to split the power between the four wheels, the quattro system uses three differentials; one between the front wheels, one between the rear wheels and one between the front and rear. The latter centre differential is necessary because the front and rear wheels (even those on the same side of the car) turn at different speeds in a corner. The differential not only prevents transmission wind-up, it also distributes engine power between the front and rear wheels.

Audi's initial choice was to split the engine power equally between the front and rear wheels. However, where the road surface is extremely slippery, the centre and rear differentials can be locked mechanically and separately by the driver. Because of the increased tyre scrub effect, the diffs should only be locked *in extremis*. Furthermore, taking tight bends or manoeuvring into a parking space on a good surface with the diffs locked could actually cause transmission damage.

On non-Torsen diff cars the driver can select to lock either the centre diff only or the centre *and* the rear diff – the latter should be selected only as a last resort. Selecting either of the diff locks causes the ABS to lock-out automatically and the ABS warning light to illuminate.

## Rear differential differences

*The WR rear differential was made all of a piece and, for some reason, this placed extra strain on the rear axle bushes. The MB casing (as here) is a slightly different design with separate 'arms' coming out to either side and it does not 'eat' bushes in the same way. The 20v rear diff is the same as the MB.*

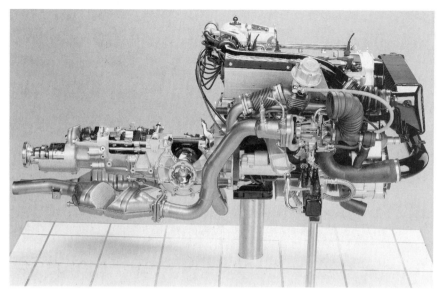

*This photo of a 20v engine also shows its gearbox back to the propshaft mounting. It is, of course, a Torsen diff 'box, the workings of which can be partly seen in the cutaway.*

*Seen in situ it makes a surprisingly dull photo for such a clever piece of equipment. Nevertheless, its pedigree is impeccable, forged first in Grand Prix and now, Audi motorsport. The earlier cars had their manually locking differential in the same place.*

## The Torsen differential

As the quattro developed, Audi realised that in certain situations it would be better to have more power to the front wheels, and in others to have more power to the rear wheels. What was really required was a continuously variable distribution of power that adapted automatically to different driving situations, different road surfaces and different weight distribution.

In searching for a solution, Audi noted three basic requirements: The new design should be dependable and backed by production experience; it had to be comparable with the existing differential set-up in terms of size and weight; it had to be relatively inexpensive.

The answer was found in the USA. An American engineer named Vernon Gleasman had developed a mechanical limited-slip differential which was being used at the time to prevent wheelspin on one side of a pair of driven wheels. The Torsen (TORque-SENsing) differential certainly had an impressive record as it had been used on the McLaren Porsche Formula 1 racing cars of both Niki Lauda and Alain Prost during the 1984 and 1985 seasons. Niki Lauda was World Champion in 1984, and Alain Prost in 1985. Moreover, for road use, its design was compact, only slightly heavier than a conventional differential and, most of all, it was dependable and maintenance-free.

Audi reasoned that a differential that worked well between two wheels on the same axle, should work just as well as a centre differential in a 4WD system. From this, they went on to develop the first self-locking (or limited-slip) differential employing the Torsen principle.

As ever, they tested the system mercilessly, not least as part of a fierce competition programme.

## How Torsen works

The Torsen differential senses when the wheels of one axle are about to lose traction and diverts engine power to the other pair of wheels before they can start to spin. This is done mechanically, but instead of bevel gears (as in a conventional differential) the Torsen differential employs six worm gears grouped in pairs. These distribute engine power between front and rear wheels with a ratio of 1:1 in normal conditions.

If the wheels of one axle should start to lose their grip and cannot transmit all the incoming power (for example, when the weight is transferred away from the front wheels under harsh acceleration) the worm gears, which are interlinked by means of spur gears, transfer excess power. The front wheels will not spin and are restrained at the same speed as the rear wheels. The torque split function between front and rear wheels is continuously variable from 75:25 to 25:75.

## Torsen and ABS braking

The advent of the Torsen differential was also important for the development of ABS braking on the quattro. On previous models, manually locking the differential automatically cut-out the ABS operation. This is because the processor that controls the ABS braking is unable to recognise wheel slip as long as there is a rigid mechanical connection between front and rear. Thus the advantage the driver may gain by engaging the differential locks was, to some extent, offset by the loss of ABS.

However, the Torsen differential is different because it locks up only under load, ie only when the throttle is open. The front and rear wheels are able to revolve independently as soon as the power is interrupted. By definition, when the driver is braking (assuming he is not attempting a rally course and indulging in some left-foot braking techniques!) he is not applying the throttle and thus the wheels are free to turn, ergo ABS still works. Like the Torsen differential itself, the ABS works without intervention by the driver.

## When the going gets tough ...

The rear differential can be still locked-up by the driver electronically by pressing a button in the centre console. As previously, this also switches off the ABS, but as soon as the car exceeds a speed of 15mph, the signal from the electronic speedometer automatically switches off the differential lock and reinstates the ABS braking.

## Practicalities

Though complex beyond belief, the relationship for the real-world quattro driver is simple – the gearbox either works, or it doesn't. It is well-known for being incredibly tough, not surprising given its military background. 100,000 miles is generally regarded as a running-in period and there are few reports of problems. The same applies to the prop shaft linking the rear diff to the gearbox. But that doesn't mean things can't go wrong, and it's worth knowing that Audi do not offer a service exchange system for the gearbox, prop shaft or differential. At current prices the gearbox is £7,000 and a prop shaft is over £1,000 – no small beer by any standards; and in many cases replacement could be almost twice what was paid for the car. Obviously it is possible to have the gearbox examined and, usually, repaired by a specialist such as BR Motorsport, but though almost certainly this will be cheaper than a complete new unit, it still won't be a cheap operation. The driveline components are expensive in themselves and very complicated.

## BRAKES

The 10v quattros originally came with servo-assisted, non-ABS braking, diagonally split for safety reasons. There were discs all round, ventilated at the front and solid at the rear. There was a pressure regulator to inhibit the rear brakes locking up during heavy braking and the rear callipers incorporated handbrake mechanisms.

## ABS

In 1984 the Bosch ABS anti-lock braking system became standard, and much better it was, too. All quattros after this date were so-fitted. In essence, ABS 'cadence brakes' in extreme situations; that is, it allows braking effect to the point where the wheel (the brake at each wheel is adjusted separately) just about locks-up and then releases the braking effect for a fraction of a second before reapplying it. Apart from the obvious benefit that you will (usually) be able to stop more quickly and thus avoid hitting something, there's the steering aspect; a car with its wheels locked is effectively out of control. A car *without* locked wheels, whatever the speed, remains in the control of the driver because steering capability is retained.

Only in extreme circumstances is there a need to turn the ABS off; for example, when driving in deep snow and the build-up of packed snow against skidding wheels would probably stop the car more quickly. However, the steering caveat remains – when you can't steer, you can't control. (ABS is automatically turned off when the diff locks are engaged.)

## Disc details

The disc sizes and thickness varied over the years as follows:

| Engine type | Chassis number | Front (mm) | Rear (mm) |
| --- | --- | --- | --- |
| WR | Up to G902400 | 280 x 22 | 245 x 10 |
| WR/MB | From H900001 | 276 x 25 | 245 x 10 |
| RR | All | 276 x 26 | 269 x 20 |

The pads varied accordingly. Remember that the RR, MB and late WR engined cars were equipped with twin pot front callipers.

This photo shows the master cylinder/reservoir to the left, with the accumulator sphere just out of shot beyond it. The ABS hydraulic modulator with solenoid valves is to the right, with the protective cover removed for photo clarity. The electronics and relays are to the front of the box, with the hydraulic valves to the rear. The modulator is generally not something repairable by the DIY mechanic. However, it is possible to check that the sensors are physically OK and getting the right kind of signal.

This diagram shows a cutaway close-up of an ABS sensor and its relationship to the sensor ring mounted on the stub axle.

Key: 1. Electric cable; 2. Permanent magnet; 3. Housing; 4. Winding; 5. Pole pin; 6. Sensor ring. (Courtesy Robert Bosch GmbH)

On each stub axle is a sensor ring, the toothed section seen here. This is often clogged with oil and road dirt and if this is the case the sensor will get confused by the information it is receiving. Use a small screwdriver to clean out all the teeth – laborious, but worth it. The hole in the inside lower part of the suspension unit is for ...

... the wheel sensor itself. As can be seen, it gets dirty and oil-covered, and cleaning it could prove to be the answer if the ABS light stays on. Use copper grease around the (cleaned) casing when replacing.

The plastic plugs and sockets are clipped into place near the callipers and it's possible for the internal connections to corrode and thus fail to make contact. Unclip them and check, spraying with WD40 or similar to prevent corrosion.

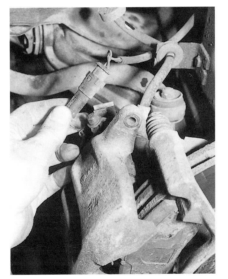

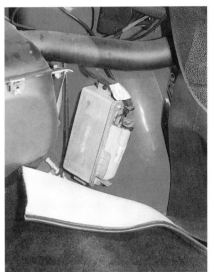

The ABS 'black box' is actually grey, and mounted in the boot, under the carpet to the right of the fuel tank.

The calliper itself is pretty much standard Audi fare. Note that each calliper mounting bolt ...

*... has a blue section at the end of the thread. This is the bolt equivalent of a nylock nut and is designed to prevent the bolts unscrewing themselves. ALWAYS replace these when you've had the calliper off for any reason.*

*The brake disc is held in place by the five bolts securing the road wheel and, with them removed, by the pressure of the pads in the calliper on the disc. It's a good idea to 'paint' around the centre of the disc (NOT the surface!) with copper grease before replacing the wheel as, on occasion, the reaction between the aluminium wheel and steel disc can make them 'stick' together. This is a nuisance in the workshop, but a disaster on the open road if you have a puncture.*

*It's difficult to imagine over-braking a quattro, and a step-up to high-performance discs is always a good idea. Certainly, if you have tuned your engine, tuning the brakes accordingly is essential. These are high performance Black Diamond grooved discs from C&R Enterprises.*

*Made from racing-type materials, the grooves keep the brake pad's friction face clean, and dust, water, etc is collected in the grooves and then thrown out by centrifugal force. Don't forget you'll need suitably high-performance pads to get the best from such good discs. Also seen in this photo is ...*

*… a Goodridge stainless steel brake hose, designed to replace the original flexible rubber hoses. The benefits are mainly that there can never be any bulging of the hose under pressure and, of course, it can't deteriorate in the same way as a rubber hose.*

*The hoses come complete with the correct size and type of fittings and new copper washer. Note the plastic cover on the union, which should be left in place until the last minute, to prevent accidental ingress of dirt. All Goodridge stainless hoses come with a lifetime guarantee and, again, are available from C&R Enterprises.*

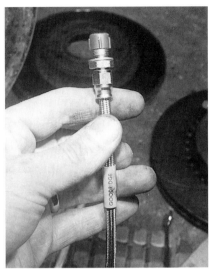

*There's a saying that racing improves the breed, and here's the proof; the AP Racing front brake system was developed from Touring Car Racing for use with road-going quattros of all types. The discs have been developed to give best retardation with minimum noise. They're drilled for added cooling. They come with precision die-cast alloy racing callipers with additional dirt seals and hard anodised coating to withstand the harsh environments encountered by road cars. The piston sizes are specially developed to give equal wear along the length of the brake pads (which also incorporate anti-rattle springs). Light alloy brake disc mounting bells and the calliper mounting brackets are machined from solid to fine tolerances on computer-controlled machining centres and are also hard-anodised. TUV-approved stainless steel brake hoses are used to adapt the new parts to the quattro's original braking system. It should be noted that the size of the new assemblies makes them unsuitable for use with standard wheels and tyres – an 8J x 17in wheel/tyre combination must be fitted.*

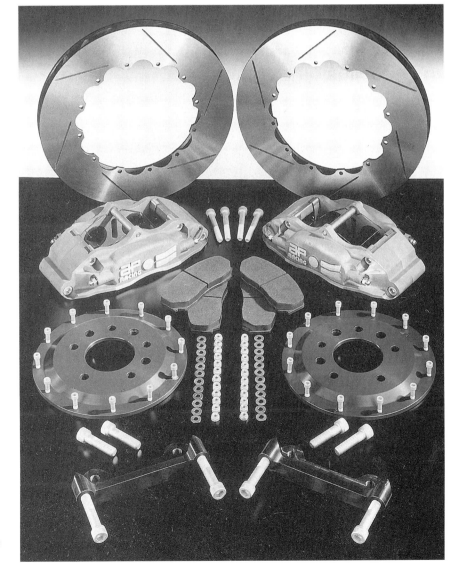

## The power of four

The 10v Torsen cars were fitted with 4-pot callipers which will fit the WR-engined cars, obviously with different pads. These are directly interchangeable with the previous 10v single-pot callipers and offer seriously improved braking performance. It may be possible to buy used 4-pot callipers but, as ever with braking components, you must be certain that they are absolutely perfect before fitting them to your car. They are available as new parts from Audi. Clearly, you will need to use the later model brake pads in these callipers.

## SUSPENSION AND STEERING

Independent MacPherson strut suspension was used all round, with combined dampers and springs. In general, Boge gas dampers were used, and to great effect.

|  | WR | MB | RR |
|---|---|---|---|
| SUSPENSION |  |  |  |
| Front toe in (+), toe-out (−) | +5° to 10° | +0.5mm to −1.0mm | +0.5mm to −1.0mm |
| Camber | −50° +/−30° | −50° +/−30° | −50° +/−30° |
| Castor | +1°30' +40' | +1°30' +40' | +1°30' +40' |
| Rear toe in (+), toe-out (−) | −10' +/−10' | −1.0mm +/−1.0mm | −1.0mm +/−1.0mm |
| Camber | −30' +/−30' | −30' +/−30' | −30' +/−30' |

Top left *For the most part, the quattro's suspension is similar or the same as that used on contemporary 80, 90 or Coupé models. Triangular bottom pressed steel wishbones were used at the front and, with it being 4WD, at the rear as well (the set-up here being more or less the front suspension turned through 180 degrees). The 20v cars featured rather better cast aluminium front wishbones which, apart from looking better, were less prone to flexing and offered better cornering and handling. It is possible to retro-fit these to the 10v cars, but the new cost is high and finding a set of good used wishbones is difficult. (Note this photo also shows the twin pot calliper front brakes fitted to the MB/RR cars.)*

Top right *The wishbone bushes all round take a real hammering from the engine's torque and regularly require replacement. Removing the wishbones is simple, but it pays to take them to your local garage who are likely to have a hydraulic press. With this, removal and replacement of the bushes takes minutes; without it, it might take you days!*

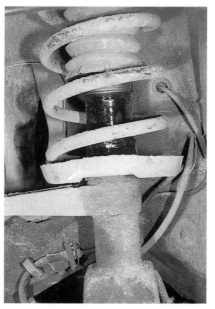

Bottom left *In the same area, the front and rear subframe bushes suffer a similar fate. This is a rear bush. The front right-hand side has a heat shield around it, which also serves to keep out the elements, oil, road dirt, etc, and thus makes it less likely to fail than the other three.*

Bottom right *Oil leakage can plainly be seen here, indicating the need for damper replacement. Dampers, like springs, should always be replaced in axle sets of two.*

Working on the suspension is well within the reach of the competent DIY owner, though setting it up definitely isn't. One of the initial problems is that the adjusting nuts on the track rods seize rock solid with monotonous regularity. Even where the track rod does not actually need replacing, that is often what is required, just to enable the suspension to be set-up. At top is an old seized track rod with a new one below.

Paul Beaurain is a Quattro Owners Club member and runs Pro Align in Northampton, a company able to keep your quattro running straight and true. The very latest, high-tech infra-red equipment is used. Special sensors are located at each wheel and then ...

... the results can be read off on a large screen, telling the operator the good news or the bad. Owners can get a before and after printout.

Most quattros came on Boge springs and gas dampers. Front dampers for the 10v are now unavailable, and Boge usually supply rear dampers for both ends of the car. The 20v was always fitted with the same dampers at front and rear. You can replace like for like when the time comes, or uprate for harder dampers and/or shorter springs. There is always a trade-off when going for a harder suspension set-up; on smooth roads, there will be much more control and less roll. However, on more bumpy surfaces, there may be a tendency for the car to jump around more, especially when cornering. And, of course, you lose some ride comfort. It's your choice, go for what you like most!

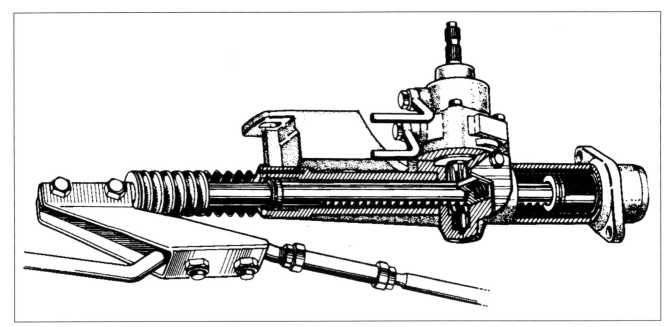

*This cutaway shows the standard rack and pinion steering set-up with inbuilt servo. The power assistance came from a hydraulic pump. The steering assistance was speed-related, which meant that at low speeds (with those large wheels and tyres to turn) there was lots of help available, but this decreased dramatically as the speed progressed, giving more 'feel' to the car.*

*The pump was always located at the front of the engine bay, to the left of the main radiator and, like the rack and pinion system, is not user-serviceable. If it leaks, replacement is the only answer (a leaking power steering pump is also an MoT failure point).*

## BODYWORK

Apart from being better built than most cars, the quattro's bodywork is no different in the care it requires. It should be washed regularly, using a quality car shampoo (not washing-up liquid, which will just pull off the wax). Waxing regularly is a good move, especially if you have a red car, as this colour fades quite badly. If you do have faded paintwork it's often sufficient to use a mild abrasive polish to cut back the 'damaged' colour and then wax over the top to protect it. If it's too badly faded, however, a respray is the only answer.

Though its exterior adornments are generally subtle, decals are used along its flanks (twin stripes) and on the door bottoms (Audi rings). As these are stick-on items, they will tend to get scuffed and ripped over the years and

eventually need replacing. All are available from Audi or from specialists such as AM cars, who offer complete kits. it is possible to get black stripes on a roll from Halfords and other accessory stores and, if you look hard enough, you might even find one of the right width and spacing. The other alternative is to buy two separate stripes and fit them individually – but getting the spacing exactly even all the way down the side of the car would be a major undertaking!

*The low front spoiler is often damaged by catching it on kerbs or sleeping policemen, etc. The only answer is to be aware of it and to take extra care where there are protrusions in the road. Because it is 'plastic' it is generally easier to fill and to touch-up any minor imperfections. The stripes along the bottom can be replaced using the same principles described later in this chapter. Note the side indicator markers which were always standard. The spoiler section is separate to the actual centre bumper piece, although both are colour coded to the body colour of the car. Contrary to popular opinion, those lovely flared wheelarches are not fibreglass (or even steel) add-ons. They are all-of-a-piece items fabricated specially for the quattro by the German company Baur.*

Door handles are an Audi failing generally. They tend to break internally and are irreparable. As doors are often 'spiked' they can be damaged in that way, too. However, they are common with the Coupé and other contemporary models, so it's usually possible to source a good handle from a dismantler and save around a third of the new price. By removing the lock it's possible to transfer the good parts to the new handle so there is no need to change keys.

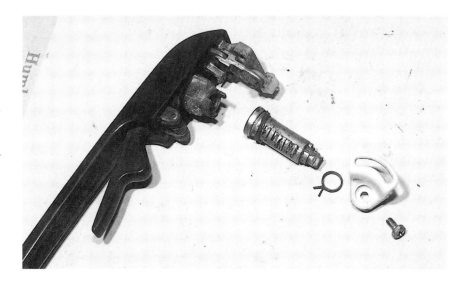

The boot lid is a shared component with the non-turbo Coupé models, though MB-engined cars had a fibreglass item. Across the back is a prismatic strip, removed here to show the positions for two foglamps – although only one was fitted for UK spec.

Again, the prismatic is the same on the Coupé, early models being red, later ones (like this) being smoked black to match the lamp clusters. Note that there are also two plastic pieces which fit above the boot-width prismatic.

**Left** *If your four-ring logo has deteriorated, peel it off (carefully so as not to take the paint with it) and fit a new set. But before you remove them, use masking tape to mark its exact position. Once the rings have been removed, clean the area and wash it liberally with a solution of washing-up liquid and water – this is one occasion when you actually want to remove the wax for better adhesion.*

**Middle left** *Though it seems odd, don't wipe the door dry, but apply the decal (it comes all of a piece) in the right position. Because the door is still wet, it allows you to move it around and get it exactly in the right position. Then use a plastic squeegee to get rid of all the water and air bubbles. Do not rush this part as it's very easy to miss a bubble or two, and they will totally ruin the effect.*

**Bottom left** *After a little tender, loving care, you'll have bright new Audi rings, just like the factory fitted. When dry, it's a good idea to re-wax the lower part of the door to compensate for using all that washing-up liquid. The decals shown here are original Audi items, sold as a pair (Part No. 111999103 BLK). It's worth noting that if your doors start to rust at the bottom (where water gets in through leaking window seals and rots from the inside out) the doors are the same as on contemporary Coupés – which opens up the market at your friendly local dismantler.*

**Bottom right** *Very few quattros will be left out in the open overnight, but even in the garage you'll find a layer of dust accumulating, especially if it is days or even weeks between drives. This dust contains thousands of harsh particles that will make tiny scratches on your paintwork. It's a good idea to use a Metex cover which is made from a unique and durable cotton fabric that is soft and non-scratching. Moreover, air can flow through the cover, thus preventing damp forming on the paintwork.*

## INTERIOR AND ELECTRICAL

The quattro came with a high specification level right from the start. Standard equipment included: Tinted (bronze) glass; laminated front screen with green anti-dazzle strip; electrically operated and heated door mirrors; electric windows; five seat belts; driver's seat height adjuster; radio/cassette deck with four speakers and leather-trimmed wheel; gear knob and gaiter.

It is often stated that the quattro is a full five seater, and whilst that's technically true it is much more at ease being a full four seater; the centre rear seat passenger has only a lap belt and has to sit on the bulge in the squab. Moreover, he'll block the driver's rear view, more important than in most cars because of the blind spots caused by the heavy 'C' pillars.

The interior is generally hard-wearing. The driver's seat especially can lose its shape as the squab bolsters wear out, though companies such as DB Car Trim can do wonders with them. Another common problem is that the seat tilt mechanism can appear to have jammed – in fact, the 'mechanism' is two levers connected to a long piece of

*Top right* Some of the early seat and trim patterns were to the '70s taste and are best viewed through your Ray-bans!

*Middle right* It didn't take long for things to calm down, and early into the '80s we had much more subdued interiors.

*Right* The steering wheel rim and gearknob/gaiter were always leather and these do require special treatment. Gliptone cleaner and conditioner are excellent choices, as they are pH neutral and won't harm the leather. Better still, the company has somehow encapsulated the rich leather aroma in the cleaner bottle, and it smells wonderful!

*Far right* Obviously, it should also be used on 20v cars (and Sports!) with their masses of leather trim.

wire, and over time the wire stretches.

Interior trim can be replaced by a visit to a specialist dismantler, as often the parts used were the same as in contemporary Audi 80/90 or Coupé models.

On 10v models, the quattro needs nothing in the way of specialist care for its interior. The carpet should be vacuumed on a regular basis to remove all the harmful grains of dirt. Ideally, protective floor mats should be used. You can clean the seats with a proprietary cleaner and the dash and other trim likewise.

## The digital dash display

The quattro digital dash has passed into legend for (a) always going wrong, and (b) being impossible to replace. Like most legends, there is only the slightest glimmer of truth to this one. There were two types of digital dashboard fitted, the WR-engined cars getting a three-piece, fluorescent green display and MB/RR cars getting an orange LED set-up, again divided into three sections. In terms of driving, it can be a little irritating on occasion, particularly at night, but by turning down the brightness and selecting speedometer only, it is much more user-friendly.

The fluorescent illuminated display shows a rev counter (a semi digital/analogue device), numerical speedometer, turbo boost gauge (0–2 bar), coolant temperature and fuel level. The brightness was controlled by a rheostat at the bottom left of the instrument console. Pressing the end of this control eliminated all displays except the speedometer. The mileage counter was semi-electrical. Also included in the dash assembly was a trip computer. This showed one display (of six) which could be selected from the rocker switch in the instrument console. It defaulted to a digital clock on start-up, but also available were; average mpg, current mpg, average mph, fuel range and elapsed time (where the display flashes '2:00' after a driving period of two hours, to remind the driver to take a break). If required, the

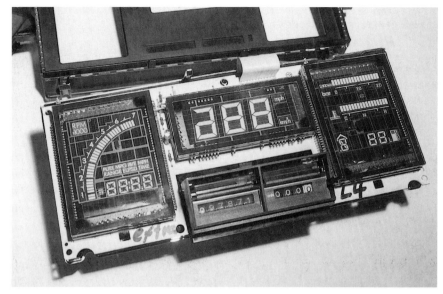

*The bright green display was divided into three sections, shown here out of the car and without the smoked cover, for clarity.*

speedometer, fuel gauge and trip computer calculations could be changed from mph/gallons/mpg to kph/litres/kpl.

## The voice

If the digital dash was unpopular, the voice synthesiser was doubly so. However, once one has become accustomed to it, there's a lot to be said for something that lets you know when, say, a brake light is out – how many of us check brake lights on a regular basis? Pressing the button on the end of the wiper column stalk with the ignition 'on' (but not with the engine running) causes the system to speak its warnings in the following order:

- Attention! Brake system defective
- Please fasten seat belt
- Please switch lights off
- Please check battery voltage
- Please check brake pads
- Please refill washer fluid
- Please check brake lights
- Attention! Radiator overheating
- Attention! Check brake fluid
- Please refuel
- Please check lights
- Brake light not working
- Attention! Check cooling system
- Attention! Check oil level

*These corresponded to three sealed glass fluorescent bulbs which are quite delicate – the pointing finger here is showing where the glass was sealed during the manufacturing process. If these are broken it's the end of the line, because replacements are very expensive. However, faults are often down to a simple electrical failure within the circuitry. Whilst you or I may look in wonder at the complexity of the display innards, Chris at Manton Software described it as '... a fairly simple piece of early digital technology ...' The display seen here is from the author's car, and one evening it simply stopped working. Chris investigated and found that a 12p transistor had failed.*

Having replaced this with a much
uprated device, he also hard-wired the
two boards (far left), replacing the usual
delicate ribbon connector as it had
started making occasional unwanted
contacts – another common occurrence.
Unless there is a really drastic problem
(with the bulbs, for example) it is usually
the case that a display can be repaired.
Moreover, whilst this is happening, it can
be given a checkover and have any other
problems rectified. The alternative
(unless you are seriously rich) is to
purchase a used unit from an Audi
dismantler, the only possible problem
being that because it is a second-hand
unit, you have no way of knowing how
long it will last or what sort of condition
it's in.

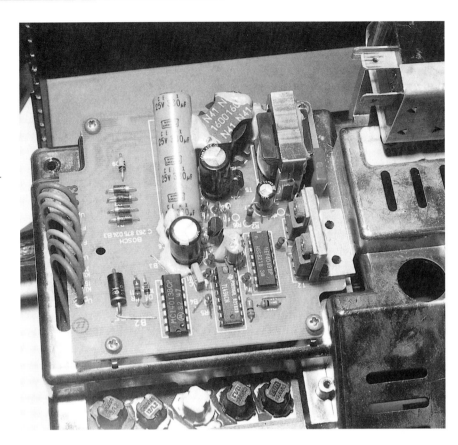

*Unlike the later dash, this had a
mechanical odometer, operated by an
electric steppermotor – the MB unit was
digital.*

## LED display

Though the design was basically the
same, the warning lamps moved to a
block in the central section and the
readouts were in LED (light-emitting
diode) format. There is a bulb behind
each of the sections which, at the time
of writing, cost around £45 each. The
functions were: Rev counter (as previously) numerical speedometer; digital
odometer and trip; fuel gauge; coolant
temperature; digital clock. There was
an onboard computer (showing average fuel consumption, average speed,
fuel range and driving time). The voice
was deleted for the LED displays.

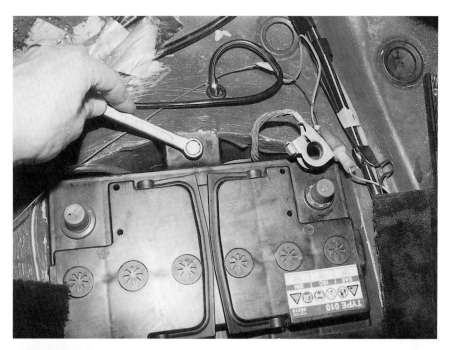

## Battery

The digital dash is just one of many electrical items on the quattro that make it essential to have a battery in good condition. A hindrance to ensuring this is that its position is Beetle-like – out of sight and out of mind under the rear seat (no room under the bonnet!) – and there's no way to avoid some element of voltage drop. It's a tight fit and care has to be taken to avoid spilling acid and/or accidentally making short circuits as it is removed/installed. It pays to check it occasionally, making sure that the terminals are clean (smear them with Vaseline) and that the cells are topped up with distilled water where appropriate.

This Hella 'Starter' is an ideal heavy-duty unit which complies with all EC regulations (it is recyclable) and produces 510A DIN. If your car is not used on a regular basis, you can help preserve your battery charge (and its life) by using a device called the Battery Sava, which effectively trickle charges it, according to the makers, for around 4p per week.

## SEAT BELTS

All five seats were fitted with seat belts as standard and, with the exception of the centre rear seat lap belt, they were the inertia reel type.

Top *Wherever else you save money, NEVER buy second-hand seat belts. You can't know whether the belts have been 'used' in an accident. If they have, they won't be any good. New belts are available from companies such as Securon, for both front and rear (including the lap-only central rear belt).*

Middle left *Check your belts on a regular basis, pulling ALL the webbing out and looking closely for signs of fraying and cuts.*

Middle right *The lower front seat mountings are at the bottom of the 'B' pillar and also behind the trim panel to the rear of the 'B' pillar.*

Bottom left *There's a screw on the arm rest to remove and another sneaky one, here, where its easily missed.*

Bottom centre *The rear seat belt mountings can be found under the seat squab (which lifts up and pulls out), at the front of the rear wheel arch (remove that piece of trim again) and also ...*

Bottom right *... just below the rear parcel shelf, accessed – as can be seen here – from the boot (after removing the carpet cover from the fuel tank).*

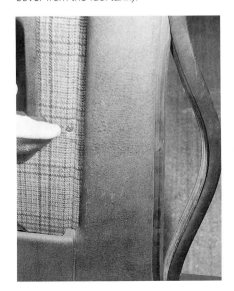

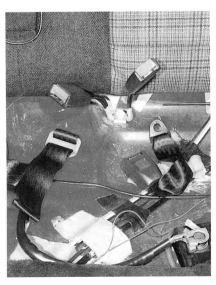

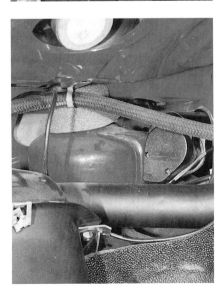

*Good tyres are absolutely vital to getting the best from your quattro – safely. Don't skimp here. If necessary, live on bread and water for a month to scrape up the necessary cash, because VR (or, better still, ZR) rated tyres are not cheap.*

## WHEELS AND TYRES

A very limited choice of wheel was offered as standard equipment on the quattro, all of which were alloy and 15in

diameter. Initially a 6J wheel was fitted and then, in 1983 for the 1984 model year, an 8J version of the same wheel was introduced. This wheel remained standard for all cars, including the 20v.

## Wheel definitions

| | |
|---|---|
| Offset (ET) | Distance in mm between the mounting surface of the wheel and the centre line. |
| Back face | Distance from the mounting face (the hub) to the rear of the wheel. |
| +Offset | Back face is located to the front of the centre line. |
| –Offset | Back face is located to the rear of the centre line. |

*You can see the difference here when comparing this new Goodyear (centre) with two tyres that had been taken off the author's car. The new tread depth is canyon-like and the difference in ride and grip (these tyres are known for being particularly sticky) was incredible. The original quattros were supplied with Goodyear or Fulda tyres as standard, though those fitted with the 8J Ronals (the R8 wheels) were almost always shod with Pirelli P7 rubber.*

*All the information you need is printed on the face of the wheel. This shows the VW part number, the width and diameter and the offset.*

Right *For a limited period when the quattro was first produced, the 7J Fuchs wheel was offered as an option. It was, of course, used by the rally team for loose surface work for the first three years of quattro competition. Quite apart from that sporting link, it looked particularly good. Though still listed on Audi's microfiche (at a price!), these are rarities, particularly in the UK. Seen here is a Fuchs wheel on the author's car fitted with a Goodyear 215/60 Eagle tyre, used for the UK winters, both to preserve the refurbished Ronals (see later) and to improve driveability. The Eagle was produced mainly for dealing with wet weather conditions. There's a real benefit in fitting this wheel/tyre combination when wet roads are the rule rather than the exception, as the steering feels a little lighter and there's much less susceptibility to aquaplaning. (Note that a Clarke pneumatic ratchet is being used with a DIY compressor, but this is NOT an impact wrench, as used by less aware tyre fitting centres!)*

Above far right *If you have a compressor, there's no excuse for not checking your tyre pressures regularly, though with a quattro there's no excuse anyway! Keep your tyres spot-on all the time, as a few psi makes a world of difference to the handling and can start to cause uneven wear patterns on that expensive rubberwear.*

Middle right *The high performance tyres needed for the quattro are usually 'handed' ie they must be fitted to specific sides of the car with the 'rotation' arrow pointing towards the front of the car.*

Right *When wheels have been fitted or refitted, always check the torque settings of the wheel bolts yourself. This S-P wrench is particularly accurate and easy to use. Tyre fitting centres often go overboard with their pneumatic tools, and wheel bolts that are too tight could prove impossible to remove with the wheel brace in the event of a puncture. It's just as important to make sure they're tightened up far enough – loose wheel bolts and 200bhp do not good bedfellows make!*

## Going up in the world?

It's a common feature on many cars to 'improve' them by fitting wider wheels and huge low profile tyres. However, the quattro really doesn't need them – it's still hard to find much wider wheels than the 8J Ronals fitted to most models, and the 215/50 section tyres are large lumps of rubber to have at each corner. Apart from the cost, going up with width or down in profile gains little, if anything. There will be an increased tendency to aquaplane and, though grip may be improved in a straight line, the car will want to 'tramline' (follow the vagaries of the road surface) even more than usual, and on unevenly surfaced corners will tend to bounce around them. So, unless you're going racing or hill climbing, the best bet is to stick to standard size wheels and tyres.

The tyre sizes, types and availability are correct at the time of going to press, but you should take into account the changing face of Euro legislation with regard to tyre specifications, particularly the 'CE' marking which will apply to all new tyres. Before purchasing tyres, always consult your tyre dealer, or even the manufacturer, to ensure that you are buying exactly the right type and size for your quattro's wheel rim.

| Standard tyre fitment | WR | MB | RR |
|---|---|---|---|
| Wheel: 6J Ronal | 205/60 x 15 | 205/60 x 15 | |
| 7J Fuchs | 205/55 x 15 | 205/55 x 15 | |
| 8J Ronal | 215/50 x 15 | 215/50 x 15 | 215/50 x 15 |
| Pressures (front/rear) | 1.8/1.7 bar | 1.9/1.9 bar | 2.2/2.2 bar |

*Those quattros not equipped with a full-size alloy wheel and tyre as a spare used 115/70 R15 spacesaver spare tyres fitted to skinny 4J x 15in ET55 steel wheels. It's worthwhile checking the pressure of this regularly, as it should be kept at a whopping 60 psi. It should never be used at more than 50mph (80kph).*

## Wheels uprate

The original wheels were so well suited to the car, it really is hard to improve on them. That said, the years take a heavy toll on their appearance. Any car used on a regular basis will soon have wheels which, despite the owner's best efforts, are stained by an etched-in water and brake dust 'ink' and scuffed around the edges. The 8J are especially prone to kerbs leaping out in front of them! Careful owners will give the wheels a quick rinse down after each journey, though if the car is used regularly, this probably isn't too practical.

Buying second-hand wheels to replace them is an option, but it's something that should be approached with caution. The odds are that they won't

*Made to make your mouth water! Lovely sticky Goodyear ZR rated tyres wrapped around a set of new 8J Ronal alloys – except that they're not new. They're refurbished and, at the time of writing, the cost was less than 10 per cent of a new wheel!*

be much better than the ones you already have. More important, you need to avoid buying cracked or dented wheels. If you're not an expert on alloy wheels, then don't buy without getting an opinion from someone who is. Of course, you could buy new wheels, but on a 10-year-old quattro they'll probably set you back more than the cost of the car itself!

*When you're having new tyres fitted and/or when you've had your wheels refurbished, make sure you ask for the balancing weights ...*

*... to go inside the wheel, rather than on the outside where they will spoil the effect. It's not hard to do, but some tyre companies take the easy way out unless you specifically request otherwise.*

These wheels were totally revitalised by the Pristine company, who can do wonders with just about any type of wheel you care to name. The first job was to put the damaged and corroded wheels into the bead blasting machine. The turntable makes sure that all of the top surface rim gets a good old blasting. Each side of the wheel gets a 2 minute blast.

The wheels were given a dip in the acid bath which removes all the last vestiges of the original paint finish. After the wheels were pressure blasted clean, they were taken to ...

... the machine room and put on to a lathe. This is computer controlled, and Pristine has the original specification of the wheels on disk. These are fed into the machine and it automatically cuts away as much corrosion and damage as is safe at exactly the correct angles.

The amount of swarf suggests that half the wheel has gone, but the actual amount of metal removed is minuscule.

The wheels then go to the pre-treatment bay, where they get a really good wash in the hot degreasing jet-blast cabinet, followed by a dunking in the cold bath, in which compressed air is used to give a swirl effect and get the water into all the nooks and crannies. They're then dunked in etch primer and finally washed in cold clear water before being taken to the oven to be baked. This obviously dries the wheels, but it also removes all traces of inherent gasses contained in the metal.

## AUDI HIGH PERFORMANCE DRIVING COURSES

Recognising that quattro owners are likely to want to get the best from their cars, Audi have set up a series of high performance driving courses at venues across Europe which, at the time of writing, include Spain, South Africa, Italy, Austria and Finland, as well as the UK where they are held at racing circuits across the country. In 1997 these included Thruxton, Oulton Park, Croft, Snetterton and the GP venues of Brands Hatch and Silverstone.

The subjects covered include: Driving theory; ABS braking; variable traction; cornering; vehicle dynamics; oversteer and understeer; a timed slalom competition and a rescue simulator demonstration.

Thousands of drivers have benefited from attendance since their inception in the early 1980s, not least because only the best instructors are used – for example, the UK team for 1997 included five-times Le Mans winner Derek Bell! Not surprisingly, the Audi A4 quattro, powered by the 2.8 litre V6 engine, is used on the courses.

In keeping with the current thinking on 'corporate entertainment', Audi also mix and match this kind of course with other sporting activities such as karting, golf, clay pigeon shooting and even helicopter flying. Information on all types of course can be obtained by ringing 01295 276701.

*Above The wheels come straight out of the oven and are powder coated while still hot, which means that the coating cures as it is applied. The powder coating is an electro-magnetic process, with a 12v positive charge coming through the gun and the wheel being earthed via the rail in the spray booth. When the spraying process is complete, the wheels go into an oven where they are baked yet again.*

*Right After being hung to dry, they are lacquered cold and then cured. The results you've already seen. A complex and effective process and one of the true quattro bargains.*

# Chapter 5

# Buying a quattro

*This chapter was produced with the invaluable help of David Preece, Chairman of the Quattro Owners Club, Adam Marsden of AM Cars and Brian Ricketts and Martin Parker of BR Motorsport.*

**SAFETY**: Always take the obvious safety precautions when checking any car, eg caution when working around a hot engine and when looking underneath a raised vehicle.

If you're not already one of the happy band of quattro owners, you'll no doubt be licking your lips at the thought of joining us. Moreover, a brief glance through any of the specialist magazines or your local *Auto Trader* will convince you even more that you should break open the piggy bank – now! Quattros are available at distinctly reasonable prices – to be running around in, say, an eight-year old supercar for the price of a brand new Lada hatchback makes a lot of sense. Unfortunately, all that glisters is not gold and you should not be lulled into a false sense of security by the fact that Audi make 'normal' saloon cars by the million. The quattro, whether 10v or 20v, is an extremely high-performance motor car with a powerful, highly tuned engine and complex transmission. The prices of some 'unique' spares reach deep into Ferrari and Porsche territory,

and the number of truly professional concerns able to work on the quattro are few and far between. Though many aspects of quattro maintenance can be tackled by the competent owner, on the whole it is not particularly DIY-friendly and you should build in a margin for professional labour into your projected ownership costs.

Do not underestimate the care required when buying a quattro. Start here and follow the rules very carefully.

## Reference point
Turbo quattros are commonly referred to by the first two letters of their engine numbers, as follows:

| WR | 2144cc | 10v | SOHC | 1980–1988 |
| MB | 2226cc | 10v | SOHC | 1988–1989 |
| RR | 2226cc | 20v | DOHC | 1989–1991 |

Quoting that you have, say, an 'MB' engined quattro can make life much simpler when ordering new or used parts, as any specialist will instantly know exactly the model you have.

## Four play
Buying a quattro is the easiest thing in the world; buying a *good* one is a bit like sipping treacle through a straw on a cold day. Like many specialist cars, most quattros have passed from owners who lavished plenty of tender loving care (and money) on them to

owners who have traded in their GTi or XR3, thinking they can run a quattro on the same sort of budget. They can't – and neither can you.

Even if quattro purchase is but a faint glimmer in your fevered imagination, now is the time to join a club – both clubs if you wish. Don't waste your fee – ask questions of fellow members and regional organisers. Go to the regular meetings they arrange and/or national meetings and/or track days. Ask more questions, pick brains (everyone just *loves* talking about their car) learn absolutely everything you can. Almost as a by-product you will probably learn of good, straight cars for sale.

## Professional checking
If you are not one hundred per cent sure of your ability to pick a good quattro from a bad one, then get some help. It's nice if you have a really competent friend who is happy to lend a hand for the price of a few beers, but if you don't, then try one of the recognised quattro specialists (see Appendix 1). Companies such as AM Cars and BR Motorsport offer a pre-purchase inspection service, the price of which could recoup itself many times if they spot a duffer that you hadn't.

## The power of two
Take along a friend who knows something about quattros (or at least about

cars). That way, while one of you is talking to the owner, the other can be examining the car in more detail without having to concentrate on the formalities. It's also helpful to have an unbiased opinion to balance out any natural over-enthusiasm you have which may well get the better of your judgement.

In general, quattros are not brisk sellers as most members of the car-buying public are frightened of their running costs. Bear this in mind when it comes to decision-making. Don't be rushed by the seller or your own eagerness. Though numbers are diminishing, there are still plenty about and plenty of owners have reason to regret a hasty purchase.

## Which model for you?

The same basic bodyshell was used throughout its 11-year life, the only major change being to the 20v floor pan to take the twin catalysts. So, in silhouette at least, all quattros are the same, but there are differences under the skin, some greater than others. So your first choice is to decide which model you want, what specification it should have and how much you want to spend. You are well advised to try at least one example of the model you have in mind and ideally, try all the models so that you can compare how the quattro has evolved. This is another area where the club may be able to help.

## Ages

There are four main 'ages' of quattro, though there were many tweaks here and there to muddy the waters a little:

1. The first imports up to 1983 (LHD only in 1981–82).
2. The digital dash, large wheeled 1983–87 cars, complete with synthesised warning voice.
3. The 1988–89 Torsen diff models with fully digital dash (but no voice).
4. The 1989–91 20v versions.

If price is no object, most would buy a 20v – they're newer, more powerful, have many galvanized body panels

and greatly reduced turbo lag. However, they are more expensive to buy and service and spares are dearer, particularly when they relate to the complex engine management system. And the price of those catalysts is eye-watering (though it is possible to delete them from the system).

However, the earlier cars are more plentiful (almost three quarters are WR-engined cars), easier for the DIY mechanic to work on, cheaper to buy and cheaper to run, and so tend to be more popular. Logically, the most practical era is 1985–89; there are lots of them and, though more refined than the very early cars, they don't carry the price/complexity penalties of the 20v models. Those with variable split Torsen differentials are technically better than the 50/50 split earlier models, but in truth, most drivers won't be able to tell the difference.

Most very early cars are now well-worn and in need of some work, if not complete restoration. By taking on such a project you'll be preserving a very important part of motoring history and gaining a very individual car. Whether your bank manager agrees with this is another matter, for restoring an early quattro will almost certainly be a real wallet-wasting experience. If they're not looking down at heel, they're probably original or already-restored cars carrying accordingly high price tickets. Again, a healthy bank balance is required, but the main benefit here is that you don't have to get involved in the wearying business of restoration.

## Mileage

With few exceptions, most first owners of quattros bought them because they had lots of miles to cover and little time to cover them in. They were very popular as high-flyer's company cars. Because of this a genuinely low-mileage quattro is quite rare, and usually carries a commensurate (high) price. Expect around 10,000 miles a year to be typical, but do not rely on a mileage indicated either by the seller or the odometer. All quattro odometers are

simple to 'clock' (turn back), even those on the second-generation full LCD digital dash. Lots of service history and consecutive MoT certificates may well back-up mileage claims, but overall you should buy the car on what you see, what it goes like and what it feels like. A low-mileage car will not, for example, have tatty and torn seats.

## VIN things

Never, ever buy a quattro from someone who hasn't got the log book (V5). The reasons for not having it range from it being swallowed by the dog, swallowed by the washing machine or the good old 'lost in the post'. If you really want the car, go back when the V5 is present, because without it you cannot verify that the engine, chassis and VIN plate details are correct.

## Paperwork

Ideally, you're looking for a full Audi service history documenting every minute of its life. Realistically, even 20v cars are getting ever less likely to have this, and if you find a genuine 10v car that has been treated this way, most motoring magazines would want to hear about it. (In fact, many motoring magazines would want to buy it!)

More likely you will find a car which has been tended by Audi early in its life (with bills to prove) but which has been serviced either by a specialist and/or DIY since then. Many jobs are well within the reach of DIY owners as long as they know what they are doing. What *you* need to know is exactly what is DIY-able and what isn't so you can check that the receipts match up.

## MoT certificates

Check the current MoT and as many previous ones as possible, if only to verify at least some of the mileages. An enthusiastic owner will keep these religiously. Having only the current certificate should ring alarm bells – it may be perfectly innocent but, equally, it may be an attempt to cover up a 'clocked' car. Mileages should be related directly to the service and replacement bills.

Remember that an MoT certificate

You need all the help you can get and the clubs are the best place to get it. There are plenty of meetings throughout the year – this is a combined effort between the two main clubs held at Woburn Safari Park in 1996.

Service history is unlikely to be complete, particularly on older cars, but any history at all is welcome and helps you verify mileages.

ALWAYS check that the chassis and engine numbers match those on the V5 (log book). The VIN plate is on the right-hand side of the car in the plenum chamber, and the chassis plate ...

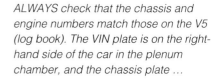

... is on the back of the front bulkhead. Check for signs that the plate or numbers have been tampered with –'ringing' is common, so take extreme care.

doesn't necessarily mean that the car is fully roadworthy now – only at the time it was issued. If that was six months ago, any number of nasties could have reared their ugly heads. As much use as the MoT certificate itself is the MoT Inspection Checklist, where the tester makes notes as he is inspecting the car. On this list could be points that are not failures now but which will require attention before the next test.

## When to buy

Plan your ownership carefully; study what there is and what you want. Ideally, buy your car in the summer months for five main reasons:

1. There's lots more light and it means you can view with some confidence in the evenings.
2. It is (or should be) warmer, so you'll be more likely to take your time and thus spot potential problem areas.
3. It should be dryer and thus you'll be more inclined to grovel around on the floor looking for underbody damage, oil leaks, worn bushes, etc.
4. Psychologically, people buy cabrios and sports cars in the summer and anything with 4WD in the winter. It follows that the prices of 4WD will be more during the winter months.
5. If the worst happens and you do buy a car that requires work, it's less hardship sorting it out when you're not knee-deep in snow and fighting a −7° wind chill factor.

## General tips

- See the car at the buyer's house – anyone trying to sell a stolen car or a 'ringer' (a car with a false identity) will usually prefer to meet you somewhere else, or come to your house.
- Many crafty thieves park outside someone else's house and just 'happen to be outside with the car' when you arrive, so you assume that the house is theirs. Always try to get inside the house if you can – asking to go to the loo is fair. If the seller hasn't got the keys ('my daughter has them and has just gone to the supermarket', etc) then be extremely wary.
- A keen owner will know where all the controls are – an 'owner' fumbling around for basics is a warning sign.
- The more paperwork, the better, especially MoT certificates, which are essential in plotting a car's true mileage.

## The buyer's tool kit

- Torch.
- Mat or carpet to kneel on when looking underneath.
- Magnet.
- Notepad with list of salient questions and points.
- Your own detailed list of what the standard specification *should* be.
- Assistant, preferably knowledgeable.
- Lock and key – to restrain your over-enthusiasm!

It should be noted that the engine number on 20v engines is situated on the manifold side of the engine in such a position that it is all but impossible to see without major surgery (to either car or buyer!). As such, 20v owners must be even more vigilant when checking the rest of the car.

## CHECKING THE BODYWORK

Have you already checked the engine and chassis numbers with the V5 (log book)? No V5? No sale! First impressions count; stand back from the car; does it look good? It should actively menace you from the driveway and crouch purposefully on its big broad tyres. It should glint in the sunlight and fire a need in you to go and find a rally track somewhere. Looks aren't everything, but a quattro that looks like it's tired out, probably is. Kneel at either end of the car and look along its flanks; areas of faulty paintwork and small 'dings' will appear that couldn't be seen from a full side-on view.

The body is quite resistant, but not impervious, to the onslaught of the tin worm. Certain parts of the earlier models were galvanized (see Reference Point below), and the 20v came with a ten-year anti-rust warranty. Even if a panel is galvanized, any damage repair not carried out properly will leave it just as vulnerable to rust as a normal mild steel panel. Because welding and working with galvanized steel is such a specialist (expensive) process, 'amateur' repairs are common.

Obvious points to check are under the front/rear wheel arches, along the large, vulnerable sills and inside the boot wells, which act as water traps. Check that the jacking points are OK – if not, the sills may have been used instead, with unpleasant consequences. Also, check around the boot hinges where serious corrosion can get a hold.

Look for the usual signs of overspray under the arches, on tyres and wheels and under the bonnet (often present after a front-end shunt). Parking 'dings' in the doors or quarter panels, or bumps and knocks on the corners of the car, are common, particularly at the rear where the chunky three-quarter blind spot makes reversing tricky. Doors can rust out along their bottom edges, but remember that they are interchangeable with contemporary coupés, so it may be possible to replace them from a specialist dismantler. Check around the door locks for signs of forced entry – spiking early Audi locks is a favoured method for thieves to gain entry. Always check the door handle operation and that of the locking mechanism – if a car has been broken into, one or both may have been damaged. Again, repair parts can usually be obtained from a dismantler.

The leading edge of the bonnet suffers from stone-chipping and most will have been touched up or resprayed. No problem, as long as it's been done well. If the paint's still wet, it was done yesterday in a last-minute spruce-up and you should wonder what else has been treated the same way. Take a good look in the headlights; the standard Cibié units are good, but the reflectors suffer from rust, and replacements aren't cheap. Flick the bonnet

Some parts of the quattro were galvanized, but the parts that weren't will rust at the normal rate. Check all the usual places, notably around the edges of the car and underneath where stone chips attack the underseal. A common place is where the front spoiler and wing meet.

Check the sill-to-front wing join and under the sill itself, which is prone to physical damage from poor parking and manoeuvring.

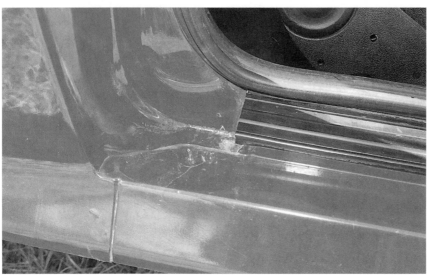

There are often signs of corrosion at the sill-to-'B' pillar join. Here, it's just surface rust, but if there are holes, it will structurally weaken the car.

The quattro sits low on the ground and floorpan damage isn't unknown. In particular, look at the undersides of the sills, especially if the jacking points have corroded – someone may have used the sill to position a jack! As you can see, the fuel pipes are exposed along the length of the car – check for damage and corrosion.

The area around the boot lid can rust and, again, it means trouble if the metal has been perforated.

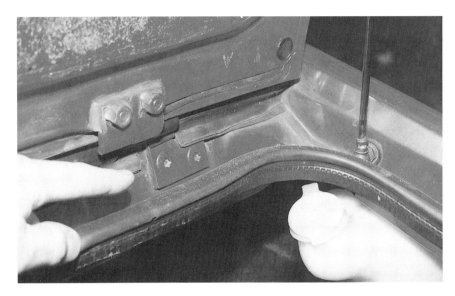

Still at the rear of the car, MB-engined cars were fitted with a fibreglass boot lid – check the ripples in the reflection. A steel boot lid where there shouldn't be one indicates the possibility of a rear-end shunt. Tread carefully.

Those headlamp reflectors are renowned for rusting. If they rust as badly as this, the lighting will be drastically reduced and it will fail the MoT. Replacements aren't cheap, but they are also used on contemporary Audi 90/Coupé models.

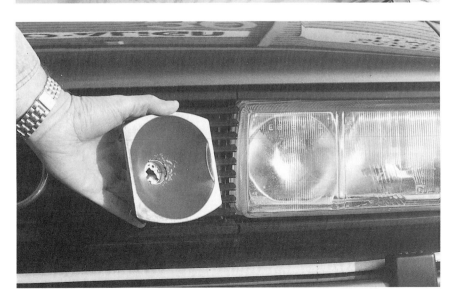

and look deep behind the headlamp area for signs of accident damage (overspray, kinked metal, new sections of wiring loom etc).

Boot lids were a shared item with the non-turbo coupé, so used replacements are not hard to find. However, from the Torsen diff models it was made of plastic, so a metal bootlid on a late model car indicates a possible rear-end shunt and a cheaper replacement.

## Security

Any quattro of any year is a prime target for the thief, whether he's a joyrider, professional 'ringer' or running an unofficial aftermarket 'spares' operation. You *must* take measures to secure your quattro, and for certain insurance policies you won't get theft cover without it. If the present owner has taken few or no security precautions, it's an extra cost for you (see Chapter 7).

## Reference point – galvanization

All modern Audis are now galvanized – quite simply, the steel cannot rust. However, though the process of galvanizing the whole range began in the mid-1980s, there has always been some confusion as to whether or not the quattro was galvanized. The official Audi line is as follows: 'Though always well-protected against corrosion, the handbuilt Ur-quattro was never 100 per cent galvanized, since its B2 body pre-dated the introduction of full galvanizing at Audi. Over the years, more and more galvanized panels were introduced in critical areas, including the floorpan and sills.'

One commonly held theory is that because the quattro was always built away from the production line, they were put in for galvanizing on an ad hoc basis. There is no hard evidence for this, although some quattros seem to rust in just about all the usual places and others, hardly at all.

## CHECKING THE ENGINE

The turbo engine really is the heart of the matter – without it the car could be

just one of many other quattros. Moreover, whilst there are ways to save money in most other areas (brakes, suspension, exhaust, etc) there are few short cuts to a good quattro engine.

The 5-cylinder Audi lump is as tough as old boots, especially the bottom end. Even with that turbo tagged on the side, all should be capable of reaching 100–120,000 miles. Remember that Audi were making the 5-pot turbo before the advent of the quattro, and carried on sticking it in the 100, 200 and 'S' models into the 1990s. The 20v version also powered the short-lived S2 and, at the time of writing, is being used as the basis for the upmarket 100 S4. It can't be all bad! Make a thorough visual check. You're looking for anything not correctly attached, working loose, etc.

## 20v

Checking a 20v demands the presence of someone who really knows what's what. The Bosch Motronic engine management system is superb but very complex and faults may be difficult to spot. Equally, problems with the 20v engine hardware are likely to be much more expensive even than on the 10v.

Look deep into the engine bay, which should be clean and free of dirty, oily gunge. If it isn't, catch the next bus home, because it shows that (a) the owner cares nothing about the car, and (b) at least some of the oil is not staying where it should – and quattro engine oil leaks can cost a packet to sort out.

## Oil and filters

Check the oil level – it should look like lager rather than Guinness. It should be changed every 5,000 miles (more often if the car is a low-mileage, 'shows only' vehicle) and it must be good stuff – supermarket own brand is not for the quattro. Most 'experts' recommend synthetic oil. It's expensive, but check out a few spares prices (original crank at £950 + VAT, for example!) and you'll see it's worth it. Can the seller show that it has had regular oil changes using quality lubricant? If not, it's a worrying debit mark. Remove the oil filler cap

and look for the white frothy 'mayonnaise' that is a sure sign that oil and water are mixing where they shouldn't be.

Official Audi oil filters – there are two – MUST be fitted. You can save money in many directions by buying pattern and non-official parts, but not here. They contain one-way valves which keep some oil up top to lubricate the valves and camshaft on cold start-up. Most aftermarket filters don't, to the obvious detriment of engine life, and if you find the car in question is not running on Audi filters it is a very worrying point. All you can hope is that it hasn't been running on them long and that, all things being equal, you can put things right if you buy the car. More important, it shows that someone is looking to save a few pounds on a very vital point – what else has been skimped?

Underneath the engine on the offside (RHD) is an oil cooler. It's fairly vulnerable and so are its twin oil pipes, which also have a propensity for corroding. Apart from the fact that it could lead to a wrecked engine, they are not cheap. Audi quote pipes for WR engines at £254 a pair, and while BR Motorsport can better that by £151, MB and 20v owners have no choice but to pay Audi £225 or £334 respectively. However, some Quattro Owners Club members have reported having individual sets made up by engineering shops for considerably less. You'll be glad you joined!

## Cooling system

All quattro turbos run very hot and need the entire cooling system to be perfect. Check the coolant level – it should be a 50/50 mix of anti-freeze and water and be either green or blue (the two most popular anti-freeze colours). If it's brown, it's probably still the original coolant and this does not bode well. The radiator will probably be clogged and the brown will be rust.

Check the condition of the radiator fins (cold engine) and don't forget there's an auxiliary radiator directly behind the centre of the grille. If they are rusting away, the cooling will be

A clean, oil-free engine bay is a good start. Check all fluid levels and the coolant hoses for cracks or splits.

A tiny split in a hose like this (close to the clamp position) could wreck a quattro engine. Pay great attention to the cooling system as all quattros run hot at the best of times and ...

... in many cases the radiator will be the one fitted at the factory. As the radiator gets past its best, the tubes block-up with rust and silt and the fins will bow out, as shown here in this typical example. Thankfully, companies such as Serck-Marston can supply off-the-shelf replacements for both the main and the auxiliary radiator.

The exhaust pipes were originally stainless but the boxes were of mild steel, so check carefully for rot. The twin-pipe system sounds rorty even when new and it's easy to mistake a holed box for a healthy exhaust note. Remember that the 20v cars featured twin catalyitic converters – difficult to check and expensive to replace.

*Typically, compression figures should be between 102 and 131 psi (7 to 9 bar). The minimum is around 73 psi, though this indicates some severe engine wear and the prospect of a rebuild looming large. Ideally the engine should be warm to carry out this test, so take care not to hurt yourself. Remove the negative wire from the coil and remove ALL five spark plugs. For 20v cars, the fuel system must be disabled to prevent damage to the catalysts. With the throttle wide open, crank the engine for at least 8 revolutions and then check the reading on the dial – this will be the max. compression obtained. The picture shows an S-P gauge, with a release button at the top which should be pressed before the next cylinder is checked. Expect all cylinders to be within 25 psi of each other. Anything well adrift indicates a problem specific to that cylinder.*

*A good compression figure will start high and build progressively. A poor figure will start low and build more slowly to a higher figure.*

*A compression test will check: That the piston rings are running free in the ring grooves and are correctly expanded out against the bore; that the head gasket seal between the cylinder head and cylinder bores does not leak; that the valves are fully seated and sealed.*

affected. Moreover, it's probably old and clogged. Check that the expansion cap is operating correctly – if it isn't pressuring the system properly, the coolant will boil up too early, causing the engine to run too hot. A new cap costs around £10 – if you're not sure about its age, build replacement into your negotiating figure.

With a cold engine, get your torch and examine all the water hoses in great detail. Bend and twist them mercilessly. This may seem harsh, but a total water loss on the motorway could easily lead to total engine loss – and all for the cost of a hose. A ten-year-old car is likely to be running on its original cooling hoses as few owners swap them until they burst.

There are more hoses than usual on a quattro because of the extra radiator sited behind the front grille. Don't forget the hoses leading to and from the heater, especially the small one just alongside the thermostat. Hoses are only available from Audi and some cost silly money.

## Start it up

Start the engine and look carefully at all fuel system components, notably the injectors, fuel distributor, fuel lines, etc. Make sure there are no leaks at all. The quattro head is prone to cracking between the valve seats and this can often remain undetected for thousands of miles. Replacement cylinder heads cost the worst part of £1,000 installed, so consider carefully. A smoking exhaust is often the result of valve guide/seals wear. This wear can be seen as smoke from the exhaust on warm tickover (blip the throttle).

White *oily*-smelling smoke at idle indicates that the turbo seals are leaking into the exhaust turbine housing. White *sweet*-smelling smoke at idle denotes anti-freeze getting into the engine via a cracked cylinder head or gasket.

The engine should not be noticeably noisy; tappet 'rustle' (WR engines only) is common when cold and the exhaust should have a deep burble to it. However, don't confuse tappet rustle

with the death-watch 'ticking' of an exhaust manifold on the way out. A small crack sounds like tappet rattle, but a manifold with serious problems can be heard in the next county. They also crack internally which sometimes results in part of the divider breaking away and going through the exhaust turbine of the turbo (thereby wrecking the turbo). A badly cracked manifold allows the engine to run even hotter than normal which can lead to early failure of the right-hand engine mounting, vibration as the engine 'bounces' on the subframe and burning of the wiring.

The manifold is difficult to fit, and an Audi manifold is mega-money. It can be welded by experts, but don't expect the weld to last too long. At the time of writing, Dialynx had just introduced a much cheaper (but still not pocket money) alternative which quattro-istes everywhere will be hoping proves reliable. It pays not to arrange a definite time to view a quattro because cracks in the exhaust manifold close up when they get hot. If the vendor has warmed it up before you get there, you won't hear it.

## Puffing and blowing

Early turbos tend to wear out or crack their casings, particularly if they are not left to idle for a few minutes after a hard drive, as they get extremely hot. Later turbos (MB onwards) give less trouble because they were water-cooled. A duff turbo isn't the end of the world (all things being equal) and specialists such as Turbo Technics can offer a reasonably priced exchange. In most cases you'll hear the turbo whistle as it gets into its stride at between 2000 and 3500rpm, depending on the car.

The standard exhaust from Audi is extremely pricey, though there are aftermarket systems available, one of the best being Scorpion's stainless version with its lifetime warranty.

The 20v models were the only quattros to be fitted with twin catalytic converters in an effort to be 'green'. This is indeed the colour you'll go when faced with a bill for a complete replacement – it makes a 10v exhaust look bargain basement. Many owners take the easy

Whichever diff-lock type you have, make sure they lock properly, with the warning lamp illuminating.

Driving the car should highlight any serious transmission problems. Look under the car for signs of obvious physical damage to the propshaft and centre bearing ...

... gearbox and diff casings. The MB casing is slightly different from that on earlier cars and rear axle bushes wear out more slowly because of it. WR cars can ruin them in 30/40,000 miles. The slight covering of oil film on this MB diff is nothing to worry about. When the whole area is caked with a thick layer of oil and road dirt is the time to get concerned.

This is the position of the diff lock actuator on the MB cars. It's in the same place on 20v models and slightly higher on WR versions. It's similar to the pneumatic central door locking motor and more prone to seizure on the latter because it doesn't have the protective shield seen here.

way out and replace the twin cats with a straight section of stainless steel pipe – AM Cars, for example, will charge you around £70 for this. Because of the catalyst emissions regulations dates, it doesn't affect the MoT test, as long as your engine is burning its fuel efficiently; the ECU should compensate quite easily for the difference, although it pays to have it checked by experts, just to be on the safe side.

There should be a large aluminium heat shield under the boot area. It's often loose (as the aluminium corrodes because of the reaction with the steel) but even if it's resting on the rear box, it should still be in place.

## Engine modifications

Power is a drug, and for many it's so addictive they have to have more. The 20v engine in particular is easy to 'chip' for more power and torque. Another common technique is to adjust the turbo wastegate. But nothing is for nothing and the cost of more 'go' comes in a lower mpg and higher rate of engine wear. So be *extremely* careful about buying a tuned car of any hue. Unless you are a fully trained engine-builder, I would not recommend buying one without specialist advice.

## Compression testing

If possible, it's a good move to run a compression test on the engine. Obviously, you'll need to take care you don't damage the spark plug threads and it's not a bad idea to run a thread chaser through before you use the compression tester.

## CHECKING THE TRANSMISSION

The quattro transmission is extremely tough; gearbox problems are very rare as are propshaft/centre bearing troubles. BUT, it's well to bear in mind that Audi do not offer an exchange gearbox or propshaft service, and a complete gearbox is currently around £7,000.

Operation was always notchy, even on brand new cars. It's also a little nosier than its FWD siblings, but not

*that* much. Loud grinding and whining noises should worry you greatly.

You shouldn't need to force any gear – just select it with deliberation – check each gear under hard acceleration and then lift off suddenly. Any signs of jumping out of gear should have you jumping in the opposite direction with your chequebook intact. Sharp acceleration, especially in third or fourth, should show up any clutch clip.

Engage the diff locks when stationary and make sure they work – don't drive any distance on tarmac roads with the locks on, as it causes axle wind-up. You should be able to tell in yards even if the diff warning light is duff. On vacuum-operated models, non-functioning locks can be caused by vacuum pipes coming adrift. Often the owners don't realise because few people drive their quattro in situations where they're required – deep mud or snow.

Check under the car for signs of physical damage to the drivetrain and for signs of excessive oil weeping.

Gearbox and drivetrain components are almost exclusively available only from Audi, which means everything is expensive. Do not ignore potential problems – if you're unsure, bring along someone who knows their stuff. Still unsure? Buy another car.

## CHECKING THE SUSPENSION, WHEELS AND TYRES

With quattro 4WD you effectively have front suspension at the back, too. None of the parts is cheap and when suspension is replaced (or uprated) you must have the car aligned by a specialist such as Pro-Align to prevent it crabbing. If you don't, it will handle badly and wear out its tyres in no time. Professional alignment costs around £100.

On older cars, the rear track rod adjusters may have seized. Replacement costs around £90 from Pro-Align and other specialists. Check for play by jacking up the car and pulling at the rear wheel. In the same area, the rubber suspension and subframe bushes, front and rear, soon get tired of

handling all that torque. Worn bushes will make the car feel like a ten-year-old Metro, and though they're not that expensive, there's plenty of them and replacement is time-consuming – especially if nuts and bolts seize in place with age. They can wear out in as little as 30,000 miles, so look in your pile of receipts (and at the bushes, of course). Clonking noises on full lock could be front strut top mounting bushes and/or drive shafts on their way out.

You will able to feel the effect of worn bushes when driving; you'll feel the 'slop' in the car during a sudden change of direction at speed (a mild swerve); if you apply the brakes at 60/70mph and the car starts to wander across the road (differentiate between brake imbalance) then it indicates that the front wishbone bushes are soft and require replacement). Like track rods, the bottom ball joints can only be tested with the vehicle jacked up so that free play can be determined.

Make the usual visual checks on dampers and springs, in that there is no sign of leakage from the dampers and that the springs have not cracked.

A clonk experienced when setting off is the usual indicator of worn axle and/or gearbox side mountings.

## Wheels and tyres

Early quattros came on either 6in Ronal wheels or, occasionally, on sought-after rally-style 7in Fuchs wheels. The hunky 8in Ronals fitted on post '83 cars look 'the business' and most owners don't bother to swap them. But their size makes them difficult to place, and most of us (guilty as charged) have scraped the odd kerb. Superficial damage just makes them look tatty, but a bent or cracked rim can be positively dangerous. New wheels are available from Audi – at a price – but companies such as Pristine can refurbish them to look as good as new for a fraction of the price.

Tyres tell you a lot about the owner. The standard tyre size for the 6in wheel is 205/60 *VR15 and for the 8in wheel it is 215/50 VR15. The quattro demands serious tyres and they *must* be at least VR rated for UK use. The author's '85

The rear suspension is almost as complex as the front (as can be seen here) and deserves more checking than usual. Expect all the rubber suspension, subframe and gearbox bushes to need replacing unless there is conclusive proof to the contrary.

Tricky to see, but check the right-hand side engine mountings which fail because of the intense heat. This allows the engine to sit down on the subframe and vibrate.

Conversely, the right-hand gearbox mounting is protected from heat and road dirt by a special shield, seen here. On the left-hand side no protection is offered and failure is more common.

Subframe bushes at front and rear (as here) often wear out thanks to the prodigious torque produced by the turbo engine.

Left *The rear suspension is basically a front set-up turned through 180 degrees. The rear track rods are common failure points. Even when they're not worn, corrosion can cause them to seize, thus preventing correct adjustment. Without this, the car will ruin its tyres and not run true.*

Middle left *Probably another torque-related problem is the propensity for 20v cars to crack the rear subframe at roughly this point.*

Bottom left *The alloy wheels are often scuffed (especially the 8J versions) with …*

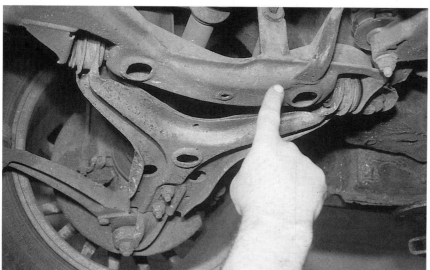

Bottom centre *… the finish lifting off on older wheels. New replacements are very expensive, although they can be refurbished by companies such as Pristine at a fraction of the cost – provided that they are not out of true (and therefore, dangerous).*

Bottom right *VR (or ZR) rated tyres will cost £600-plus for a set of four, so tread depth and wear patterns are important. Being 4WD, quattro alignment has to be set-up by specialists such as Pro-Align. However, Martin Parker reckons that all quattros scuff the insides of their front tyres like this, even when they're spot-on. The spare was always a space-saver.*

quattro is currently running on Goodyear *ZR rated rubber; not cheap but they stick like gravy to your favourite tie and they're one of the best ways to keep your quattro from becoming an impromptu off-roader.

A quattro with mix-'n'-match tyres, especially of dubious origin or speed-rating reveals an owner who can't afford to keep it the way it should be kept. Ask yourself, where else has he (or she) saved money? At the very least, you'll have to allow for the cost of replacement with suitable rubberwear. Check the tyres and treads carefully. If the tread is wearing unevenly (front and rear, don't forget), it will probably need specialist alignment at a company such as Pro-Align, Northampton.

## CHECKING THE BRAKES

The quattro has always had a disc at each corner (with ABS from the '84 model year), and they should stop the car with ease and confidence. Lack of stopping power, fading and graunching noises are all worrying signs. The rear wheel callipers often seize, so lift the rear wheels individually to check. Check that the handbrake is fully operational, as it can seize on one wheel (occasionally both wheels!) It could be a corroded cable (around £30 plus fitting) but it could be a complete rear calliper required, which is much more expensive.

Check the condition of the discs (usually obvious through the Ronal wheels) and that the pads have plenty of meat on them. New discs are fairly cheap from VAG and there are many uprates worth considering, notably Black Diamond discs and pads from specialists such as C & R Enterprises. Make sure the ABS light goes out. It could be a faulty wheel sensor, but it could be related to the expensive ABS hardware.

Where possible, check the general condition of the brake pipes and hoses, looking for rusting of steel pipes and splits or signs of wear in rubber ones.

*The VR speed rating is suitable for 130+mph and the ZR is rated at 150+mph.

Check that the brake fluid level is correct and that the fluid looks clean – it should be changed every two years, or less if the car is used infrequently.

## CHECKING THE INTERIOR

The interior trim is generally hard-wearing, even though of strange design at times – early trim was lurid, to say the

*Make sure that the discs are not scored and that the pads have plenty of meat on them. The callipers (especially the rear) often seize. The ABS warning lamp should operate correctly.*

*Inside the car the trim is generally hard-wearing, though the driver's seat in particular often suffers from sagging seat squab bolsters.*

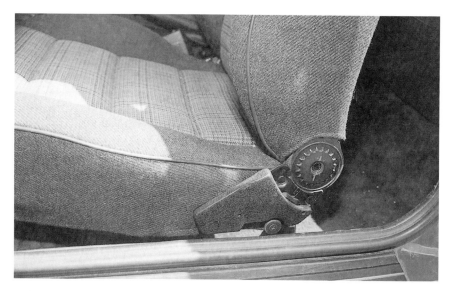

*The plastic seat trim here is often missing, having been kicked a thousand times by clumsy rear-seat occupants.*

*The door map pockets are the same as those on Audi 90/Coupé models from the same era and all suffer the same problem – the edges pull away from the self-tapping screws and they're usually secured only by the large central screw.*

*Relatively simple things, such as electric windows and door mirrors (the switchgear for which is shown here), are savagely expensive to replace. Make sure they work properly.*

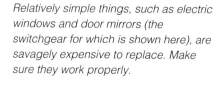

*Check that all electrical items work, in particular the digital dash (where appropriate).*

least. High mileage seats can split around the edges and the padding on the squabs has a habit of falling apart, especially on the driver's side. The cockpit in general is up to Audi's usual high standard, and a 12-year-old car should look more or less like new. Much of the interior decor is the same as that of contemporary coupés, so Audi-only dismantlers are a possible source of replacements.

Make sure all electrical items – such as electric windows and door mirrors – work, because Audi's official replacement prices are high, although it is sometimes possible to replace from a dismantlers.

Trim that has obviously been hacked about in order to fit accessories should be viewed with caution, particularly if the accessories have then been removed.

Unless you have proof to the contrary, budget to replace all seat belts – the average life is around five years, and there's no way of testing belts without destroying them. Companies such as Securon offer good aftermarket belts.

## Digital dash

If you're looking at a digital dash model, make sure you know what functions it should have and then check that it has them. Should this model have a voice synthesiser? If so, make sure its 15 functions work correctly – switch on the ignition and press the button on the end of the stalk, and she'll talk you through the warning messages (see Chapter 4). Early reasoning was that they could not be repaired, but specialist companies, such as Manton Software, can usually work on them. The early green dashes used three fluorescent glass 'tubes' for the displays, and if these are damaged, the only answer is *very* expensive replacement.

The later type orange dashes (Torsen-diff cars onwards) were LCD and featured a fully electronic speedometer. Again, repair is usually possible. A non-functioning 'section' (there are three) usually means a blown bulb at around £45 a time.

## 'DRIVING TEST'

Do NOT drive any quattro until you have run all the previous checks. For example, you might find a damaged tyre tread, bent wheel or serious suspension defect that would render it unsafe. Equally, you might find an oiled-up engine bay or tatty interior that shouts: 'run away as quick as you can!'

### Engine

Turbo lag was said to be conquered by the 20v – it wasn't. The gap between putting your foot on the throttle and getting the power delivered is a feature of all turbo cars. The difference between the very first quattros and the last models is the length of the gap; it was originally measured on a calendar, whereas the DOHC motor was almost, but not quite, instantaneous. Most quattro drivers find working the engine and turbo to their own advantage part of the quattro driving experience – a perverse reaction of the kind known only too well by Porsche 911 aficionados. Certainly, on post '83 models it should be no real problem to anyone prepared to become involved in the act of *driving*.

To check the engine for piston ring wear, get the car up to speed then change down a gear and take your foot off the accelerator, using the engine as a brake. When it has almost come to a standstill, put your foot back on the throttle pedal and accelerate. If there's a cloud of blue smoke from the exhaust as you look in the mirror, an engine rebuild is probably required. If the car smokes after it has been standing a while (say, idling at traffic lights), this is a sign that the valve guides are worn or the turbo seals are leaking on the inlet side.

The car should feel taut, almost like a racer, and should rattle your teeth down bumpy 'B' roads – the standard suspension was hard, to say the least. It should go where it's pointed, and corners should be able to be taken at speeds simply not possible in your average FWD hot-hatch. For most owners, the section of the brain that lives behind the door labelled 'survival'

takes over long before the loss of grip. But remember, most quattro accidents are 'biggies' because the driver is invariably travelling 20–40mph quicker than if he were in another car.

After your drive, let the engine idle a while before you switch off (a necessity on WR engines without a water-cooled turbo). Flip the bonnet and make a visual check that everything is OK – listen for hissing hoses and/or expansion filler cap. If the engine is hot enough (it should be) make sure that the thermo-fan for the injectors is operating.

### Transmission

The quattro transmission is legendary for being bullet-proof, but remember that serious transmission problems can cost twice the purchase price of the car to put right.

The gearchange was always 'notchy' straight from the factory and requires some mental adjustment when changing from a conventional car. The 'slop' common in 2WD vehicles is simply not there, so there should be no delay when you release the clutch – unless you've got too few revs on and are bogged down in the pre-turbo zone. For those who know, it's like the difference between a chain-drive and a shaft-drive motorcycle. Even after 100,000 miles the gearbox should still feel fresh and accurate.

All gears should locate properly; try slowing rapidly and applying sudden bursts of acceleration in the gears – especially 1st, 2nd and 3rd, as the most used gears. If it jumps out of gear, there is serious expense ahead. All quattro 'boxes whine somewhat, so it pays to know what to expect and what degrees of whine are too much. Don't confuse this with horrible graunching noises. Try the diff lock(s). Whichever model you're trying, when a diff lock is engaged a warning light should come on and, if you listen closely, you should be able to hear the pneumatic hiss on early models. If the light doesn't illuminate it could be a bulb failure or, more commonly, a jammed differential actuator. But don't guess – get out and look under the car – because what you don't need are deep differential problems.

## Brakes

When you start the car the ABS warning light should illuminate and then go off. If it doesn't, there's a problem – do not drive the car until it's solved. Selecting a diff lock should cut out the ABS operation, signified by the illumination of the warning lamp. (Remember that it is an MoT failure for the ABS light not to be working and so to drive a car in this condition is illegal.)

Try the brakes as soon as you can. On cars with the Autocheck system the warning light should go out fairly quickly after the first press of the pedal. At any speed the brakes should bring the car to a halt without drama and in a straight line any pulling to left or right is not good.

## The 'walk away' option

Chairman of the Quattro Owners Club, David Preece, reckons there are about

*Driving is the ultimate test of any quattro, but you should be sure the car is safe and thoroughly roadworthy before you get this far.*

a thousand right-hand drive quattros still around in the UK, so you can afford to be picky – *really* picky. Just think about the cost of replacement parts; a couple of good tyres will cost you over £300, an exhaust system upwards of £350 and replacing some of the complex electronics doesn't bear thinking about. And whilst some components are shared with lesser Audis, many are unique and can only be purchased from Audi at the price they care to name. As they tend to price things in lire and then drop a £-sign in front, you cannot afford to let your guard down! At the end of the day, if the car isn't *exactly* what you want and your gut feeling doesn't say 'yes', then say 'no' and walk away. There are plenty for sale; go pick a good one.

## How much?

If you're good at valuing string by the piece, then you're in with a chance. Each model must be judged very much on its general condition and any history. However, once you get below £5,000 you're in tricky territory and could easily spend as much again to get the car right. There's no doubt that the quattro is a coming classic and that restoration

is worthwhile, but you've *got* to buy at the right price. Many owners believe that a 'classic' is worth silly money, whatever its condition. This may become the case in 30 years time when there are only four left, but not now. Once again, make the most of your Club membership and ask for advice – there's a wealth of expertise here.

## Extras value?

The quattro always came with a high specification, so advertisements listing 'elec windows, central locking, elec door mirrors' mean little – they all had them, and from the Torsen-diff cars a sunroof was standard, too. Added accessories are usually worth little, if any, extra money; and if they are not pukka Audi extras they can often have the effect of bringing the price down.

## Last but not least

You've found a good one; it's straight, clean and goes like it should. It seems to have the right history and the owner appears genuine. Now it's time to find a phone (or dig around in your glovebox for the mobile) to contact HPI Equifax. These good people will relieve you of £30 or so, for which they will check the

things you can't, notably the Stolen Vehicle Register, whether it's been a write-off stolen and recovered, whether there is finance owing against it (or any other number it's been registered under – very important) and various other vital aspects.

## Buying from dealers

Ur quattros are few and far between at official Audi dealers, though some still dabble occasionally. Buying from a non-Audi dealership, it's best to stick to specialists and Club 'friends' who know their stuff. *Bloggs Prestige Motors* is probably not the best place to buy a quattro.

## Warranty

Warranties are not always what they appear to be. Some cover breakdowns only, and then only if the problem can be shown to have started after the sale. As this is usually not the case or impossible to prove, you could be paying extra for less than nothing.

## When I get you home ...

Having bought your quattro, it is important to carry out certain rituals before you succumb to the understandable desire to get out on to the roads and have fun. If you're buying an older model (most quattros at the time of writing) then the odds are that it has not seen any serious servicing in two or three years.

Regardless of what the previous owner says, your first job is to change the two oil filters (one engine, one turbo) using ONLY pukka Audi filters; these have non-return valves which prevent all the oil draining back into the sump and the top of the engine starting 'dry'. Replace whatever black oily stuff is in the engine with top quality synthetic oil.

If the cost of this necessity worries you either (a) don't buy the car or (b) negotiate £50 harder in the deal!

Next, take a good look at the air filter. The odds are it will be clogged, which is no good at all for the engine. Again, replace it. If your pre-purchase examination revealed down-at-heel coolant, replace it; at least a 50/50 water/anti-

freeze mix is required. Dig deep and use Audi's top-notch stuff designed specifically for high-performance engines. Check the tyre pressures to ensure they're spot-on.

## BUYING A SPORT QUATTRO

Hardly cheap at the launch (£51,000), Sport prices rocketed to insane levels during the late 1980s, but they have eased off since them. Even so, you'll be extremely lucky to see one advertised for much less than £40,000, and a well-looked-after, low-mileage example could be upwards of £60,000.

If you are set on buying a Sport take heed of the following advice:

- DO NOT do so until you have an unequivocal report on the vehicle which includes any known faults and (very important) that it is what it purports to be. It is well worth the while of clever car thieves to put some effort into making a stolen or written-off car look like the real McCoy. Specialists such as AM Cars, BR Motorsport or Historic Motorsport will be able to help here.

- You should be well aware of the staggering cost of spare parts. At the time of writing, a petrol filler flap costs £120, a distributor cap £300 and the composite bonnet can be put on special order at a tad over £11,000 – unpainted! Naturally, this will make getting insurance a work of some endeavour. Moreover, having even a minor accident could easily result in the car being declared a write-off!

- Unless you are purchasing to add to your collection of exotic classics, drive before you buy. With its LHD driving position, peaky powerful engine and massive wheels and tyres, it can be more than a handful, especially on the UK's crowded roads.

## QUATTRO BUYING CHECKLIST

This checklist should be used as a basic guide in conjunction with the more detailed sections in this chapter.

| | |
|---|---|
| Location. | Try to view at owner's home. Meeting in car parks, etc is suspicious – car may be stolen. |
| Is the log book (V5) present? | STOP NOW! Do NOT buy a quattro without seeing the V5 (see next comment). |
| Check the name/address, number of owners, engine, chassis and VIN numbers, etc on the V5. | Any discrepancies should be ironed out before continuing. |
| Is there at least some service history, invoices, etc? Ensure that the mileages tally. | Enthusiasts tend to keep every scrap of information. The less there is, the more you should worry. |
| Are there MoT certificates? Ensure that the mileages tally. | Again, enthusiasts hoard these, and if available they will give some idea of the true mileage. |
| Is it raining or has it rained recently? Has the car just been washed? | Bear this in mind – water makes any car's paintwork look better than it is. |
| Are you viewing in fading light? | You really can't inspect a car properly in the dark or half-light. |

| | |
|---|---|
| Look hard all around the car. | Check along its flanks for accident damage, and inside boot and engine bay for minor bumps – check for signs of overspray, etc. |
| Look in the engine bay. Check oil and coolant level. | Dirty oil or brown coolant are worrying signs, as are oil leaks and a generally scruffy bay. |
| Look under the car. | Check for oil leaks from engine, transmission or dampers. Look under wheel arches and along sills for damage or rust. Check exhaust condition. |
| Wheels and tyres. | Check wheels for serious damage – expect minor scuffs. Check tyres for legal tread, uneven patterns, sidewall damage, etc. |
| Look at brake discs and pads through wheels. | Damaged and/or scored discs and badly worn pads mean no test drive until replaced. |
| Interior trim | Check condition is commensurate with mileage. Look for signs of abuse. |
| Interior functions | Make sure EVERYTHING electrical works, especially the digital dash (where fitted). |
| Start car and let it idle. | Car should start easily and idle cleanly straight away – if not, could be fuel-injection or electronic problems. |
| Drive the car if possible on a selection of road surfaces. | Check all gears engage and stay there. Listen for untoward noises from engine/suspension. |
| Braking. | Brakes should stop the car quickly and in a straight line. Check ABS light operation (where fitted). |
| After the test drive. | Let engine idle for a few minutes then blip the throttle – a puff of blue smoke indicates engine wear and lots of expense. |
| HPI/AA check. | A phone call to HPI or AA Data Check is essential and will reveal if the car has been stolen, written-off, etc, even against a changed 'personal' number plate. |
| The deal. | Like an auction, set your budget beforehand and stick to it. Know replacement prices and use them as a lever to get to your price. Offset against any spares included in the deal. |

# Chapter 6

# Tuning

*My thanks to Brian Ricketts of BR Motorsport and Ian Sandford of Superchips for their help with this chapter.*

The engine's power and torque is only a part of the tuning equation. Clearly, if the car goes more quickly it needs to stop more quickly, too. So, you'll need to uprate your brakes! Also, its likely the suspension will have to be uprated as well.

For anyone uprating a car in a serious way, it is advisable either to go on one of Audi's specialist quattro training days or a track day organised by one of the clubs – or both!

Before starting, be aware that it's no use tuning an engine that is on its last legs. According to Brian Ricketts, an engine that has covered up to 50,000 miles and which has been well treated (correct oil, etc) should be OK to tune. Between 50,000 and 100,000 miles, he would expect to have to strip and examine the engine, checking crankshaft bearings and almost certainly replacing the valve guides. Over 100,000 miles the engine will need serious attention; a full strip down to find and replace worn parts and rebore, with new pistons where required. A tip from The Master: *Fitting new piston rings in worn bores does not work on the quattro engine!*

*At BR Motorsport much attention is paid to the cylinder head – this MB head has been gas-flowed with reprofiled valve seats, etc.*

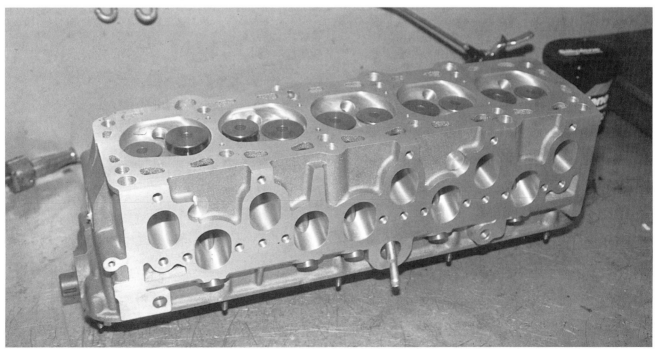

Also be aware that once you have altered your car in any way you must tell your insurers. Not doing so could lead to a subsequent claim being rejected.

## BR MOTORSPORT

BR Motorsport, run by GTi Engineering founder Brian Ricketts, is one of the prime movers in quattro servicing and tuning in the UK and claims to handle more quattros than anyone else in an average year.

Because of the relatively simple nature of the fuel injection and ignition systems on the WR- and MB-engined cars, tuning is quite limited. BRM list the following at the time of writing:

### WR – 260bhp

Hybrid turbocharger with standard exhaust turbine fitted with bigger compressor, giving more boost throughout the rev range. This increases the usable rev range from 5000rpm to 6500rpm.

### MB

The larger turbo from the RS2 can be fitted. It starts to boost at 1500rpm and gives good power all the way up to a heady 7000rpm.

### WR and MB – 240bhp

Fully gas-flowed cylinder head with reprofiled valves and seat, gas-flowed inlet and exhaust manifolds fully matched to ports in head. This gives better driveability and more torque whilst reducing turbo lag. Turbo boost starts at 2200rpm and 1800rpm on the WR and MB respectively, where the standard figures are 2800rpm and 2200rpm.

## 20v OPTIONS

As ever, the 20v car with its Bosch Motronic engine management system lends itself more readily to tuning. BRM can offer the following conversions.

### 258bhp

Reprogrammed ECU fitted with 2 bar

boost pressure, transducer, higher boost settings and optimised ignition, fuel settings. BRM quote an improvement of ten per cent in fuel economy.

### 262bhp

Reprogrammed ECU fitted with 2.5 bar boost pressure, transducer, higher boost settings and optimised ignition, fuel settings. Because of the extra torque the engine develops, stronger con-rods are fitted as part of the conversion.

### 300bhp

Reprogrammed ECU with special turbo boost controller, special exhaust manifold and hybrid turbocharger, special air cleaner system, stronger con-rod bearings.

### 320bhp

As above, but with fully gas-flowed cylinder head, reprofiled valves and seat, fully matched inlet and exhaust manifolds.

## CHIPS WITH EVERYTHING

With modern cars 'chipping' is the norm when it comes to obtaining more power. However, the opportunities are very limited with the early WR quattros

when it comes to changing the electronics to gain performance. In essence, the ECU can be reprogrammed to allow a little more boost pressure. According to Superchips MD Ian Sandford, this is typically raised from around 10 psi to 14 psi. However, he points out that where the original figure is lower (because of engine wear, etc) the uprated figure will be correspondingly lower. The aim of the boost increase is mostly to improve the mid-range power and torque – on a good engine Ian would expect to see an increase of around 35bhp.

From the 1988 model, when the 2226cc MB engine was introduced, there was a different ECU fitted and this means that it can be re-mapped more comprehensively.

The 20v Ur quattros were equipped with the ultra-modern fully electronic Bosch Motronic engine management system and these are the most responsive of all to this form of engine tuning and Superchips has available a wide range of 'chips' and uprates for them.

*Superchips produce a range of standard replacement chips for owners who feel confident that their car is up to scratch and capable of fitting it themselves.*

# Tuning

This 12-year-old WR-engined car was given a power uprate by Superchips technician Dave Tinsley. He checked the existing boost pressure using a special gauge which was connected to one of the pipes from the manifold. It shouldn't be taken from the wastegate pipe or any other which is only atmospheric pressure. The car was showing around 6 psi, as opposed to around 10 psi when new.

Dave said that the stainless pipe which runs from the wastegate under the manifold to the turbo is notorious for coking up. It's difficult to reach (which is why it gets ignored) and results in reduced boost pressure and, of course, reduced performance.

He checked all the turbo pipes and connections, a vital procedure where extra boost is the aim – poor connections can be blown off altogether.

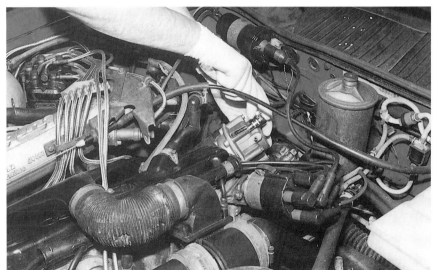

He removed six nuts from the top of the wastegate cover. The last two have to be removed whilst holding the cap, because the pressure ...

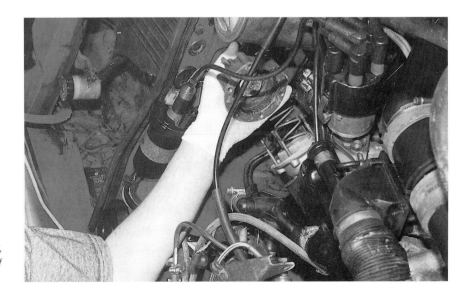

... from the spring underneath could blast it off as the nuts come off the last few threads. He applied lots of easing agent as these studs often corrode and snap. A broken stud could be drilled out, though there would be a danger of swarf falling down the wastegate.

Far left *Dave drilled out the protective cap in the centre of the wastegate to give access to the Allen-headed adjuster screw. He used a heat gun to melt the factory-applied Loctite and make removal possible. Note that the WR engine wastegate top is different from that of the MB engine – they are NOT interchangeable.*

Left *Inside the wastegate cap there's a plate attached to the screw – it often corrodes solid and needs encouraging free. Here is a complete breakdown of the cap parts, together with the replacement spring (on the right). They're the same height, but the new spring exerts much more pressure. Clearly, the more pressure this spring has, the harder it is for the wastegate to come into play and the more boost gets to the engine.*

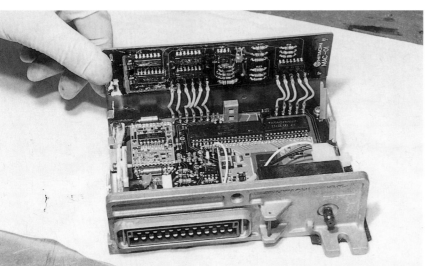

*Though the early ECUs can't be 'chipped' in the unplug and plug-in way that the Motronic 20v cars can, Superchips are able to modify this one to accept the higher level of boost expected.*

*Having replaced the ECU in its hideaway position under the lower right-hand side dash panel …*

*… Dave and Ian then did the road test – it's a hard job, but someone's got to do it! By running their own calibrated boost gauge inside the car, they were able to check exactly what was happening. During the ten-mile test they stopped several times to make adjustments. In this case the engine was running nicely up to 12 psi. Driving the car, the benefit of the uprate was particularly noticeable in the improved throttle response and reduced lag.*

## Power

The maximum standard power outputs for the WR and MB engines is 200bhp, and for the 20v it is 220bhp. It has to be remembered that this is taken at the flywheel, and by the time the power hits the tarmac it will be reduced, because of the transmission and other friction losses. On a normal front or rear-wheel drive car it would typically be around 15 per cent. With 4WD it is greater, probably around 20–25 per cent, depending on how well the car is set-up.

The following figures are the maximum Superchips expects to find on a perfect engine. Older engines have less boost to start with and so have their boost increased by less.

MB engines feature an electronic boost control system in the ECU – con-

| | Engine | | |
| | WR | MB | RR (20v) quattro and S2 |
| --- | --- | --- | --- |
| Additional work | Wastegate spring | N/A | N/A |
| ECU (std) Reference | 447 905 383C | 857 905 393 | 0262 203 451. 6462. 6259. 0261 293 188. |
| | | | 6093. 0261 200 453/484. 6139. 6261. |
| | | | 6530. 6560. 0261 203 643. 8375. |
| Type | Hitachi | Hitachi | Bosch |
| Standard psi | 10 | 11.5 | 12 |
| Uprated psi | 16 | 14.7 | 16 |

*(Courtesy Superchips)*

trols a solenoid in the wastegate. This is disconnected electronically and another board added in line between the ECU and boost sensor.

Power isn't everything, as Ian pointed out: 'The power figures are relative to boost pressure and not rpm. Therefore an increase of 30bhp does not mean that 200bhp becomes 230bhp. Boost pressure tends to fall off towards the top end of the rev range, so the 30bhp gain will probably come around 1000rpm lower, with maximum power gain probably being around 15bhp. This means that the driveability of the car improves and its urge is considerably better.'

# Chapter 7

# Security

You don't need to be told how desirable your quattro is, and neither does the thief. It remains high on any 'hit-list' and, unfortunately, it is remarkably easy to steal. This is because it was built in the early '80s using late '70s thinking and technology. Car crime then was a fraction of the problem it is today and the locks can easily be overcome by any average thief. It may go against the grain to have to spend out to secure your car properly, but unless you do you stand a very good chance of losing your quattro altogether. Not much of a choice, really.

When it comes to testing security products, there are currently two bodies: Thatcham, which is insurance-industry backed, and Sold Secure, a non-profit making organisation which has the support of the Home Office and the Police. They work on similar lines, but Thatcham products, for obvious reasons, tend to have more effect on insurance premiums. Sold Secure 'recognises' rather than approves products and does not have categories in the way Thatcham does.

## THATCHAM

This is the Motor Industry Repair Research Centre based at Thatcham in Berkshire. It classifies those products which meet its requirements into four basic Categories:

## Category 1 (combined alarm/immobiliser)

Alarm with full perimetric and volumetric detection, and stand-by power supply. Immobiliser isolating a minimum of two circuits, passively armed, with anti-scan, anti-grab codes. A top Category 1 system on your quattro will definitely improve your chances of keeping it and put a spring in the step of your insurers. It can sometimes actually pay for itself straightaway through preferential insurance premiums. In most cases it could be expected to be 'in profit' within three years.

## Category 2 (electronic/ electromechanical immobiliser)

Immobiliser isolating a minimum of two circuits, passively armed, with anti-scan, anti-grab codes. A two-circuit immobiliser of this nature should be seen as the minimum requirement for your quattro.

## Category 2>1

(Category 2 devices which can be upgraded to Category 1 with the minimum of effort)

## Category 3 (mechanical immobiliser)

Physical immobiliser isolating a minimum of one operating system. Easy to arm and disarm. Attack resistance to five minutes minimum using a comprehensive range of hand tools. Can be permanently fitted, or temporary DIY (temporary DIY mechanical immobilisers are listed as devices intended as supplementary security or security appropriate to lower risk vehicles). Realistically, a Category 3 device is not suitable for any quattro model.

## Q (miscellaneous)

The 'Q' category was created for those security products which were seen to be excellent ways of protecting a car but did not fall into the categories above. These include vehicle tracking systems using GPS (global position satellite) technology, security window film, smoke alarm systems, in-car security cameras, etc. Though Thatcham does not actually approve the products in the same way, it will provide a report as to the test results for use by the security product manufacturers as they see fit.

## INSURANCE

Stopping the thief getting access to your car is good news, but most insurers will want to know that you have securely immobilised your car before they'll issue cover notes (some will provide cover but delete theft cover while the vehicle is not immobilised). In order to have the best protection, a

Thatcham-approved device is probably the best option. Certainly, many insurers will insist that any security products fitted have Thatcham approval, so you may not have any choice in the matter. In many cases there will be an insurance discount which will offset the cost of alarm installation. The ABI (Association of British Insurers) reckon that, on average, owners can look to recoup the whole cost of alarm installation within three years.

## GETTING PHYSICAL

Along with many cars from its era, Audi door locks are notoriously easy to 'spike' – the thief drives a sharp metal implement just under the handle to gain access to the locking rods.

It also pays to consider those valuable alloy wheels and expensive low-profile tyres. A set of locking wheel bolts is essential. In an independent test, Carflow's Trilocks came out the best overall.

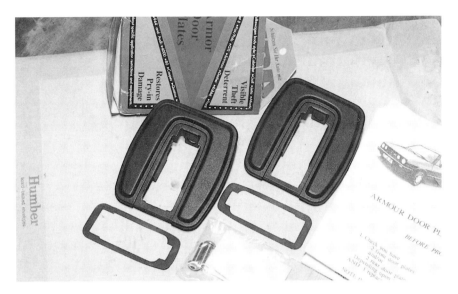

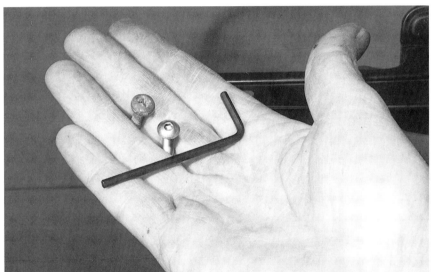

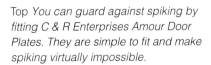

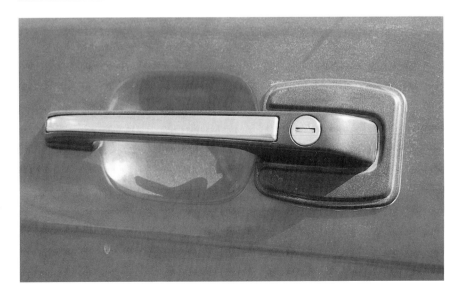

Top *You can guard against spiking by fitting C & R Enterprises Amour Door Plates. They are simple to fit and make spiking virtually impossible.*

Middle *The kit includes Allen-headed stainless steel screws (in place of the original Philips head screws) for fixing the door handles, which makes removing them less easy.*

Bottom *In place, the black finish blends neatly with the rest of the car. They look good and, by golly, they do you good!*

## The sound of breaking glass

One of the weakest areas on your quattro is the side glass. Unlike the front windscreen, it is not laminated, so it's extremely easy to break. Even if the doors are deadlocked, the thief could still gain access to your car. Moreover, many brazen thieves are actually breaking the windows and stealing from a car whilst the driver is still in it – typically when the car is in heavy traffic at a junction. Not surprisingly, women are the chief target.

Most car manufacturers are investigating the use of laminated glass (like the windscreen) for the side windows, but this will only affect new cars. The option here is to fit a special film to the inside of the glass which inhibits breakage. Two currently available are Toad Secur-Fix and Armaglass 369.

In both cases the film is virtually invisible and sticks to the inside of the side glass, front and rear. When struck from the outside the glass will craze but won't break until it has been struck noisily many, many times. However, when pushed from the inside (say in the event of an accident) it simply falls out, thus allaying any fears owners may have about being trapped inside their car.

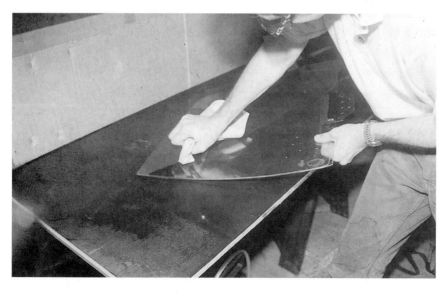

Top *This shot of a Thatcham tester attacking a filmed side window shows how the glass shatters but does not break.*

Bottom *Autofilm Direct have a number of mobile installers who can fit the film at your home or work. All the glass has to be removed from the car and scrupulously cleaned using a squeegee and de-ionised water.*

Armaglass 369 was one of the first products to be tested under the Thatcham 'Q' regime. The film is made-up of three laminated sheets (like ply-wood) which form a layer just 369 microns thick. Thankfully, the test car was not a quattro (an unsuspecting BMW was pressed into service) and comparisons between treated and untreated glass were made. The table below shows the results:

| Tool used | Standard window | | Armaglass 369 | |
| --- | --- | --- | --- | --- |
| | Secs | Blows | Secs | Blows |
| Spark plug ceramic | 4 | 4 | 32 | 31 |
| Automatic centre punch | 4 | 4 | 33 | 22 |
| Fire brick | 0.5 | 1 | 17 | 5 |

At around 30 seconds the testers gave up because no thief will stand ham-mering glass for this length of time. He will expect it to break within a few sec-onds so that he can steal and be gone. As an added bonus, in the event of an accident, the film will hold together any broken side windows, which prevents the car filling with frag-ments of glass.

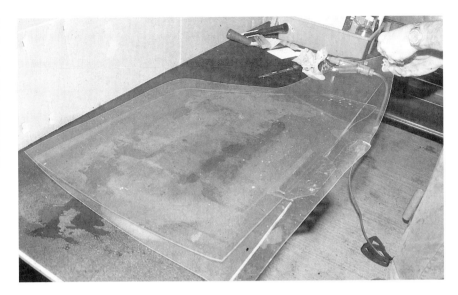

Top *Then the film was cut from the roll to the basic shape of the window.*

Middle *After that it was yet more cleaning and pressing the film down firmly into place before ...*

Bottom *... trimming it exactly to size. It is virtually impossible to tell the film is present – unless someone tries to break it, of course.*

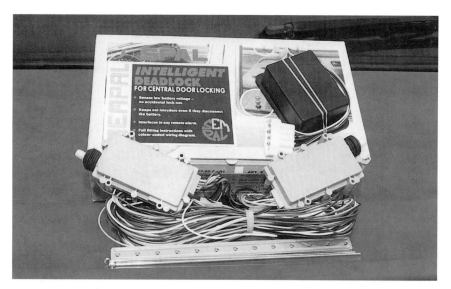

## CENTRAL DEADLOCKING

To steal your car most thieves will force entry, but those wishing to steal from it will simply break the glass and lift the locking knob. Not only does this open the door in question, but the door on the other side of the car and gives access to the boot opening handle on the 'B' pillar. Many modern Audis are fitted with deadlocking systems which prevent the locking knobs from being raised or the locking mechanism from being operated – either from inside or outside the car.

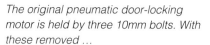

Top *Sempal make an aftermarket central deadlocking system suitable for your car, which won't break the bank, and it's a simple DIY fit. It has a variety of fail-safes to prevent you being accidentally locked out, and to thwart the electrically clever thief. And because the driver's door cannot be opened, the boot cannot be opened either!*

*The original pneumatic door-locking motor is held by three 10mm bolts. With these removed …*

*… the motor can be removed and stored either for replacement when you sell the car or for sale to another owner.*

*Sempal's technical whizzkid Matthew Morris installed this system, making sure all electrical joins were soldered.*

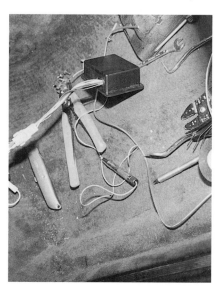

*This is the ubiquitous 'black' box which houses the brains of the system. It was mounted neatly up under the dashboard and cable-tied securely in place. It will work with any remote-controlled alarm or immobiliser (or even just remote central locking).*

# Security

## ELECTRONIC ALARMS

A Thatcham Category 2 immobiliser should be seen as a minimum installation and ideally you should opt for a Category 1 system. For those with a cashflow problem, a Category 2>1 system, as already described, offers immobilisation now with the option to upgrade with the minimum of fuss when funds allow.

### Are alarms worth it?

Regardless of what cynics say, a siren sounding as a thief is trying to steal your car (or from it) will not add to his peace of mind. Stealing cars is not difficult, but it does carry the inherent risk of getting caught, and with so many cars still not alarmed at all there's really no need for the thief to add to that risk. It's highly recommended that you opt for a battery back-up siren (with an internal battery which will power the siren should the leads from the car's battery be cut) and run a slave siren inside the car in order to give the thief some more grief. It will also act as a back-up should the underbonnet siren be attacked by thieves working in teams.

It's also a good idea to add interfaces to link in the alarm to the electric windows and central locking (many

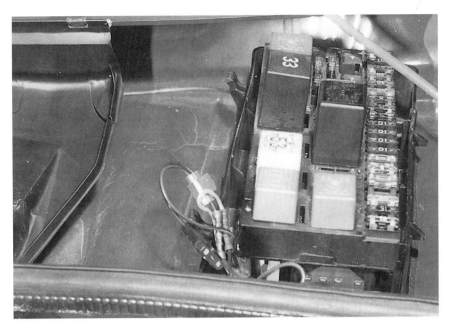

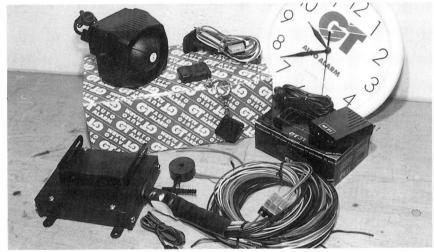

*Top Bad news, here. Self-stripping type connectors and alarms don't usually mix, especially in harsh under-bonnet conditions. This alarm was fitted to the car when it was bought, but removing and binning it was the only course of action, especially given those iffy looking crimped connectors and wiring stuffed haphazardly into the fuse box. It was a fairly low-spec unit and very badly fitted.*

*Middle The basic GT Auto Alarm GT16T system – not so basic, as the main alarm/immobiliser control unit has some 36 wires coming from it!*

*Bottom A common mistake is to try to install an alarm around the interior fittings. Top technical man Blair knew otherwise, and a great deal of the car was stripped so that the job could be done properly.*

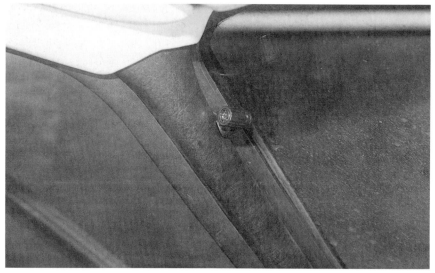

systems include an interface for the latter as a matter of course). It's more convenient and means you can't forget to close all windows/doors. Given the cost of wheels and VR/ZR-rated tyres, it's a good idea to fit a movement sensor so that the alarm triggers if the car is jacked-up to remove them.

## They always false alarm!

No, they don't. A quality alarm, installed and properly set up by a *real* professional will simply not false-alarm. The sirens you hear going off at 4 am every morning are usually either cheap systems and/or DIY-installed and/or set-up to be too sensitive. Shown here is a GT Auto Alarm installation of their GT16T Thatcham Category 1 system on a WR-engined quattro. The installers were Blair McWilliam and Peter Mouncer.

Top *Most of the units were positioned awkwardly (for the thief) under the dashboard. Note also the second siren (in the centre) designed to give the thief a headache, even if he had overcome the underbonnet unit.*

Middle *Some form of interior sensing is required; in this case ultrasonic. A sender and receiver were positioned at the tops of the 'A' pillars. Some manufacturers favour microwave sensors, although these are usually best used on larger or open-top vehicles where wind movement may be a problem.*

Bottom left *As with the Sempal locking, Blair made sure that all electrical connections were soldered.*

Bottom right *The GT Auto Alarm system is unusual in that the remote control can be integrated with the ignition key. As can be seen here, it's a neat way of doing things and makes life much easier.*

## Turning the pagers

A pager alarm works in the same way as usual, but the remote control unit also includes a receiver. If the system is triggered in your absence, the pager will pick up a signal from the unit (via a screen-mounted aerial) and beep and flash to warn you. The range depends on the model you choose and the area you're in. Credex VTA have a very powerful unit which can operate up to 2.2km distance, though this was not approved for use in all EC countries.

Meta's version is EC approved, but its power and range has to be regulated to a maximum of 1km. A pager's range is at its best in open countryside and at its worst in built-up areas. Whilst it won't actually stop a thief attacking your car, if you arrive on the scene soon after, it could make the difference between a damaged car and a space where it was parked. However, remember that car thieves are outside the law, and that generally it is not advisable to take them on physically. Whether you're beeped by a pager or just happen across someone attacking your car, your presence in the area will be enough to make most thieves run off. Do not be tempted to 'have a go', instead take note of their descriptions and contact the police immediately.

## TAG, YOU'RE IT!

Many quattros are stolen to break up for spares. With the cost of new parts as it is, there's a huge market. Datatag is a system of marking component parts of the car to make life harder for the professional thief. A sticker in the window alerts the thief that some parts of this car have been marked or tagged. The deterrent effect of this cannot be overemphasised because no thief can afford to have *traceable* components on his premises. The code numbers are registered on a central computer and when you sell the car, they can be transferred to the new owner for a small fee. The system was originally developed jointly by Yamaha and AEG for use with motorcycles where statistics show that tagged bikes are *ten times* less likely to be stolen.

*This is Meta's pager remote control unit in trendy red see-through finish.*

*The first part of the system is to etch a security code number into glass components, such as the windscreen, side glass (more tempting for the aftermarket thief if it has 'quattro' in it) or ... headlamps, and it can also be used to etch ...*

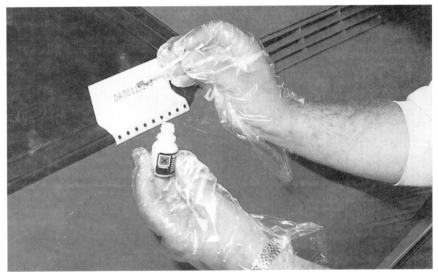

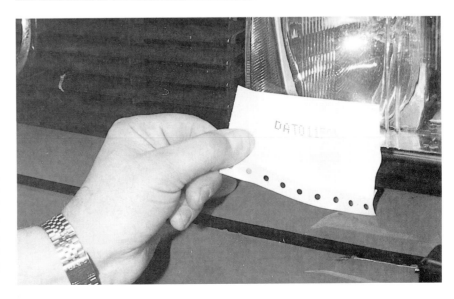

*... hard plastics such as the front and rear spoiler and door mirrors, etc.*

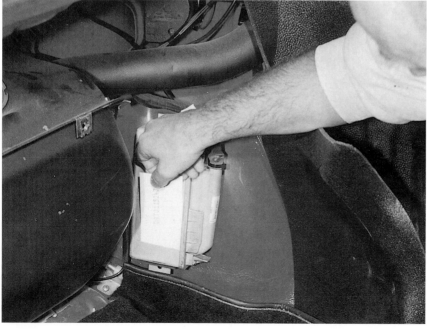

*Items such as ECUs for engine management or, as here, ABS braking, can also be marked. These parts are highly saleable on the illegal second-hand market.*

Even items like your valuable welder or compressor in your garage can be marked and listed in the same way.

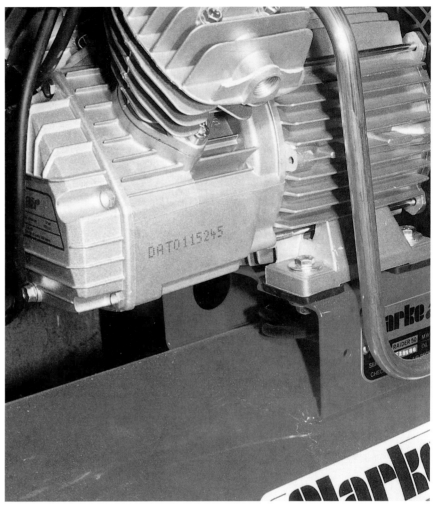

The second part involves hiding tiny plastic 'tags' (actually tiny microchip transponders) on the vehicle. Because these are impervious to heat, petrol pressures, oil and most acids, they can be positioned just about anywhere. There are several sizes and types and locating them would be virtually impossible – especially as a thief will never know exactly how many he's looking for.

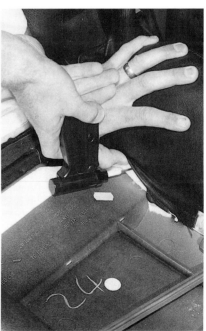

The various tags can be inserted into seats and upholstery or even ...

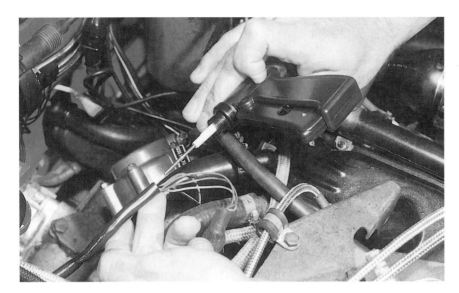

*... up inside the wiring loom. A thief may well swap an engine, but how many would swap the whole loom?*

*The credit card version can be fitted under the roof lining which means it can be read by a scanner from the outside.*

*This tiny tag was silicone glued into the centre of the alloy wheel. Crafty, eh?*

## The thiefproof car?

Sorry, but it doesn't exist, unfortunately.
Nothing will prevent your car being
stolen by a determined gang of thieves
but, if you put enough obstacles in their
way, you may make your car sufficiently
hard work that they go elsewhere.

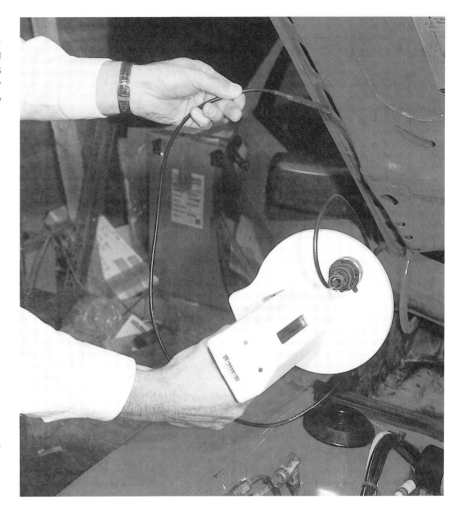

*When 'read' by a special scanner the
tags transmit the code number which is
logged against your name. In this case
the scanner has been fitted with a flexible
probe which is being used to check for a
tag stuck into place in the bonnet
pressing.*

# Appendix 1

# Workshop procedures and safety first

As already discussed, working on your quattro is not, for the most part, beyond the realms of the average DIY enthusiast owner. Many mechanical and interior servicing and repair tasks can be carried out given a reasonable level of equipment and skill. However, it's important to take a leaf or two from the professional mechanic's book of safety. A logical approach to DIY motoring is essential, as are the correct procedures and the use of the right tools for the right job.

## Preparations

When you're working on your car, always make sure that someone knows where you are, and ask them to check up on you on a regular basis – it could be your life-saver.

- Wear overalls, not least because there are less likely to be loose items of clothing to get caught in moving parts.
- Impose a NO SMOKING rule in your workshop at all times.
- Remove watches and jewellery where possible.
- Use barrier cream on your hands and arms before starting work on your car. Long-term contact with engine oil can be a health hazard.
- Keep things tidy – a workshop with cables and pipes running all over the floor is a recipe for disaster.

- Read the instructions! It's best to do this in the warmth of your living room. You'll be more likely to skip bits in a cold workshop.
- When cleaning components DON'T use petrol (gasoline). Use white (mineral) spirit, paraffin (kerosene) or purpose-made industrial cleaners.
- When using any power tools, or even hand tools where there is the danger of flying fragments (chiselling a seized nut, for example) wear goggles to protect your eyes, especially when using grinders, etc.

## The camera never lies

If you're working on particularly complex items, make notes and diagrams of where the various component parts should go. Alternatively, use a camera or even a video camera to show a dismantling procedure and replacement order. Using a camcorder enables you to give a 'commentary' as well. Don't think that you'll remember everything – it's amazing how much the memory fades. For those of us with day-jobs, complex removal and replacement tasks could easily take a week or more, during which it is very easy to forget exactly what went where.

## Under the car

You simply cannot be too careful when working under your car – 20 people die every year as a result of a car falling on them!

- Never work under your quattro when it is supported *only* by a jack. Use additional support from securely placed axle stands.
- Protect your eyes and hands using goggles/gloves.
- Don't attempt to loosen high-torque nuts or bolts while the car is off the ground. Torque them up when the vehicle is back on the floor.
- Don't touch any part of the exhaust, manifold or catalytic converter, before ascertaining that they are cold.
- Catalytic converters get extremely hot, so don't park over dry grass, oily rags or any other material which may catch fire from the heat. Never run a catalyst-equipped engine without the heat shield in place.
- Although engine and transmission fluids should be warm in order to drain them properly, ensure that they are not hot enough to scald.

## Under the bonnet

- Remember that the quattro engine bay is considerably warmer in use than that of the average car. Allow for this at all times when you have to work on it.
- Make sure that the gearbox is in neutral before starting the engine.

- Don't leave the key in the ignition while you're working on the car.
- Always remove the coolant filler cap with a cold engine. If you have to do it when the engine is warm, do it slowly, with a cloth for protection. Undo slightly and let the cap settle at the first indentation. This will release the pressure and steam – but remember that the steam will be even hotter than the escaping coolant.
- Keep brake fluid and anti-freeze off your paintwork. Wipe up spillages straight away.
- Never siphon fluids, such as anti-freeze or petrol (gasoline) by mouth – contact with skin as well as inhalation can damage your health. Use a suitable hand pump and wear gloves.

## General safety notes
- Take care not to inhale any dust, especially brake dust, which may contain asbestos.
- Wipe up oil or grease spillages straight away. Use oil granules (cat litter will do the job) to soak up major spills.
- Use quality tools – an ill-fitting spanner could cause damage to the component, your car and, of course, to you!
- When lifting heavy items, remember the rule; bend your legs and keep your back straight. Know your limitations – if something is too heavy, call in a helper.
- Time is a vital element in any workshop. Make sure you've got enough to finish a job; rushed work is rarely done right.
- Children are naturally inquisitive but don't allow them to wander unsupervised round or in your car, especially if it is jacked up.

## Finishing
When you've finished, clean up the workshop and clean and replace all your tools. You'll reap the rewards in time saved next time out and in tools that last much longer and work much better.

## Fire
Always carry a fire extinguisher in the car and have another one available for use in your workshop. Choose a carbon dioxide type or, better still, dry powder, but never a water type extinguisher for workshop use. Water conducts electricity and, in some circumstances, could actually make an oil- or petrol-based fire worse. Check the instructions for use before you need to use it and always direct the jet at the base of the flames.

Naked flames (when using gas welding equipment, for example) are an obvious threat, but petrol and its vapour can be ignited even by a spark. This could be caused by something as simple as a short circuit. This is why you should always disconnect the battery earth terminal before starting work. Other problem areas include sparks from a grinder or the striking of two metal surfaces against each other, the bulb in an inspection lamp or even a central heating boiler starting up.

## Mains electricity
Mains power tools should be used with care outdoors. Use the correct type of plug with correct and tightly-made connections. Where applicable, make sure that they are earthed (grounded).

Use an RCD (residual circuit breaker) which, in the event of a short circuit, cuts the power immediately to reduce the risk of electrocution. RCDs can be purchased from most DIY stores quite cheaply. Take special care when working in damp conditions, especially if you are using a mains extension lead. Wherever possible, work indoors and/or use battery-powered tools.

## Fumes
Never run your quattro in an enclosed space – the exhaust fumes contain deadly carbon monoxide which can kill within minutes – and this applies equally to 20v models fitted with catalytic converters. Treat all chemicals with great care, and this includes petrol. Many cleaning agents and solvents contain highly toxic chemicals and should not be used in confined spaces or used for long periods without a

break. Wear gloves when working with chemicals, and if any is spilled on your skin rinse it off with water immediately.

## High tension ignition
Touching parts of the ignition system with the engine running (or being turned over), notably the HT leads themselves, can lead to severe electric shock, especially if the vehicle is fitted with electronic ignition. Voltages produced by electronic ignition systems are much higher than normal and could prove fatal, especially to those with pacemakers.

The likelihood of an electric shock is more pronounced in wet or damp conditions, when a spark can 'jump' to an earthing point – you! When performing a task which requires the engine to be running (setting the timing, for example) take great care not to touch any ignition components.

## Plastic materials
Working with fibreglass and other similar 'plastic' materials is opening up a whole new area of safety awareness. It is vital that the instructions for use be followed to the letter in order to avoid a dangerous situation developing. Substances such as polymers, resins and adhesives produce dangerous fumes (both poisonous and flammable) and skin irritants. In particular, do not allow resin or two-pack hardener to come into contact with the skin. Make sure such materials are clearly labelled and stored safely away from the reach of children and/or under lock and key.

## The battery
Most batteries give off a small amount of highly explosive hydrogen gas, so you should never allow a naked flame or a spark near your battery. Always disconnect the battery earth terminal whenever you are working on your car to remove the possibility of an accidental electrical short circuit. When charging the battery, remove both negative and positive leads. Unless otherwise advised, loosen the filler caps to allow excess gasses to escape.

The battery electrolyte level should

be kept topped up (using only distilled water) to the point specified on the side of the battery. If any electrolyte is spilled, wipe it up immediately and wash off skin where applicable – it is highly corrosive. If you need to remove your battery, wear rubber gloves and goggles, always keeping it upright.

## Petrol safety

Petrol is a highly flammable, volatile liquid and should be treated with great respect. Even its vapour will ignite at the slightest provocation. When not actually in your fuel tank, it should be kept in metal cans (or approved 'plastic' cans) and stored where there is no danger of naked flames or sparks. Cans should have a ventilation hole to prevent the build-up of vapour. If you work in an inspection pit, extra care is required as petrol vapour is heavier than air and will tend to build-up in the bottom of the pit.

## Engine oils

There is some danger from contaminants that are contained in all used oil and, according to some experts, prolonged skin exposure can lead to serious skin disorders. You can offset this by always using barrier cream on your hands and wearing plastic or rubber gloves when draining the oil from your engine or transmission.

## Oil disposal

Never pour your used oil down a drain or on to the ground. Environmentally it is very unfriendly and will render you liable to action from your local council. In most EC countries, including the UK, local authorities must provide free Oil Banks as a safe means of oil disposal. If you're unsure where to take your used oil, contact your local Environmental Health Department for advice, or ring the Oil Bank Line on freephone 0800 663366 for details of your nearest bank. To save transporting old oil five litres at a time, use a large drum (say 25 gallons) as interim storage. When it is full, take it for safe disposal.

## Fluoroelastomers

Many items found on modern cars (eg oil seals, gaskets, diaphragms, and 'O' rings) appear to be rubber, but in fact are made from a synthetic substitute which contains fluorine. The materials are called fluoroelastomers and, if heated to more than 315°C, they can decompose in a dangerous manner. Indeed, some decomposition can occur at temperatures of around 200°C. These temperatures would normally only be found on a car if it were to be set alight or if it were 'broken' by a vehicle dismantler using a cutting torch.

When there is any water present, including atmospheric moisture, the heated fluoroelastomers produce extremely dangerous by-products. The Health and Safety Executive says: 'Skin contact with this liquid or decomposition residues can cause painful and penetrating burns. Permanent irreversible skin and tissue damage can occur.'

Clearly, this is important to note if your car has caught fire, even if only partially, or if it has been stolen and 'fired' by the thieves. Even more caution is required if you are searching for used parts in a vehicle dismantlers.

Observe the following safety procedures:

- Never touch blackened or charred pieces of rubber or anything that looks like it.
- Allow all burnt or decomposed fluoroelastomer materials to cool down before inspection, tear-down or removal.
- Ideally, don't handle parts containing decomposed fluoroelastomers. If you have to, wear goggles and PVC protective gloves whilst doing so. Never handle them unless they are completely cold.
- Contaminated parts, residues, materials and clothing, including protective clothing and gloves, should be disposed of by an approved contractor to landfill or by incineration according to national or local regulations. Oil seals, gaskets and 'O'-rings, along with contaminated material, must not be burned locally.

# Appendix 2

# Chassis number interpretation

Audi's method of chassis number *appears* complex, but when you know what to look for its actually quite simple. This chart and sample number shows what it all means. Taking the fictitious chassis number of WAUZZZ85ZEA123456 as an example, it breaks down as follows:

| | |
|---|---|
| WAU | Manufacturer's mark |
| ZZZ | Filler |
| 85 | Model type |
| Z | Filler |
| E | Model year (A = 1980) |
| A | Production plant (Ingolstadt) |
| 123456 | Chassis number |

From this and the listing below we can see that it is an Audi quattro turbo (which were all model type 85) produced in the 1984 model year.

## Chassis numbers

These chassis numbers relate to those cars imported to the UK during the model years listed.

### 10v

1980 85 AA900
1981 85 BA90099
1982 85 CA900
1983 85 DA900
1984 85 EA900
1985 85 FA900
1986 85 GA900
1987 85 HA900
1988 85 JA900

### 20v

1989 85 KA900
1990 85 LA900
1991 85 MA900

## Model years

Audi's model years always started the year before – hence a 1988 model would actually be introduced in September 1987. It's always wise to remember that dealers would be unlikely to have sold off their stock of the previous model to coincide exactly with the new one. As a result, it would be possible to see a car registered in, say, January 1988, but actually be a 1987 model, having been built prior to August 1987.

When considering specifications, it is also vital to consider that there are many cases of the last of one run getting items not due until the following year. For example, in theory, the gas strut-supported bonnet came in with the MB-engined cars, but some were fitted to WR-engined models. Conversely, the quattro side window lettering was deleted before the digital dash cars, but early models still featured it, as remaining stocks were used up.

# Appendix 3

# English/ American terminology

| English | American |
|---|---|
| Accelerator or throttle pedal | Gas pedal |
| Aerial | Antenna |
| Anti-roll bar | Stabiliser or sway bar |
| Bonnet | Hood |
| Boot | Trunk |
| Bottom gear | First gear |
| Bulkhead | Firewall |
| Cam follower or tappet | Valve lifter or tappet |
| Carburettor | Carburetor |
| Catch | Lock |
| Clearance, free-play | Lash |
| Crownwheel | Ring gear or differential |
| Disc (brake) | Rotor or disk |
| Drop arm | Pitman arm |
| Dynamo | DC Generator |
| Earth (electrical) | Ground |
| Exhaust manifold | Header |
| Fault finding/ diagnosis | Trouble shooting |
| Float chamber | Float bowl |
| Gear lever | Shift lever |
| Gearbox | Transmission |
| Gudgeon pin | Piston or wrist pin |
| Halfshaft | Axle shaft |
| Hand brake | Parking brake |
| Headlamp dipswitch | Headlight dimmer |
| Hood | Soft-top |
| Indicator | Turn signal |
| Interior lamp | Dome lamp |
| Layshaft (gearbox) | Countershaft |
| Motorway | Freeway, turnpike |
| Number plate | License plate |
| Paraffin | Kerosene |
| Petrol | Gasoline |
| Petrol tank | Gas tank |
| 'Pinking' | 'Pinging' |
| Propeller shaft | Driveshaft |
| Quarterlight | Quarter window |
| Remould or retread (tyre) | Recap (tire) |
| Reverse | Back-up |
| Rocker cover | Valve cover |
| Saloon | Sedan |
| Seized | Frozen |
| Shock absorber | Damper |
| Side indicator lights | Side marker lights |
| Side light | Parking light |
| Silencer | Muffler |
| Sill panel | Rocker panel |
| Spanner | Wrench |
| Split pin | Cotter pin |
| Steering arm | Spindle arm |
| Sump | Oil pan |
| Tappet | Valve lifter |
| Thrust bearing (or release bearing) | Throw-out bearing |
| Top gear | High gear |
| Track rod (steering) | Tie-rod |
| Transmission | Drive train |
| Tyre | Tire |
| Vice | Vise |
| Wheel nut | Lug nut |
| White spirit | Mineral spirit |
| Windscreen | Windshield |
| Wing or mudguard | Fender |

# Appendix 4

# Useful names and addresses

With a performance car like the quattro you need to know the names of specialist companies who can help you maintain and/or tune your car to your liking. Here are a few, most of whom have been instrumental in the production of this book and all of whom enthuse as much as the owners about the quattro.

## SPECIALIST COMPANIES

### AA Data Check
(0800) 234999
Essential quattro pre-purchase checks, including write-off, stolen vehicle and finance-owing register. (See also HPI Equifax.)

### AG Products
Distributors of the Battery Sava.

PO Box 575
Ascot
Berks SL5 9XS
(01344) 24131

### AM Cars
All things quattro, including warranted sales, service, tuning, new and used spares.

Station Road
Ilminster
Somerset TA19 9BL
(01460) 55001

### Audi UK Limited
Audi importers and source of O/E parts and equipment.

Yeomans Drive
Blakelands
Milton Keynes MK14 5AN
(01908) 679121

### Audi Only
A specialist dismantler offering parts at much-reduced prices.

Unit 1
Bathdale Trading Estate
Booth Hill Lane
Oldham OL1 2JT
(0161) 628 3340

### Audiparts
A specialist dismantler offering parts at much-reduced prices.

Unit 11
Hockcliffe House Garage
Watling Street
Hockcliffe
Beds LU7 9ND
(01525) 210978

### Autofilm Direct
Producers of Armaglass 369 protective security window film.

Grays Farm Road
St Pauls Cray
Kent BR5 3BD
(0800) 018 6232

### Bain Hogg
A specialist classic insurer with direct links to the Quattro Owners Club.

Falcon House
The Minories
Dudley
W. Midlands DY2 8PF
(0990) 708090

### BR Motorsport
Specialists in quattro servicing, spares and tuning.

8 Berrington Road
Sydenham Industrial Estate
Leamington Spa
Warks CV31 1NB
(01926) 451545

### Carflow Products Limited
High quality locking wheel bolts.

Leighton Road
Leighton Buzzard
Beds LU7 7LA
(01525) 383543

## C & R Enterprises

A range of tuning products for the quattro, including Black Diamond brake discs/pads, Goodridge stainless hoses and security Armour Door Plates.

Units C1–C4 Lake Street
Radford
Nottingham NG7 4BT
(0115) 978 5740

## Clarke International

A wide range of DIY workshop equipment including MIG/ARC welders, compressors and pneumatic tools, hoists, grinders, drills, etc.

Hemnal Street
Epping
Essex CM16 4LG
(01992) 565300

## Credex Ltd

Distributors of VTA pager alarm and smoke screen system.

Friesland
Coulsdon Lane
Chipstead
Surrey CR5 3QG
(01737) 556602

## Datatag

High security method of marking a vehicle and its components.

See Ross Autotronics.

## DB Car Trim

A company specialising in the renovation and repair of VW/Audi seats and trim, including leather.

Cornford Road Garage
Marton
Blackpool
Lancs
(01253) 761252

## Demon Tweeks

A wide range of tuning and motor sport spares, including stainless exhaust systems.

75 Ash Road South
Wrexham Industrial Estate
Wrexham
North Wales LL13 3UG
(01978) 664466

## Dialynx Performance

Complete range of Audi-alternative spares and servicing for the Ur quattro; notably their replacement exhaust manifold. Mail order service.

Unit 3
Bagbury Park
Lydiard Millicent
Swindon
Wilts SN5 9LU
(01793) 772245

## Draper Tools Ltd

Suppliers of all kinds of hand tools and distributors of Metabo power tools.

Hursley Road
Chandlersford
Eastleigh
Hants SO5 5YF
(01703) 266355

## Goodyear Great Britain Limited

A wide range of quality tyres suitable for all models of quattro and all weather and road conditions.

Stafford Road
Wolverhampton
West Midlands WV10 6DH
(01902) 22321

## GT Auto Alarm (UK) Ltd

Producers of a wide range of quality alarms/immobilisers, many to insurance (Thatcham) standard.

GT House
Berrington Road
Sydenham Industrial Estate
Leamington Spa
Warks CV31 1NB
(01926) 882382

## Halfords

Many common electrical and other service parts (wiper blades, etc) suitable for quattro, including Metex dust covers.

See under Car Accessories in your local *Yellow Pages*.

## Hella Ltd

A wide range of quality electrical and associated equipment, including spark plugs (Beru) ignition leads, batteries, starter motors, alternators, aerials and all kinds of bulbs and lighting.

Wildmere Road Industrial Estate
Banbury
Oxon OX16 7JU
(01295) 272233

## Historic Motorsport Ltd

Quattro specialist company operated by David Sutton, who was responsible for the Audi Sport UK rally quattros in the 1980s.

18 Lanchester Way
Daventry
Northants NN11 5PH
(01327) 300677

## Hoyle, Terry

Originally involved with the Audi Sport UK rally quattro team, Terry now runs this business specialising in engine tuning, rebuilding, etc.

Unit 2 Stepfield
Freebourne Industrial Estate
Witham
Essex CM8 3TH
(01376) 501100

## HPI Equifax

Essential quattro pre-purchase checks, including write-off, stolen vehicle and finance-owing register. (See also AA Data Check.)

Dolphin House
PO Box 61
New Street
Salisbury
Wilts SP1 2TB
(01722) 422422

## Livingstones Insurance

A specialist classic insurer with direct links to the Quattro Owners Club.

5 Coronation Avenue
Yeovil
Somerset BA21 3DX
(01935) 706258

## Manton Software

All types of electrical repair, including digital dash.

28 Hills Close
Great Linford
Milton Keynes MK14 5DA
(01908) 675916
E mail: 101546,674@compuserve.com

## Meta

Alarms, immobilisers and pager alarms.

See Ross Autotronics.

## Performance Car Services

A specialist Bosch-approved agency run by VAG-trained David Abbott, offering Audi-style maintenance and tuning operations at good rates.

54 Barton Road
Water Eaton
Milton Keynes MK2 3BN
(01908) 270503

## PP Video

Suppliers of motoring videos including (currently) four Audi-based titles.

The Storehouse
Little Hereford Street
Bromyard
Herefordshire HR7 4DE
(01885) 488800

## Pristine Ltd

Alloy wheel refurbishers to original standards, colour-coding, polished finishes, etc.

Newport Road
Woburn Sands
South Milton Keynes
Bucks MK17 8UD
(01908) 282628

## Pro-Align

Specialist in quattro wheel/suspension alignment and repair/replacement. Operated by Paul Beaurain, Quattro Owners Club area representitive.

30 Ross Road
Northampton NN5 5AX
(01604) 588880

## Quattro Corner

Quattro spares at discount prices.

97 Presthope Road
Selly Oak
Birmingham B29 4HL
(0976) 832676 (mobile)

## Richbrook International Limited

Dis-car-nect security device/battery saver and aluminium gear knobs.

11 Wyfold Road
London SW6 6SE
(0171) 381 0777

## Ross Autotronics

Distributors for Meta and Datatag high security products.

Wainwright Road
Shire Business Park
Worcester WR4 9FA
(01905) 756900

## Sachs-Boge (UK) Ltd

Importers of Sachs and Boge dampers/springs and other suspension equipment.

Eldon Way
Crick Industrial Estate
Crick
Northamptonshire NN6 7SL
(01788) 822353

## Scorpion

A range of British-made stainless steel exhausts for all quattro models.

See Demon Tweeks.

## Securon Ltd

Aftermarket seat belts.

Winchmore Hill
Amersham
Bucks HP7 ON2
(01494) 434455

## Sempal

Currently the only aftermarket central deadlocking system available.

The Commercial Centre
Sherrif Street
Worcester WR4 9AB
(01905) 617544

## Serck-Marston

Specialists with branches across the UK, offering all types of quattro radiators off the shelf with free testing service. Also anti-freeze, water pumps, inter-coolers and exchange turbochargers.

2100 The Crescent
Solihull Parkway
Birmingham Business Park
Birmingham B37 7YE
(0121) 717 0007

## South Hereford Audi

Franchised Audi dealers, enthusiastic about quattros; deals for Quattro Owners Club members.

Centurion Way
Roman Road
Hereford HR1 1LQ
(01432) 352424

## Superchips Ltd

Specialists in electronic tuning, with motorsport connections.

Buckingham Industrial Park
Buckingham MK18 1XJ
(01280) 816781

## Sykes-Pickavant

A wide range of high quality
mechanical and bodywork hand tools.

Warwick Works
Kilnhouse Lane
Lytham St Annes
Lancs FY8 3DU
(01253) 721291

## Thatcham (Motor Insurance Repair Research Centre)

Insurance industry testing centre for
vehicle security products.

Colthrop Lane
Thatcham
Newbury
Berks RG19 4NP
(01635) 868855

## Toad Innovations

A wide range of security products,
including Secur-Fix window film.

The Quorum
Barnwell Road
Cambridge CB5 8RE
(01223) 214555

## TSR Performance

Performance spares, tuning, servicing
and accessories for the Ur quattro.

Units 5 & 6
Transform Estate
Wylds Road
Bridgwater TA6 4DH
(01278) 453036

## Turbo Technics

Turbocharger replacement and repair.

17 Gallowhill Road
Brackmills
Northampton NN4 0EE
(01604) 764005

## Wayside Garages

Franchised Audi dealers, enthusiastic
about quattros, with special rates for
club members.

4 Denbigh Road
Bletchley
Milton Keynes MK1 1DF
(01908) 641535

## CLUBS

### The Quattro Owners Club

David Preece
Well Cottage
Longley Green
Suckley
Worcs WR6 5DU
(01886) 884475
Internet site –
WWW.YRL.CO.UK/quattro/

### Club Audi (with quattro register)

Campion House
1 Greenfield Road
Westoning
Beds MK45 5JD
(01525) 750500

### Quattro Club USA

7700 Quattro Drive
Chanhassen
MN 55317
USA
E mail: http://www.quattroclubusa.org/

### Club Audi Australia

Simon Ansell
7 Monomeath Avenue
Canterbury 3126
Victoria
Australia
03 9830-1575 (fax 03 9830-1069)

## THE INTERNET

The advent of electronic communica-
tions means that even more information
is to hand. There are hundreds of web
sites world-wide with quattro connections, though it can sometimes take a
little patience to get to the ones you
want. Some relate to clubs, others to
dealers, others still to individuals wanting to share their enthusiasm. There are
cars and parts for sale and current
motor sport links, and it's often the case
that a tricky problem can be one that
someone out there has already solved
and taken the trouble to put the answer
on the Net. One of the best places to
start is with a search engine such as
YAHOO! (HTTP://WWW.YAHOO.COM)
or ALTA VISTA(HTTP://WWW.ALTAVISTA.
DIGITAL.COM) entering Audi quattro
as the search criteria.

## MAGAZINES

### *Volkswagen Audi Car* and *The Audi Magazine*

Campion House
1 Greenfield Road
Westoning
Beds MK45 5JD
(01525) 750500

### *VW Motoring*

Warners Group
The Maltings
West Street
Bourne
Lincs PE10 9PH
(01778) 393313

## MISCELLANEOUS

### Audi High Performance Driving Courses

(01295) 276701

### Audi Sport Merchandising Services

(01483) 797979

# Index

Alcoa 38
Arrii, Annie 48, 51
**Audi**
  A4 quattro & S4 44, 45
  Avant RS2 39, 40, 42
  Avus quattro 39, 41
  Coupe and Coupe quattro 24, 43
  S2 44, 45, 92
  Sport quattro 33, 34, 35, 36, 37, 93,
    94, 95, 145
  Spyder quattro 38, 39, 41, 96
  TT & TTS 40, 41, 42, 96
  80 and 80 quattro 20, 24, 43
  90 and 90 quattro 24
  200 Turbo 18, 19, 20
Auto Union 12, 13, 14

Baur 38
Bensinger, Jorg 17
Biela, Frank 16, 17, 64, 65, 66
Bintcliffe, John 64, 65
Blomqvist, Stig 16, 50, 52, 53, 82
**Bodywork & fittings**
  Bodywork, door furniture 114, 115,
    116
  Checking bodywork when buying
    131, 132, 133
  Fitting new door 4-ring logos 116
  Galvanization 134
  Original dimensions 21
  Windscreen wipers (RHD) 24
  20v floorpan 75
**Braking**
  ABS 21, 107, 108
  Callipers 112
  Checking when buying 141, 144

Disc & pads removal & uprate 109,
  110, 111
  Goodridge hoses 111
Brundle, Martin 65

Cecotto, Johnny 64
**Cooling**
  Anti-freeze (coolant) 98
  Basic description 97
  Checking when buying 134, 135
  Radiator removal & bleeding 98
  Radiator replacement 99, 100, 101
Cresto, Sergio 53

Daimler Benz 14
DKW 11, 12, 13, 14, 15

**Electrical**
  Battery 120
  Checking headlamps for rust 133
  Spark plugs/leads 72, 73
Elford, Vic 20
**Engine**
  Checking when buying 143
  Compression – checking 73, 136
  Oil and filters 71, 134
  Oil cooler/hoses 70
  Servicing 10v 71
  Specification 10v WR 68
  10v MB 68, 69
  20v 73
  Tuning 138, 147, 148, 149, 150, 151
  Turbocharger 71, 76, 136
Eriksson, Kenneth 53
**Exhaust**
  Basic description 102

Catalytic converter 75, 104
  Checking exhaust when buying 135
  Exhaust manifold 71, 72
  Replacing with a stainless steel
    system 102, 103,

Fiala, Ernst 17
Ford 9, 63
**Fuel system**
  Air sensor 80
  Bosch K-Jetronic fuel injection 76,
    77
  Bosch Motronic engine management
    74, 75, 77
  Components & description 80, 97
  Fuel distributor 80
  Fuel injection 74, 76
  Fuel injectors 80
  Fuel pump 78
  Leaded and unleaded fuel 76
  Trouble-shooting guide 97

GTi Engineering 32
Gumpert, Roland 50

Haywood, Hurley 61, 62
Hertz, Arne 48, 49
Hertz, Wilhelm 15
Historic Motorsport 32
Hockenheim GP circuit 17
Holsher, Michael 39
Horsch 11, 12, 13

**Interior & electrical**
  Care, repair and description 21, 117,
    118, 119, 120

Checking interior when buying 141, 142, 143
Digital dash, description and repair 118, 119, 120
Seat belts 121

Jelinski, Frank 65
Jensen Interceptor 18

Kottulinski, Freddy 20

Lancia 9
Lloyd, Richard 64, 65

Marsden, Adam 129
Menu, Alain 65
Mikkola 16, 18, 33, 48, 49, 50, 51, 53, 81, 84
Moss, Stirling 65
Mouton, Michèle 16, 33, 48, 50, 51, 52, 53, 63, 81
Müller, H.P. 14
Munga 14, 19

NSU 15

Paris Dakar Rally 18
Parker, Martin 128, 140
Piech, Dr Ferdinand 17, 38
Pikes Peak (USA) 63, 83
Pirro, Emanuele 16, 17
Pons, Fabrizia 51
Popow, Issay 38
Porsche, Ferdinand 12, 13, 15
Preece, David 128, 144

Prices 32
Prinz (NSU) 15, 40

Ricketts, Brian 20, 32, 64, 128, 147, 148
Röhrl, Walter 16, 48, 51, 52, 53, 61, 63, 65, 83, 84
Rosemeyer, Bernd 13, 14, 65

Sandford, Ian 147, 148, 150
Santos, Joaquim 53
Schmidt, Werner 17
Schmucker, Toni 18
**Security**
Central deadlocking 156
Door lock protection 153
Electronic alarms/immobilisers/ pagers 157, 158, 159
Electronic tagging 159, 160, 161, 162
Overview 152
Side glass uprate 154, 155
Smith, Martin 38, 40
Sold Secure 152
Stockmar, Jurgen 20
Stuck, Hans 13, 65
Stuck, Hans-Joachim 16, 61, 62, 63, 64, 65
**Suspension & steering**
Checking suspension when buying 139, 140
Steering 114
Suspension specifications & uprate 112, 113,
Sutton Motorsport, David 32

Thatcham 152

Thomas, Freeman 40
Tinsley, Dave 149, 150
Toivonen, Henri 53
**Touring Car Audis**
Audi A4 quattro Supertouring 64, 66
Audi V8 quattro 63, 64, 65
Audi 80 Competition 64
Audi 80 (MK2) 65
Audi 90 quattro IMSA GTO 61, 62, 63, 85
Audi 200 quattro TransAm 61, 62
**Transmission**
Basic description, gear ratios 104, 105, 143
Differentials 105, 106, 137, 143
Torsen differential 29, 42, 106, 107
Treser, Walter 48

Unser, Bobby Snr 63

**Volkswagen**
Beetle 15
Iltis 17, 19
Vorsprung durch technik 10

Wanderer 11, 12, 13
Wankel rotary engine 15
**Wheels & tyres**
Checking when buying 138, 140
Wheel/tyre care 122, 123
Wheel/tyre specifications and uprate 124, 125, 126
Wickham, John 64
Wilson, Malcolm 63
Witterman, Franz 48